God's Good Earth

God's Good Earth

The Case for an Unfallen Creation

Jon Garvey

CASCADE *Books* · Eugene, Oregon

GOD'S GOOD EARTH
The Case for an Unfallen Creation

Cascade Books
An Imprint of Wipf and Stock Publishers
199 W. 8th Ave., Suite 3
Eugene, OR 97401

www.wipfandstock.com

PAPERBACK ISBN: 978-1-5326-5200-4
HARDCOVER ISBN: 978-1-5326-5201-1
EBOOK ISBN: 978-1-5326-5202-8

Cataloguing-in-Publication data:

Names: Garvey, Jon.

Title: God's good earth : the case for an unfallen creation / Jon Garvey.

Description: Eugene, OR: Cascade Books, 2019 | Includes bibliographical references and index.

Identifiers: ISBN 978-1-5326-5200-4 (paperback) | ISBN 978-1-5326-5201-1 (hardcover) | ISBN 978-1-5326-5202-8 (ebook)

Subjects: LCSH: Natural theology. | Religion and science. | Redemption. |

Classification: BL240 .G28 2019 (print) | CALL NUMBER (ebook)

Manufactured in the U.S.A.   01/11/19

To my parents, Geoff and Doreen Garvey,
who taught me to think,
and to F. G. Gilbert-Bentley,
who taught me to think outside the box.

Contents

Section 4—The Application

Acknowledgements

MANY THANKS FOR IDEAS, discussion, and encouragement are due (with the usual caveats about the residual errors being mine). Nick Needham was not only the conversation partner who started me investigating the history of the theology of creation, but also pointed me to many of the primary sources and continued to provide more as he discovered them. Ted Davis first suggested I should write a book on it, but also passed my name on to Keith Miller, to whom thanks are due for running with my contribution to his own project. Ted also suggested significant improvements to the manuscript, as did Richard Middleton, to whom I also owe a huge debt of gratitude for believing in the project enough to approach publishers on my behalf.

Valuable support of various kinds has also come over several years from my colleagues at *The Hump of the Camel* blog: Merv Bitkofer, Sy Garte, and Edward Robinson. Thanks are also due to Preston Garrison, Tim Mc-Mahon, Joshua Swamidass, and Vincent Torley.

My wife Cynthia has kept the coffee flowing abundantly over the years and encouraged my strange obsession, which is kept in balance by the observation of a Christian musician friend that I always keep in mind: "It's the kind of work I'm very glad somebody else is doing."

Introduction

Glory, from Him who moves all things that are.
Penetrates the universe and then shines back,
Reflected more in one part, less elsewhere.

—DANTE ALIGHIERI (1265–1321)[1]

THE IDEA THAT THE natural creation is fundamentally damaged because of the fall[2] of humankind was to me, for nearly fifty years, one of those unquestioned axioms of the faith, like the crucifixion or the existence of sin. It is usually called "the traditional view." Creationists emphasize it as the explanation for the existence of natural disasters, carnivorous animals, parasites, disease, and death.

Most Christians of course, even Creationists, the majority of the time don't think about origins and get on with life and faith here and now. If someone gets ill, or there is a destructive hurricane, immediate divine judgement for individual or corporate sin will usually be discounted as the cause nowadays. But the catastrophic effects of sin on the whole natural order *in general* are often taken for granted by believers. "Natural evil," including everything from man-eating tigers to tsunamis or asteroid collisions, is seen as the outworking of the cosmic effects of the fall of humanity. Charles Haddon Spurgeon expressed what is still common currency, in a sermon of 1868:

> Creation glows with a thousand beauties, even in its present fall-
> en condition; yet clearly enough it is not as when it came from
> the Maker's hand—the slime of the serpent is on it all—this is

1. Alighieri, *Divine Comedy,* Cantica 3: *Paradiso,* Canto 1, 320.

2. "Fall" is not the biblical term, but it does at least convey the significance for human history of the events of Genesis 3. The Bible's equivalent is "the Curse" (Rev 22:3— its scope is one of the key questions we will tackle), which differs in demonstrating God's active judgement on sin rather than a passive human decline to a lower state. One could also refer to it as "exile," since the banishment from Eden is closely equivalent to Israel's exile from the promised land.

not the world which God pronounced to be "very good." We hear of tornadoes, of earthquakes, of tempests, of volcanoes, of avalanches, and of the sea which devoureth its thousands: there is sorrow on the sea, and there is misery on the land; and into the highest palaces as well as the poorest cottages, death, the insatiable, is shooting his arrows, while his quiver is still full to bursting with future woes. It is a sad, sad world. The curse has fallen on it since the fall, and thorns and thistles it bringeth forth, not from its soil alone, but from all that comes of it.[3]

The existence of death before the fall is one major reason for the rejection of evolution by Young Earth Creationists. How could Adam, in his innocence, have been in fact walking over cruel sufferings and shattered bodies resulting from billions of years of evil?

Such a negative view of the world has also survived in the thinking of those who do espouse old earth chronology, though it poses obvious problems in that context. One of the more orthodox and intellectually rigorous theistic evolution theorists, Robert John Russell, sounds very much like Spurgeon when, after pointing out some of the wonders of creation, he adds:

But life is also torn by the pain of hunger, cold and bodily wounds; threatened by hurricanes, drought and earthquake; vulnerable to bacterial and genetic diseases; a fierce combat zone in the Caribbean tropics and the African savannah. Most living creatures are caught up in the endless cycles of predation that compose the food chain, and most animals are fated to an agonizing death.[4]

Intelligent Design theorist William Dembski, who despite his doubts about Neo-Darwinism holds to an old earth, writes:

The young-earth solution to reconciling the order of creation with natural history makes good exegetical and theological sense. . . . I myself would adopt it in a heartbeat except that nature seems to present such strong evidence against it.[5]

To reconcile the fall with an old, corrupted earth he proposes a creation whose fallen nature is a retrospective "Plan B" reflecting God's foresight of sin, an idea not completely unique in the history of theology.[6]

3. Spurgeon, *Creation's Groans.*.

4. Russell, *Cosmology,* 249.

5. Dembski , *The End of Christianity*, 55.

6. John of Damascus (c. 675–749), *Exposition of the Orthodox Faith*, book 2: "For He Who knew all things before they were, saw that in the future man would go forward

But most "old earth" Christians can't accept the convoluted idea of the fall's acting retrospectively, and so cannot regard natural evil as a result of humankind's sin. This includes in particular supporters of theistic evolution, or "Evolutionary Creation," who tend simply to attach other causes to the same pessimistic view of nature, such as the randomness inherent in evolution, or the inevitability of suffering when God allows "freedom" to his creation. R. J. Russell, for example, like Spurgeon and Dembski, claims that the biblical witness teaches:

> Suffering, disease and death are the universal consequences of an inestimably tragic and singular event, the Fall.[7]

But he goes on:

> This historical/theological explanation of the two sides of life as created and only consequentially evil is severely challenged by Darwinian evolution, where natural selection and with it death and extinction, is integral to what drives evolution and thus become constitutive of life.[8]

Very largely as a result of this, and partly in response to atheist critiques, theodicy (the pursuit of justifying God's goodness in the face of evil) is also a central concern of most theistic evolution discourse about nature. For many the detachment of the evils in creation from Adam's first sin has contributed to rejecting the idea of a historic fall altogether. With its traditional theological origin rejected, sin may then be seen as a consequence of natural evil rather than its cause.

In this respect, then, theistic evolutionists tend to be in accord with the most hard-line of adaptationist Neo-Darwinians like Richard Dawkins. If selfish evolution has always been carried on by selfish genes, then who could be surprised that the end result is selfish humans?

The ramifications of this for the shape of Christian faith are profound. It becomes almost impossible not to make God the author of evil, rather than Satan or humankind, unless he is effectively banished from responsibility for

---

in the strength of his own will, and would be subject to corruption, and, therefore, He created all things for his seasonable use, alike those in the firmament, and those on the earth, and those in the waters. . . . But even now wild beasts are not without their uses, for, by the terror they cause, they bring man to the knowledge of his Creator and lead him to call upon His name." He follows Theodoret of Cyrrhus (c. 393–c. 458) in this. The difference in Dembski's approach is that he sees these things as evils: St. John and Theodoret see them as *remedies* for evil.

7. Russell, *Cosmology*, 249.

8. Ibid., 250.

his creation. This encourages a view of a distant God presiding over a more-or-less autonomous nature, a view that has been called "semi-deism."[9]

But this is not a book about theodicy. Justifying God's goodness in the presence of evil has been a preoccupation of much mainstream philosophical theology of the last century, with analytic philosophers of religion like John Hick,[10] Richard Swinburne,[11] and Alvin Plantinga[12] tackling it largely as an issue of logic outside time and history. In reaction to this, some scholars such as Kenneth Surin[13] and Terrence Tilley[14] complain that the whole enterprise, carried on in the tradition of Leibniz's response to the skeptical Enlightenment framing of the issue as an argument for atheism,[15] is the wrong place to start.

Tilley dismisses theodicy as a pursuit altogether, and Surin, following Jürgen Moltmann and others, approaches it from the angle of a theology of the cross. Both point out, though, that the use usually made of ancient writers like Augustine, Irenaeus, or Aquinas wrenches them out of the specific contexts in which they wrote about God's goodness and the existence of evil, and that criticism gets a little closer to what I am attempting here. I am interested in God's interaction with the natural world in history, not in theory.

The aim of this book is far more restricted than theodicy, then, although it necessarily has some cross connections to it. In the first place, the field I wish to explore is entirely what is called "natural" or "physical" evil, that is what occurs in the nonhuman world, and in particular with respect to its origins in the doctrine of creation. It is significant that theodicies of natural evil were not even thought necessary for a major period of the church's history, a point to which I shall return in due course.

---

9. Coined by science historian Reijer Hooykaas, the term is also used by Christian population geneticist David L. Wilcox, who writes: "[F]or those who have committed themselves by faith to nature's autonomy, the idea of intelligent direction of natural causes is simply incomprehensible (even for those who believe in God). For them, a 'god' who acts in nature would be the ultimate intruder in a closed system." (Wilcox, *God and Evolution*, 47.)

10. Hick, *Evil and the God of Love*.

11. Swinburne, *Providence and the Problem of Evil*.

12 Plantinga, *God, Freedom and Evil*.

13. Surin, *Theology and the Problem of Evil*.

14. Tilley, *The Evils of Theodicy*.

15. Typically framed as a syllogism and attributed to the Greek philosopher Epicurus:
   If an omnipotent, omniscient, and omnibenevolent god exists, then evil does not.
   There is evil in the world.
   Therefore, an omnipotent, omniscient, and omnibenevolent God does not exist.

Although as both a Christian and a professional in life science I have been always been interested in the subject of the natural world, I started studying more seriously the interface between science, especially origins science, and creation doctrine just a few years ago. I was rather astonished to realize, as I examined Scripture again, not so much that the effects of the fall on the natural world had been exaggerated, but that the "traditional view" *in its entirety* lacks any solid biblical support whatsoever.[16] As a serious student of the Bible for half a century it made me rather ashamed to realize how much I had taken a thoroughly erroneous view for granted. Such is the hidden power of pre-existing worldviews on biblical interpretation!

A second surprise came when, in correspondence with a scholar of church history, Dr. Nick Needham, of Highland Theological College, Scotland, we began to discover in the primary sources that the idea of a fallen creation had been almost unknown, with very few exceptions, in the earliest centuries of the church. Rather the goodness of creation, here and now, was actually a distinctive of early Christianity's message. Further research showed that this "optimistic" tradition remained mainstream until theologians began to focus on "natural evil," just 500 years ago, and indicated some possible reasons for the change.

This project arose from that discussion, when I was asked by paleontologist Keith Miller (author of *Perspectives on an Evolving Creation*) to contribute a chapter (essentially chapters 6–8 of the present work) to a book on natural evil. Other authors included Sam Berry, George Murphy, Bob White, Denis Lamoureux, and Michael B. Roberts.

When the book failed to gain a *BioLogos* grant or a publishing deal, it was rescheduled for a special edition of the American Scientific Affiliation journal *Perspectives on Science and Christian Faith*, but since I was asked to shorten my piece by 50 percent for this I withdrew it from the project.

I subsequently decided to expand it to book length in order to include the key biblical material, and some considerations from a scientific viewpoint, hoping that it may form a readable, but informed and multi-faceted, treatment to move the origins discussion and the evangelical understanding of creation theology forward.

In this arena I am hoping to challenge some of the underlying *assumptions* now made in the discussion of natural evil, particularly within the evangelical Christian tradition, about what Christianity itself has taught on it, both from within its biblical foundation, and in its theological history.

---

16. This discrepancy was noted by one of the earliest theistic evolutionists, Rev. Charles Kingsley (Kingsley, *Natural Theology*). It seems to have escaped modern Creationists, Intelligent Design theorists, and theistic evolutionists alike.

I also go on to challenge, from a scientific viewpoint, some of the frankly hyperbolic expressions of the depravity and savagery of nature that have been with us since Darwin and tend to be taken as axiomatically valid. Surin, discussing the current pursuit of theodicy already mentioned, says rather ironically:

> The tasks . . . are perhaps best undertaken in the tranquility of the theodicist's study (a perusal of the writings of the theodicists will tend invariably to confirm the suspicion that the study is very much the theodicist's domain).[17]

I suggest the same is true for many of the biologists (and theistic evolutionists) who wax most indignant against the cruelties of nature—I have observed that they tend to be lab-based molecular biologists or population geneticists (and sometimes theologians!) rather than field-based zoologists who actually work with nature "in the raw" and who are usually filled with admiration for it.

All this leaves untouched the question of *why* God allows "natural evil," for those who wish to pursue what is probably unanswerable; certainly Scripture studiously avoids attempting any such answer beyond faith in the goodness of the God who reveals himself in history. Indeed, the fact that both Judaism and Christianity are based on God's self-revelation through historical events should alert us to the need to discern God's views on what is evil, and what is not, *from* such revelation and not from abstract reasoning. But my arguments may, perhaps, clarify a little of the "what" of the matter; that is, what God would have to explain, if he were actually accountable to us, rather than the reverse, the reverse being what Christianity crucially teaches.[18]

When such a central doctrine of Christian faith—the creation—is involved, it seems important to present the true position of biblical and historic church teaching as clearly as possible, to which purpose this book has been written. This is even more important when one considers the cultural situation, particularly in America. I am going to argue that nature is not nearly as red in tooth and claw as has been supposed for several centuries, but the aggressive culture wars associated with "the nature of nature" certainly make up for any deficiency in nature's savagery.

Evolution has become, and will remain for a little while to come, I suppose, a front line for the pursuit of militant materialistic atheism against

17. Surin, *Theology and the Problem of Evil*, 20.

18. I always treasure the words of one blog commenter who wrote, "Classical theology needs a theodicy like a fish needs a bicycle." The remark depends on an appreciation of critiques like Tilley's.

all forms of religion. Indeed, a surprising proportion of the apologetic for evolution is, and has always been, theological, and especially theodical.[19] Sadly, some particularly bad theology has been employed in combating this (on the Creationist side), or in seeking to accommodate to it (on the Theistic Evolution side) with both parties accepting the premise that creation *is* full of evil. It has to be a worthwhile goal to take an authentic view both of what science and Christian doctrine actually reveal about the world, because long after all these local battles are forgotten, Christians will still be living in God's creation, and will still be taking the Bible as their authority. If either is seriously misinterpreted, many evils result.

The plan I follow in this book is as follows.

In Section 1 (chapters 1 to 5) I survey the relevant biblical material broadly, if not exhaustively.

In Section 2 (chapters 6 to 8) I move on to the history of the doctrine of nature, with reference to the fall, through the last 2,000 years, to show how the balance shifted from a strongly positive view of the goodness of creation to a seriously negative one. I also look at possible reasons why the "traditional view" rose to prominence, around the sixteenth century.

In Section 3 (chapters 9 to 12) I look at "natural evil" as evidenced within the world itself, and within the science that observes it, and why nature is now so widely *perceived* as cruel and malevolent, when once it wasn't. This is in part a study of how ideas become plausible or implausible over time as worldviews change, and how evidence comes to be considered significant or to be disregarded.

Lastly, in Section 4 (chapter 13) I sketch out the differences it makes to Christian life and hope to accept either the "traditional view" that creation is tainted by the fall, or the view I have presented, that it is not; and the difference it makes to be freed from false ideas about a corrupted created order, in terms of our worship, witness, and plain *enjoyment* of God's good earth.

Lastly, I will touch on the Christian hope for the future, and how it involves not an escape from an evil creation to an uncreated heaven, but the renewing of a good creation as a better one, of the naturally empowered (*psuchikos*) as the spiritually empowered (*pneumatikos*), of the perishable as the imperishable—of the old order as the new heavens and the new earth.

The Christian gospel, like soccer, can be loosely described as game of two halves—creation and redemption.[20] Both, at root, are christological.[21]

---

19. Dilley, "Charles Darwin's use of theology."

20. The analogy, though not the gospel narrative, is spoiled when the third major theme—new creation—is factored in.

21. Col 1:15–23.

Although the main description of creation takes up only two chapters of the Bible, and the rest is primarily about God's redemption, they are inextricably intertwined, and both teaching and assumptions about creation are woven into the whole scriptural narrative from Genesis to Revelation. That is, not least, because it is the creation that, in the end, is the object of redemption.

But how we understand what this means in turn depends on how we have understood the nature of God's creation. A misunderstanding of creation is bound to impact on our understanding of redemption, and it is my contention that the innovation of a theology of "fallen nature" over the last few centuries has seriously damaged the message of Christianity to humankind. It includes introducing a pessimistic view of the world, as it is, that has done untold harm in areas normally not considered "religious," including science, the arts, and politics. That has achieved the very opposite of Christ's instruction to be "salt and light" to the world: by denigrating the goodness of Christ's creation, we have made him even more unwelcome on his own, good earth.

I hope this book may, at least, persuade others not only that we have been seeing the world in a wrong way for too long, but that it matters.

Section 1—The Bible

Chapter 1—God's Relationship to Creation

O let the Earth bless the Lord : yea, let it praise him, and magnify him for ever.

O ye Mountains and Hills, bless ye the Lord : praise him, and magnify him for ever.

O all ye Green Things upon the Earth, bless ye the Lord : praise him, and magnify him for ever.

O ye Wells, bless ye the Lord : praise him, and magnify him for ever.

O ye Seas and Floods, bless ye the Lord : praise him, and magnify him for ever.

O ye Whales, and all that move in the Waters, bless ye the Lord : praise him, and magnify him for ever.

O all ye Fowls of the Air, bless ye the Lord : praise him, and magnify him for ever.

O all ye Beasts and Cattle, bless ye the Lord : praise him, and magnify him for ever.

—PRAYER OF AZARIAH[1]

Yahweh as Creation's Governor

A NUMBER OF BIBLICAL passages are habitually cited to support the doctrine of a fallen creation, of which the most important are in the first three chapters of Genesis. However, before I deal with those in detail, it will be instructive to look at what the Bible says about God's relationship with the

1. *Prayer of Azariah (Bendicite), vv52–60, from Book of Common Prayer (1662).*

3

natural creation in our world *as it is*—the world after the fall of humankind. I will deal with the usual key passages in the next chapter.

I propose to bypass, for the most part, God's relationship to human agency, although it is important in its own right, in order to concentrate on the nonhuman creation, which is the matter in question. In Scripture, God's sovereignty over nature is not sharply distinguished from his sovereignty over human affairs, but the aim of this study is to point out that what happened to humankind in the garden did *not* spread to the rest of the world, the "irrational creatures."

Another reason for steering clear of the interface between sovereignty and sinful human will is that, particularly amongst theistic evolutionists, there is a chronic confusion between "free will" and various concepts of "autonomy" applied improperly to inanimate nature, a confusion that I do not propose to perpetuate here.[2] For both of these reasons I will concentrate on the creation apart from humanity.

As is generally the case, the Old Testament is the best source from which to establish the basic foundations of biblical religion, on which the gospel is built. And a good place to start this study, for our purposes, is the list of blessings and curses associated with the Mosaic covenant.

It is now pretty well accepted in Old Testament scholarship that the Jewish "law" or *torah*, the first five books of our Bible (the *Pentateuch*), has a close affinity with ancient near eastern treaty documents, and particularly with those of the Hittites in the second millennium BCE.[3] The pattern of Israel's covenant with Yahweh follows that of the treaties that powerful kings would make with their vassals.

The book of Deuteronomy, which consists largely of Moses's discourse to Israel as they prepare to cross the Jordan, follows the pattern of such a treaty in its entirety. The pattern in the rest of the Pentateuch is broken up with law codes, narrative, and so on, but one can still discern part of the pattern of such a covenant document in the account of Moses on Mount Sinai in Exodus, and in Leviticus. The covenant is also restated in the book of Joshua.

Old Testament and ancient near east scholar John H. Walton gives the basic elements of an ancient near east treaty as follows:

2. Theistic evolution tends to follow naturalism in excluding *teleology* within living things, yet espouses "Nature's" ateleological *autonomy*. For the sake of argument I follow them on the first aspect here, though both Scripture and the latest biology imply a degree of inherent teleology in nature.

3. Kitchen, *Reliability of the Old Testament*, 283–94. Quite probably other nations had such treaties at the time: the Hittites' are those that have come down to us, giving the most convincing geo-historical setting for the Pentateuchal covenants.

Introduction of the speaker

Historical prologue

Stipulations

Divine witnesses

Curses and blessings[4]

In the Exodus account of the making of the covenant, the first heading (introduction of the speaker) is limited to 20:2.

> "I am the LORD your God, who brought you out of Egypt, out of the land of slavery."

The historical prologue occurs in 19:3–6, in which God describes how he has brought Israel to himself, out of Egypt, and offers them the covenant—that they will be his treasured possession if they are faithful to him.

The stipulations are primarily the Ten Commandments of 20:3–17. A typical ANE treaty would, at this point, have items such as the paying of tribute, providing military support, and showing general faithfulness to the king making the treaty. The Ten Commandments, however, being part of a treaty with God as King rather than with an earthly ruler, instead embody faithfulness to Yahweh in the "first table," and faithfulness to brother-Israelites in the "second table."

Their role as covenant stipulations explains their global scope and ethical basis. They are not "laws" as such, for they would be practically unenforceable. Instead they stipulate what kind of people the Israelites are to be, if they are to stay faithful to the gracious covenant God has made with them, having rescued them from Pharaoh's power. And, like the treaties made elsewhere in the ANE, Israel's copy is kept for reference in the temple of their god—in this case, of course, the two tables of stone kept in the ark of the covenant in the tabernacle.[5]

Coming to the matter in hand, the Ten Commandments are backed up by a series of blessings and curses, just as were ANE treaty stipulations. Walton says that even in these political treaties, it was the gods who were the agents who would bless compliance or, more often, punish violation.[6] The biblical blessings and curses are most clearly set out in Leviticus 26, though they are also seen in Deuteronomy 28 and Joshua 24. First the blessings:

---

4. Walton, *Ancient Israelite Literature*, 101.

5. Exod 25:10–16; Deut 10:3–5.

6. Walton, *Ancient Israelite Literature*, 104–5.

³ "'If you follow my decrees and are careful to obey my commands, ⁴ I will send you rain in its season, and the ground will yield its crops and the trees their fruit. ⁵ Your threshing will continue until grape harvest and the grape harvest will continue until planting, and you will eat all the food you want and live in safety in your land.

⁶ "'I will grant peace in the land, and you will lie down and no one will make you afraid. I will remove wild beasts from the land, and the sword will not pass through your country. ⁷ You will pursue your enemies, and they will fall by the sword before you. ⁸ Five of you will chase a hundred, and a hundred of you will chase ten thousand, and your enemies will fall by the sword before you.

⁹ "'I will look on you with favor and make you fruitful and increase your numbers, and I will keep my covenant with you. ¹⁰ You will still be eating last year's harvest when you will have to move it out to make room for the new. ¹¹ I will put my dwelling place among you, and I will not abhor you. ¹² I will walk among you and be your God, and you will be my people. ¹³ I am the LORD your God, who brought you out of Egypt so that you would no longer be slaves to the Egyptians; I broke the bars of your yoke and enabled you to walk with heads held high.'"[7]

Note how much of this has to do with nature's provision. And then come the (rather longer) curses:

¹⁴ "'But if you will not listen to me and carry out all these commands, ¹⁵ and if you reject my decrees and abhor my laws and fail to carry out all my commands and so violate my covenant, ¹⁶ then I will do this to you: I will bring on you sudden terror, wasting diseases and fever that will destroy your sight and sap your strength. You will plant seed in vain, because your enemies will eat it. ¹⁷ I will set my face against you so that you will be defeated by your enemies; those who hate you will rule over you, and you will flee even when no one is pursuing you.

¹⁸ "'If after all this you will not listen to me, I will punish you for your sins seven times over. ¹⁹ I will break down your stubborn pride and make the sky above you like iron and the ground beneath you like bronze. ²⁰ Your strength will be spent in vain, because your soil will not yield its crops, nor will the trees of your land yield their fruit.

²¹ "'If you remain hostile toward me and refuse to listen to me, I will multiply your afflictions seven times over, as your sins

7. Lev 26:3–13.

deserve. ²² I will send wild animals against you, and they will rob you of your children, destroy your cattle and make you so few in number that your roads will be deserted.

²³ "'If in spite of these things you do not accept my correction but continue to be hostile toward me, ²⁴ I myself will be hostile toward you and will afflict you for your sins seven times over. ²⁵ And I will bring the sword on you to avenge the breaking of the covenant. When you withdraw into your cities, I will send a plague among you, and you will be given into enemy hands. ²⁶ When I cut off your supply of bread, ten women will be able to bake your bread in one oven, and they will dole out the bread by weight. You will eat, but you will not be satisfied.

²⁷ "'If in spite of this you still do not listen to me but continue to be hostile toward me, ²⁸ then in my anger I will be hostile toward you, and I myself will punish you for your sins seven times over. ²⁹ You will eat the flesh of your sons and the flesh of your daughters. ³⁰ I will destroy your high places, cut down your incense altars and pile your dead bodies on the lifeless forms of your idols, and I will abhor you. ³¹ I will turn your cities into ruins and lay waste your sanctuaries, and I will take no delight in the pleasing aroma of your offerings. ³² I myself will lay waste the land, so that your enemies who live there will be appalled. ³³ I will scatter you among the nations and will draw out my sword and pursue you. Your land will be laid waste, and your cities will lie in ruins. ³⁴ Then the land will enjoy its sabbath years all the time that it lies desolate and you are in the country of your enemies; then the land will rest and enjoy its sabbaths. ³⁵ All the time that it lies desolate, the land will have the rest it did not have during the sabbaths you lived in it.

³⁶ "'As for those of you who are left, I will make their hearts so fearful in the lands of their enemies that the sound of a wind-blown leaf will put them to flight. They will run as though fleeing from the sword, and they will fall, even though no one is pursuing them. ³⁷ They will stumble over one another as though fleeing from the sword, even though no one is pursuing them. So you will not be able to stand before your enemies. ³⁸ You will perish among the nations; the land of your enemies will devour you. ³⁹ Those of you who are left will waste away in the lands of their enemies because of their sins; also because of their ancestors' sins they will waste away.'"⁸

8. Lev 26:14–39.

For our purpose the key thing to notice here is that Yahweh, as well as human enemies, uses the creation as his reliable and obedient agent both for blessing *and* for cursing. In fact, the very same elements are used in both ways. And so in the blessings section, we read that God promises to send regular rains and bring forth crops from the soil. He will grant Israel peace, and remove wild animals from the land (which in practice, of course, means they will go to live elsewhere). He will also grant them fertility, and dwell among them.

If they break the covenant, however, he will bring defeat, wasting diseases, fevers, and anxiety. He will withhold rain and bring famine, send wild animals against them, and destroy them with plagues.

Now, unlike some other episodes in the Bible, such as the plagues of Egypt, these actions are not presented as signs, or miraculous interventions against the usual run of things, but as the way that God routinely manages the nation he has established and brought into covenant relationship. Israel will *always* be experiencing either God's blessing or God's punishment, and most often these will be manifested through God's deployment of the powers of the natural creation.

A key doctrinal point can be made quite clearly from this: one reason for Yahweh's creation of the natural order is so that it will be his instrument of government *for* the world, and especially for the human world that is the prime focus of his concern. The things in the world exist not, primarily, for their own sake, but in order to serve Yahweh's governing purposes day by day.

The blessings and curses demonstrate that everything in creation does, indeed, do God's bidding quite willingly to achieve his ends. According to what he commands, the weather will either be beneficial and productive, or violent and destructive. The wild beasts will either withdraw harmlessly into uninhabited places, or act as marauders in town and villages, according to his purpose. The bacteria and parasites (if we may view things in that modern manner) will be harmless or will produce epidemics, just as he wills.

God, then, actively commands all aspects of nature, and whether these act benignly or wreak destruction depends on the outworking of God's sovereign justice and mercy. Nature itself, therefore—by which we mean nature in the world *after* the fall—must surely be regarded as "good," for it is utterly obedient to the will of its maker.

We may well conclude that, had humankind not become guilty of sin, God would employ the elements more uniformly benignly towards us, always bringing blessing rather than cursing. But the fact that they do not reflects the change in *our* relationship with God to one of enmity,[9] and not a change in the character of the elements themselves.

Now the collection of blessings and curses in Leviticus brings these elements of creation together in one place, but there are a multitude of other passages that show how God actually exercised his lordship over nature through Israel's history. There are many more to show that his active rule, through an obedient nature, is not confined to his dealings with the covenant people, but characterizes his rule over the world as a whole.

Weather

The weather, in particular, is said in Scripture to be God's agent of government:

> [3] He makes the clouds his chariot
>   and rides on the wings of the wind.
> [4] He makes winds his messengers,
>   flames of fire his servants.[10]

For example, Psalm 65 describes God's care for the land through his control of rainfall:

> [9] You care for the land and water it;
>   you enrich it abundantly.
> The streams of God are filled with water
>   to provide the people with grain,
>   for so you have ordained it.
> [10] You drench its furrows and level its ridges;
>   you soften it with showers and bless its crops.
> [11] You crown the year with your bounty,
>   and your carts overflow with abundance.
> [12] The grasslands of the wilderness overflow;
>   the hills are clothed with gladness.
> [13] The meadows are covered with flocks
>   and the valleys are mantled with grain;
>   they shout for joy and sing.[11]

The book of Job, in a remarkable passage in chapters 36–37, not only describes the hydrological cycle accurately, but shows that God's judicial use of the weather is broader than Israel both geographically,

9. Rom 5:10; Col 1:21.

10. Ps 104:3–4.

11. Ps 65:9–13.

> [31] This is the way he governs the nations
>   and provides food in abundance,[12]

and in the range of divine purposes it serves: it provides abundance (36:28, 31; 37:13), punishes sin (37:13), or simply shows his glory (36:29–30; 37:4–8). In some cases his reasons, as well as his methods, for bringing the weather that he does remain mysterious and simply excite wonder (37:14–18). The last, in particular, reminds us that part of God's sustaining work is in keeping the systems of the world running smoothly quite apart from issues of justice towards humanity—what we would consider to be "maintaining the natural order."

Other examples of God's complete control of the weather include his sending of an east wind to drive back the Reed Sea (Exod 14), sending thunder and rain out of season to highlight Israel's sin (1 Sam 12:18), showing his sovereignty against Baal (a storm god) by bringing and ending drought through Elijah (1 Kgs 17–18), and commanding wind, earthquake and fire in order to instruct Elijah (1 Kgs 19). He is also responsible for snow, frost, hail, and insupportable icy winds—and then for melting them again with his word and with the breeze (Ps 147:15–18). In the New Testament too Paul tells the Lystrans that God witnesses to himself by giving them rain, crops, plenty, and joy (Acts 14:17).[13]

Crops

The weather, as some of the passages above indicate, is inextricably linked to times of plenty and famine. And crops themselves are uniformly said to be under God's control in Scripture. Even before the settlement in Canaan God blesses Isaac with an exceptional crop (Gen 26:12–14), and makes both Laban and Jacob rich by blessing their livestock (Gen 30:27–43; 32:9–15).

The seven years of plenty followed by seven years of famine, described in Genesis 41 and the ensuing chapters, is explicitly explained by Joseph when interpreting Pharaoh's dream to be what *God* is about to do. In this case God's purposes are described in some depth, and are complex. God is honored by the fulfillment of the prophecy, and through Joseph's good management. Joseph himself is honored, making him able to benefit his family to the point of their settling in Goshen. Pharaoh's power increases through the changes in land ownership in Egypt. The malevolence of Joseph's brothers is

---

12. Job 36:31.

13. Other weather references include Job 38:23–30, 34–38; Ps 29:3–9 (where the elements are actually God's voice); Jer 10:12; Jonah 1:4; Hag 1:5–11.

turned to God's intended good. And, of course, the course determined for Israel's history at the time of God's covenant with Abraham (Gen 15:13–14) is fulfilled, and the Covenant preserved. God's management of nature is therefore not to be seen in a simplistic way as the caprice of a bad-tempered deity, but as the ongoing business of wise government.

Even the Jubilee law is predicated on God's undertaking to give triple harvests to allow the land to lie fallow (Lev 25:20–22). His rule is an active one in every way.

The elements are never independent of God

Now there are instances in Scripture where natural phenomena of extreme weather, famine, and so on are mentioned without any specific references to God's actions or intentions. But it should not be understood from this that these things "just happen" apart from God's will. That would be alien to the whole Hebrew worldview. Rather, when things are described phenomenologically, without reference to divine intent, we are to suppose that God is going about his "own business" and that his particular motives are hidden from us, or are just irrelevant to the narrative.

And so the famine of Genesis 12, which takes Abraham to Egypt, and that of chapter 26, which takes Isaac to Abimelech, cannot be ascribed to "chance" or forces alien to God in the light of what is revealed about the great events of the famine sent by God in Joseph's time, even though the earlier situations appear to threaten the covenant. God is at work even in these.

In a similar way the storm that shipwrecks Paul in Acts 27 is presented as a happenstance, and so could be taken as a convulsion of uncontrolled nature (see chapter 4), or even as Satan's attempt to prevent Paul getting to Rome—though the latter is not in the least hinted by the text. Yet the storm is set in the context of Paul's whole apostolic calling, and of several prophecies regarding his trip to Rome, and within a theology and literary theme of Christ's sovereignty over all things because of his glorification, including over the chaos that goes with "sea" in Hebrew thought.

On the one hand, such a storm was a normal seasonal possibility, although not anticipated by the experienced sailors. Yet Paul prophesied it, with its catastrophic results on the voyage, when they reached Fair Havens in Crete: and predictive prophecy is usually about what *God* is going to do. God's control is such that he undertakes to save all 276 people on board, through a foretold shipwreck, only on condition that (in a rather allegorically charged way) they all stay on board with Paul. The storm becomes the very means by which God is glorified in Malta, and the means by which

Paul gets to Rome. It would seem to belong within the realm of "mysterious providence" better than within any idea of nature working against God.

Regarding this passage one must also note the close, and probably deliberate, parallel/contrast with the story of Jonah. Jonah was an unwilling prophet fleeing from God; Paul, a faithful apostle braving everything to go where God wanted him, despite prophetic warnings from God that his death would ensue. In Jonah, the storm is overtly sent by God. Why would Paul's not be also?

Another instance, back in the Old Testament, of a major disaster not accorded great theological significance is the earthquake during the reign of King Uzziah. This was severe enough to have left destruction levels in archaeological sites of that period.[14] The earthquake is referenced as a time marker in Amos 1:1-2 (whose initial oracles had come two years before). There is little sign that the earthquake is regarded as judicially significant there apart, perhaps, as a rumbling warning of future judgement. The same earthquake is mentioned historically in Zechariah 14:5—also in relation to God's future judgement. Such catastrophes may occur, then, without clear "messages" as to their divine purpose, but never apart from God's intentions, albeit hidden. The elements are doing God's bidding, not bucking his rule.

A few passages in the Old Testament do speak of God's ability to rescue from the elements, as if he were in conflict with them. Such is Psalm 46:

> [1] God is our refuge and strength,
>   an ever-present help in trouble.
> [2] Therefore we will not fear, though the earth give way
>   and the mountains fall into the heart of the sea,
> [3] though its waters roar and foam
>   and the mountains quake with their surging.[15]

Yet even here the psalm ends with an invitation to see the works of Yahweh, "the desolations he has brought on the earth." Similarly, in Psalm 75:2-3, God's judgement is expressed in terms of an earthquake, but its destruction is held in check by his holding the earth's pillars firm. God's power over the wildest elements, not their rebellion against him, is what is in view in such passages.

Another infrequent theme that, superficially, might suggest a natural element opposed to God, is the occasional reference to the sea monster Rahab and God's subduing of it (Job 9:13; 26:12; Ps 89:10; Isa 51:9). Whilst these few references certainly refer to the Canaanite myth of the subduing of the chaotic primordial ocean at creation, they appear to represent

---

14. Kitchen, *Reliability of the Old Testament*, 53.

15. Ps 46:1-3.

the borrowing of a graphic folktale rather than of pagan theology. "Rahab" may well loosely represent the theme in Genesis 1 of "chaos" (*tohu wabohu*) being pushed aside to bring order, and the term is also used figuratively of Egypt, as the "monster" that God comprehensively defeated when he delivered Israel across the Reed Sea (Ps 87:4; Isa 30:7). But old comparisons of Genesis 1 with the battle between Marduk and Tiamat in the Babylonian *Enuma Elish* are now seen to be invalid.[16] Monotheistic sovereignty pervades these accounts.

There is a strong reminder of this in Jesus's calming of the storm on the Sea of Galilee. The word used by Jesus in all three Gospel accounts, "rebuke," is that used in the Septuagint version of Psalm 104, in which God's creative power over primal disorder, not his quelling of an evil rival, is in view:

> [5] He set the earth on its foundations;
>   it can never be moved.
> [6] You covered it with the watery depths as with a garment;
>   the waters stood above the mountains.
> [7] But at your *rebuke* the waters fled,
>   at the sound of your thunder they took to flight;
> [8] they flowed over the mountains,
>   they went down into the valleys,
>   to the place you assigned for them.[17]

God's first work here is to cover the earth with waters, and his second to "rebuke" them into separating the oceans from the land, on the third day of the Genesis creation account. Jesus likewise is controlling his own creation, not opposing an alien one. And so there is no sense in which nature's elemental forces are ever portrayed with any rebellious attitudes against God—he remains their ruler, and they remain his instruments for blessing or cursing.

One more word on the elements, and that is on the idea that *Satan* might ever control them.[18] The person of Satan appears only sketchily in the Old Testament, but once (and once only) he is said to exercise some control over nature. That is in the story of Job, which although clearly set as a theological discourse rather than as *reportage*, nevertheless employs serious theology.

In Job chapter 1 Satan sends a destructive fire (v16) and a mighty wind (v19), and of course in chapter 2 the most famous boils in history (2:7). But it's essential to understand that Satan is represented here as a morally

16. Walton, *Ancient Israelite Literature*, 34–38.

17. Ps 104:5–8.

18. See chapter 5 for a more detailed treatment.

ambiguous, but obedient, "son of God" (i.e., a member of the "heavenly council") who acts only under the direct permission of God, and as the rest of the book shows, ultimately in a mysterious way for Job's blessing. It therefore seems no coincidence that the tools he uses, especially in the first chapter, are those most commonly associated with God's own judgements: the fire is "the fire of God," and the "mighty wind" is like those everywhere else ascribed to God's agency.

Health and disease

Good health is one of the Covenant blessings promised to the children of Israel, and it is specifically contrasted with the ill health of the Egyptians they have left behind (Exod 15:26; Deut 7:15)—don't believe all those fit-looking people in idealized Egyptian art! Those diseases, God says, he himself had "brought on the Egyptians"—not meaning the final plagues before the Exodus, but the general state of the nation Israel had inhabited for four centuries. We might refer to it as "an unhealthy climate." The pattern of routinely blessing and cursing is evident, once more, in God's treatment of the nations apart from Israel, even though not in covenant relationship.

In like manner, under the covenant curses and in other contexts, God is said to be the direct cause of sicknesses and diseases. Those covenant curses are mentioned elsewhere in imminent or actual fulfilment (e.g., Jer 14:12; Ezek 14:19–20; Amos 4:9–10). In Habakkuk 3 the glorious coming of God in deliverance is *marked* by sickness:

> [3] God came from Teman,
>   the Holy One from Mount Paran.
> His glory covered the heavens
>   and his praise filled the earth.
> [4] His splendor was like the sunrise;
>   rays flashed from his hand,
>   where his power was hidden.
> [5] Plague went before him;
>   pestilence followed his steps.[19]

But other examples of God's active use of ill health in governance include the disease put on Pharaoh's household because of Sarah (Gen 12:17), the sterility put on Abimelech's wives (Gen 20:17), and tumors inflicted on the Philistines for taking the ark of the covenant (1 Sam 5:9–12). Even the Levitical laws refer to the treatment of spreading mildew

---

19. Hab 3:3–5.

in a house as enlisting priestly help for an affliction that God himself has caused (Lev 14:34).

Lest we think that the idea of God using illness in his (righteous) judgement is restricted to the Old Testament, we should remember Paul's attribution of weakness and sickness, and even death, to chastisement for the abuse of the Lord's Supper (1 Cor 11:30–32).

As in the case of the "elements," though, there are instances in both the Old and New Testaments of illnesses being treated as mere happenstance. For example, King Asa had bad feet (2 Chron 16:12), King Hezekiah had life-threatening sepsis (Isa 38:1–22), Paul got sick in Galatia (Gal 4:13), and Epaphroditus nearly died from a disease possibly caught visiting Paul in prison (Phil 2:25–27). And Timothy had many ailments.[20]

Like Job's boils, Jesus himself attributes diseases to the agency of Satan (e.g. Luke 13:16), whom he is committed to defeating. And yet even then there are hints that God's "active" permission, and mysterious providence, are as operative here as in the case of Job: in John chapter 9, when the disciples ask Jesus whose sin caused a man to be congenitally blind, Jesus emphasizes that "this happened so that the work of God might be displayed in his life."[21] Jesus makes no attempt either to blunt the mystery of God, or to exonerate him as the sole final cause of all things.

Wild animals

Considering that the wild beasts are the part of creation most often considered to have become corrupted in the fall of humanity, they are remarkably commonly used by God in his government of the world.

Wild animals bringing direct blessing are comparatively rare, but one notable exception is the pair of ravens, largely carnivorous birds, which God sends to feed Elijah during the drought, and which obediently bring him bread and meat until their instructions change (1 Kgs 17:4–6).

As for judgements, perhaps it is worth taking a whistle-stop tour through the animal kingdom to give examples of those creatures which God names as his agents:

Gnats (Exod 8:16–18)

Flies (Exod 8:20–31)

Locusts (Exod 10:1–19; Joel 1–2; Amos 4:9, 7:1)

20. 1 Tim 5:23.
21. John 9:3.

Frogs (Exod 8:1–14)

Snakes (Num 21:4–9)

Birds (Jer 15:3)

Dogs (Jer 15:3)

Bears (2 Kgs 2:23)

Generic wild beasts (Jer 15:3; Ezek 14:15–16)

In addition to these, the general judgement of God himself is likened figuratively to another menagerie of fierce creatures:

Lions (Isa 31:4; Jer 4:5, 5:6)

Wolves (Jer 5:6)

Leopards (Jer 5:6)

Birds of prey (Isa 46:11)

Snakes (Jer 7:17)

It is incongruous to consider God identifying his own actions with such creatures if, as the "traditional view" says, they are corrupted and evil. That is especially so since most of the animals he uses, or emulates, in judgement are the carnivores alleged to result only from sin. If, however, as the old theologians said, each of God's creatures reveals some aspect of God's character, then each has its appropriate place in his works. There is, after all, "a time for everything, and a season for every activity under heaven."[22]

God's care of creation "for its own sake"

Although I have shown above that God's creation should be seen as the instrument he has designed for his own use, and which now faithfully serves his purposes in his kingly government of the world, this is not to suggest that he is careless of its welfare. In that sense he is both a careful workman looking after his tools, and a kind husbandman, having regard to the welfare of his stock. Anything less would be quite alien to the biblical concept of his loving character. The clearest descriptions of his care towards the nonhuman creation are in passages from Job, and in the Psalms.

22. Eccl 3:1.

Job

In Job chapter 12 the animals are called to witness their dependence on God's care moment by moment:

> [7] "But ask the animals, and they will teach you,
>   or the birds in the sky, and they will tell you;
> [8] or speak to the earth, and it will teach you,
>   or let the fish in the sea inform you.
> [9] Which of all these does not know
>   that the hand of the LORD has done this?
> [10] In his hand is the life of every creature
>   and the breath of all mankind."[23]

But a key passage comes later in chapter 38, in which God is showing Job the wisdom of his dealings with his world, at this stage stressing his care—even workmanlike pride—in the details of what he has made.

> [39] "Do you hunt the prey for the lioness
> and satisfy the hunger of the lions
> [40] when they crouch in their dens
> or lie in wait in a thicket?
> [41] Who provides food for the raven
> when its young cry out to God
> and wander about for lack of food?
>
> 39 "Do you know when the mountain goats give birth?
>   Do you watch when the doe bears her fawn?
> [2] Do you count the months till they bear?
>   Do you know the time they give birth?
> [3] They crouch down and bring forth their young;
>   their labor pains are ended.
> [4] Their young thrive and grow strong in the wilds;
>   they leave and do not return.
>
> [5] "Who let the wild donkey go free?
>   Who untied its ropes?
> [6] I gave it the wasteland as its home,
>   the salt flats as its habitat.
> [7] It laughs at the commotion in the town;
>   it does not hear a driver's shout.
> [8] It ranges the hills for its pasture
>   and searches for any green thing.

---

23. Job 12:7–10.

9 "Will the wild ox consent to serve you?
  Will it stay by your manger at night?
10 Can you hold it to the furrow with a harness?
  Will it till the valleys behind you?
11 Will you rely on it for its great strength?
  Will you leave your heavy work to it?
12 Can you trust it to haul in your grain
  and bring it to your threshing floor?

13 "The wings of the ostrich flap joyfully,
  though they cannot compare
  with the wings and feathers of the stork.
14 She lays her eggs on the ground
  and lets them warm in the sand,
15 unmindful that a foot may crush them,
  that some wild animal may trample them.
16 She treats her young harshly, as if they were not hers;
  she cares not that her labor was in vain,
17 for God did not endow her with wisdom
  or give her a share of good sense.
18 Yet when she spreads her feathers to run,
  she laughs at horse and rider.

19 "Do you give the horse its strength
  or clothe its neck with a flowing mane?
20 Do you make it leap like a locust,
  striking terror with its proud snorting?
21 It paws fiercely, rejoicing in its strength,
  and charges into the fray.
22 It laughs at fear, afraid of nothing;
  it does not shy away from the sword.
23 The quiver rattles against its side,
  along with the flashing spear and lance.
24 In frenzied excitement it eats up the ground;
  it cannot stand still when the trumpet sounds.
25 At the blast of the trumpet it snorts, 'Aha!'
  It catches the scent of battle from afar,
  the shout of commanders and the battle cry.

26 "Does the hawk take flight by your wisdom
  and spread its wings toward the south?
27 Does the eagle soar at your command
  and build its nest on high?
28 It dwells on a cliff and stays there at night;
  a rocky crag is its stronghold.

²⁹ From there it looks for food;
    its eyes detect it from afar.
³⁰ Its young ones feast on blood,
    and where the slain are, there it is."²⁴

It seems hard to conceive how anyone could read this and still think that God considers his creatures to be corrupt in any way. He is equally enthusiastic about the carnivores whose prey he procures (lions, ravens, hawks, and eagles) as the herbivores (mountain goats, wild donkeys, wild oxen, ostriches, and horses). He delights in the quirky stupidity of his ostriches, and glories in the very untamability of his donkeys and wild oxen. His showcase example of a horse is, of all things, a warhorse.

At Job 40:15 God begins his long descriptions of *behemoth* and *leviathan*. *Behemoth* might be the hippopotamus, or perhaps the elephant, and *leviathan* the crocodile rather than the mythical sea monster of that name. But the whole point is that, whatever their identity, these are the most dangerous and unfriendly of all creatures—and yet these are the very characteristics in which God exults as their maker and custodian. There is no sense of God's simply being able to master "fallen monsters" better than can humanity: "Who has a claim against me that I must pay? Everything under heaven belongs to me."²⁵

Psalms

Psalm 104 is another important passage about God's intimate care of his creatures, which once more shows no distinction between fierce and gentle. He directs his streams of water to feed all things—wild donkeys, birds, cattle, crops, wild goats, and rock hyrax. He brings night specifically so the forest hunters and the lions can get their prey whilst humankind rests. He cares for all the creatures in the sea, even the leviathan he "formed to frolic there."²⁶ They all look trustingly on God for their food, who governs their birth, death, and replenishment.

In Psalm 65 God's care of the land through the rainfall not only benefits humankind, but nature too "shouts for joy and sings,"²⁷ as though nobody had told it that it was supposed to be corrupted. And this is not surprising since Psalm 145 tells us that God is loving to all he has made, feeding them at the proper time and satisfying all their desires.

24. Job 38:39—39:30.

25. Job 41:11.

26. Ps 104:26: in this case perhaps "leviathan" signals the whale, several species of which are seen in the Eastern Mediterranean.

27. Ps 65:13.

God the householder

To draw together this picture of God's relationship to his natural creation, Scripture often speaks of the Lord as a landowner. In Leviticus 25:23 he reminds Israel, in the context of social justice, that he is the landowner of Canaan, and they only his tenants. Psalm 50:10 extends his ownership to the beasts of the forest and the cattle on a thousand hills. Jeremiah 27:5 tells us that this proprietorship extends to the whole world, since he created its people and all its animals, and that he gives the earth to whoever he pleases (in this case, unfortunately for Judah, to the Babylonians). Deuteronomy 10:14 extends his ownership even to the highest heavens.

But there is a danger that this description can summon up the image of an "eastern potentate" exercising absolute despotism over an empire from a distance. Apart from the fact that the average eastern potentate was a good deal more in touch with his people than, say, a US President, the "king" image may lead us to forget just what a hands-on kind of care has been shown in the passages I have cited.

A complementary image, with a good basis in the creation narrative itself, is of God as a householder, with the world as his household or farmstead, and humankind as his children (though the "house" in Genesis 1 is actually a temple[28]). Now those of us who are the heads of families know that, although our house provides a roof over our head, and produce for the table, it's primarily a home for the nurture of a family.

We may give our growing children increasing responsibilities, just as Psalm 8 tells us that God has delegated the rule of earth's creatures to humanity, and we also give them house rules to follow and discipline them when they don't follow them, just as we have seen that God judges the world daily through the creation. But at least until our children are close to adulthood, they have little understanding of how much we do to run the whole household on their behalf, and that we allow nothing into it that will detract from that.

The children are unaware of our regular maintenance, of our paying the bills, and of our making sure there is always food on the table. If there are pets it will usually be the householder who thinks about their vaccinations and problems (or perhaps working livestock is a better analogy than

---

28. The temple imagery in Genesis 1 was identified by the unconventional sixth-century monk Cosmas Indicopleustes (*Christian Topography*), a fascinating (and illustrated!) read, but he has received little credit for what, in recent years, has become increasingly recognized by many scholars as a key theme. A full account of its use in Genesis is set out in Walton, *Genesis 1 as Ancient Cosmology*, but the centrality of the theme in Hebrew thought right up to New Testament times can be found in, for example, Beale, *The Temple and the Church's Mission;* Middleton, *A New Heaven and a New Earth;* and Wright, *Jesus and the Victory of God.* See the further discussion in chapter 4.

pets, like the backyard chickens that provide eggs as well as enabling us to train the children in their proper care).

Just as in God's world, there is a sense in which our house exists "for its own sake"—we care for it because it is valuable, maybe even beautiful, and fill it with beautiful things. Houses even make some kind of statement about their owners, just as the glory of creation speaks of God's own majesty. But in the end, it is the family—the kids—around whose development the home revolves, or should. The house is an instrument, or a whole set of instruments, for their benefit, albeit that it is loved and cared for in its own right.

A household is also a personally established world, and not a public institution. It's vitally important to retain the truth that God is the *sole* Creator (Isa 44:24, 45:18; Jer 27:5, Amos 4:13; John 1:3, Col 1:16; Heb 1:3). The biblical picture we have covered really leaves no place for the idea, common in theistic evolution, that God delegates to creation the ability to help create itself[29] (which is a pretty incoherent idea philosophically anyway[30]). But neither does it leave a place for creation to be partly a work of "sin," and still less of Satan, contra the quotation from C. H. Spurgeon in the introduction to this book.

Nothing in what we have examined in this chapter, covering the whole sweep of Old and New Testament teaching about the creation as it is, gives any hint that some other agent has corrupted the natural world, nor that God himself has altered its nature for the worse because of human sin, nor that it has corrupted itself. If God uses it for harm, it is because of humanity's desert, not because of nature's corruption. We now need to turn to examine the Scriptures that are most often cited to claim the opposite. As Terence Fretheim puts it:

> What is important to stress here is that such consequences are the effect of *creaturely* irresponsibility and God's judgemental response and not that of some evil forces.[31]

---

29. "I prefer to see the same history in the light of a God who desires to share aspects of his nature with his creation, notably including his creativity. Just as he has made humans to be creators (with a little 'c'), he has given the rest of our world the gift of being instrumental in its own creation through the process of evolution." Tice, *Oxygen and Co-Creation*. Tice is a geobiologist.

30. "Nothing can be the efficient cause of itself" (Aquinas, *Summa Theologiae,* Part 1:2:A3). "But whereas one understood an evolution in which the less issued from the greater wherein it was contained, that form of evolution in which the greater continually springs from the less is incomprehensible. It at least deserves no more to be called e-volution"(Gilson, *From Aristotle to Darwin,* 103).

31. Fretheim, *God and World,* 45.

Chapter 2—Scripture on the Fall

But I cannot deny that I find still lingering here and there certain of the old views of nature of which I used to hear but too much here in London some five-and-thirty years ago. . . . that this Earth did not reveal the will and character of God, because it was cursed and fallen; and that its facts, in consequence, were not to be respected or relied on. This, I was told, was the doctrine of Scripture, and was therefore true. But when, longing to reconcile my conscience and my reason on a question so awful to a young student of natural science, I went to my Bible, what did I find? No word of all this. Much—thank God, I may say one continuous undercurrent—of the very opposite of all this.

—CHARLES KINGSLEY (1819–75)[1]

Adam and death

AS WE TURN TO the passages of Scripture most often cited when considering the "fallen creation" the most useful place to begin will be the stern warning God gives Adam when he is placed in the garden.

> [15] The LORD God took the man and put him in the Garden of Eden to work it and take care of it. [16] And the LORD God commanded the man, "You are free to eat from any tree in the garden; [17] but you must not eat from the tree of the knowledge of good and evil, for when you eat from it you will certainly die."[2]

It is unnecessary for this discussion to spend too long discussing the exact nature of the tree. Like others John H. Walton, after an in-depth word

1. Kingsley, *Natural Theology*.
2. Gen 2:15–17.

study, concludes that "good and evil" is a merism (i.e., including all that lies on the spectrum between extremes), indicating "discerning or discriminating wisdom."[3] This is consistent with Eve's observation that the fruit was "desirable for gaining wisdom."[4] In fact, The Jewish historian Josephus, writing in the first century, also refers to it as "the tree of wisdom,"[5] and so does the Jewish philosopher Philo.[6]

Since wisdom is something both desirable and later offered as a gift by God (see Proverbs chapters 1–9) we must suppose that God always intended that wisdom should sooner or later be learned by Adam through communion with him in the garden (as *torah* was later to be imbibed in childhood for adulthood[7]) rather than being seized prematurely. After all, "the fear of Yahweh is the beginning of wisdom,"[8] and it was the due fear of God that was lacking in the act of taking the forbidden fruit. Paul, commentating on the fall, indicates that what was gained as "human wisdom" was, in fact, folly:

> [22] Although they claimed to be wise, they became fools . . . [9]

In any event, it is noteworthy that the warning was given to Adam alone, and the penalty for disobedience—death—was given to him alone too. The focus on Adam himself in this is maintained throughout the Bible, for though Eve is the one deceived into eating, it is Adam whose punishment is linked to it,[10] who alone is named as the one excluded from the

---

3. Walton, *Genesis*, 170–72.

4. Gen 3:6.

5. Josephus, *Ant.* 1:40 (Maier, *Josephus*, 20).

6. "For, as [Moses] intimates, it is *prudence*, and this is the science of knowing, through which good and beautiful things and bad and ugly things are distinguished; and (the science of knowing) all things which are contrary to each other, of which the one is of a superior order, and the other of an inferior order. Now the wisdom which is in this world is not God but is truly the work of God; it sees nature and studies it. But the wisdom which is in man sees with dim eyes, confusing one thing with another, for it is weak in seeing and understanding purely, simply, clearly each thing by itself alone. Wherefore with man's wisdom a kind of deception is mixed, in the same manner as to the eyes certain shadows are often an impediment to catching sight of unmixed and pure light." (Philo, *Questions*, 11.)

7. "These commandments that I give you today are to be on your hearts. Impress them on your children. Talk about them when you sit at home and when you walk along the road, when you lie down and when you get up. Tie them as symbols on your hands and bind them on your foreheads. Write them on the doorframes of your houses and on your gates." (Deut 6:4–9.)

8. Prov 1:7.

9. Rom 1:22.

10. Gen 3:17.

garden and from eternal life[11] and who is said later to be the one through whom sin and death entered the world.[12] So there is a sense in which Eve seems to share his punishment under some kind of "federal headship" model, rather than in her own individual right. The text itself does not make any comment about Adam's offspring sharing his punishment, but they clearly *do* die, and the sharing of all humankind in his death (and in his sin) is explicit by the time of the New Testament.

So Adam certainly has some kind of archetypal role for humankind. But no such representative role is indicated for him, anywhere in Scripture, towards any *other* part of creation than humanity. Adam alone, and consequently Adam's race, incurs the penalty of death for disobedience.

The nature of the penalty of death is sometimes disputed, a distinction being made between physical and spiritual death. Although there is some theological use in the distinction, neither the Genesis story nor the main NT texts have much to say on the distinction: in Revelation the "first" and "second" deaths are both pictured simply as death, the latter following the general resurrection. So the NT, in the light of Christ's resurrection, clearly views the idea of eternal life as both a spiritual *and* physical matter. And the Genesis text, by tying the tree of life closely into communion with Yahweh in the "midst of the garden," also links the two inextricably.

In any case, the context of Genesis within ANE literature shows that physical death is clearly in mind, since that is the concern of comparable texts. For example, in the *Eridu Genesis,* Ziusudra (the equivalent of Noah) is granted eternal life as a reward after the flood, and in the later *Epic of Gilgamesh* the hero visits him (under his alternative name of Upnapishtim) in an unsuccessful attempt to live forever as well. Another such failure is that of Adapa the sage, in the eponymous myth, who appears to be duped by his patron god Ea into not eating the food of eternal life when he is offered it. "Living forever," and not just "living spiritually," are clearly in mind.

This leads us to a sharp contrast the Bible makes with the parallel ANE literature, which is that, uniquely, Adam *loses* eternal life, or at least free access to it, rather than failing to gain it. The tree of life in the garden is not forbidden him,[13] and the penalty of his death comes as a result of his exile from the garden into the land of Eden, the place of his creation before being placed in the garden, for "he must not be allowed to reach out his hand and take also from the tree of life and eat, and live forever."[14]

11. Gen 3:22–24.

12. Rom 5:12; 1 Cor 15:21–22. See also 2 Esdras 3:5–26; Wis 2:23–24.

13. Gen 2:9, 16.

14. Gen 3:22.

The implication must be that humankind has no innate immortality, but only that granted by God, and in fact, assuming the tree of life to be at least partly metaphorical, eternal life is gained only in communion with God, the very thing broken by Adam's disobedience. Humanity, then, was created mortal, but may overcome death through relationship with God. This leads us to consider the case of animals, which according to the "traditional view," did not die before the fall.

If this were the case, then either Adam would have been alone in needing to eat from the tree of life to avoid death (a strange situation for the one made in God's image and likeness), or all the animals in the world also must have had access to the tree of life. This makes no sense whatsoever in material terms, if we are to imagine snow leopards, kiwis, jellyfish, and even earthworms migrating to Mesopotamia, on a regular basis, for their dose of life. Remember that there was just one tree of life, in one garden small enough to be cultivated by a single human couple, in one small corner of the Near East. And for the animals to have incurred death after the fall, Adam's exile would have had to apply to them too—something on which the text is as silent as it is about their implication in Adam's sin.

One other feature from the text itself also demolishes such an already bizarre interpretation (though an inevitable one, given animal deathlessness before the fall). And that is that the creation ordinance allocating food to humanity and animals, which I shall discuss below, allowed if taken literally the eating of fruit from trees for humanity, but not animals.[15] They would have been forbidden access to the fruit of the tree of life anyway.

There are no grounds whatsoever, then, in Genesis 2–3, for suggesting that any creature other than Adam and Eve ever had exemption from natural death, nor was threatened with death together with Adam, nor incurred that penalty along with him. Mortality was their natural state, as we shall see below. The New Testament goes along with this in speaking only of the resurrection of *human beings* to new life in the age to come. We therefore simply have no warrant from the Bible for suggesting that animal death came through the sin that condemned Adam to death.

The serpent, Eve, Adam, and curses

Apart from the exaction of the penalty of death, promised in Genesis 2:17, through Adam's exile from the garden, Genesis 3 contains the scene of God's additional judgement on the three guilty parties in the case. These too, I will show, give no support whatsoever for the idea of a fallen creation.

15. Gen 1:29–30.

The first to be confronted by Yahweh is the snake:

> [14] So the LORD God said to the serpent, "Because you have done this,
>
> "Cursed are you above all livestock
>   and all wild animals!
> You will crawl on your belly
>   and you will eat dust
>   all the days of your life.
> [15] And I will put enmity
>   between you and the woman,
>   and between your offspring and hers;
>   he will crush your head,
>   and you will strike his heel."[16]

Exactly how the identity of the snake was understood by the original author of Genesis is hard to gauge with certainty in the "mythic" language of the genre employed. But it is clear that later biblical writers detached it entirely from the animal realm and equated it both with Satan's agency (e.g., Rev 12:9) and Satan's human agents (e.g., Matt 3:7; 12:34). The prophecy of enmity between the woman's seed (v15) and that of the serpent therefore has some clear prophetic import in later Scripture, beyond simply that of snakes biting people and getting trodden on. Since snake gods were common in the ANE, some anti-pagan sentiment may well be included in the text, but that need not concern us, being at best obscure.

What does concern us is the sentence, in v14, that the snake would be cursed to crawl on its belly and eat dust. This seems to be regularly taken by Creationists not only as an indication that the snake lost its legs in the deal, but that it offers a template for widespread changes in the rest of the animal kingdom. This, to be frank, is sheer fantasy.

A snake without legs would be essentially (with apologies to any taxonomists reading this) a lizard.[17] And it was a snake, not a lizard, which tempted Eve in the story. John Walton points out that, like eating dust, the expression "crawl on your belly" indicates merely humiliation:

> . . . he is going to be docile, rather than in an attack position. The serpent on its belly is nonthreatening, whilst the one reared up is protecting or attacking.[18]

---

16. Gen 3:14–15.

17. The Cretaceous varanids (or a similar group) are thought to be the (legged) ancestors of snakes.

18. Walton, *The Lost World of Adam and Eve*, 130.

So the net effect of this curse on the world of nature, outside the spiritual arena, is nothing more than a loss of status for snakes. It isn't even condemned to eat meat—just dust! In any case, there would be no justice in punishing the entire animal kingdom with anatomical changes for the fault of one demonically affected reptile.

Eve is next up for judgement:

> [16] To the woman he said,
> "I will make your pains in childbearing very severe;
>   with painful labor you will give birth to children.
> Your desire will be for your husband,
>   and he will rule over you."[19]

Although an increase in physical suffering during labor may be indicated here, it's also possible that general problems in family life, parallel to the apparent "war of the sexes" at the end of the verse, may be intended. After all, in Eve's own life we read of how her sin leads to the murder of her second son by her first, whom she also loses to exile to the land of Nod. Both would have been far more painful occurrences to her, as a mother, than childbirth. In any case, nothing whatsoever in this verse affects any part of nonhuman nature.

That leaves the sentence pronounced on Adam himself:

> [17] To Adam he said, "Because you listened to your wife and ate fruit from the tree about which I commanded you, 'You must not eat from it,'
>
> "Cursed is the ground because of you;
>   through painful toil you will eat food from it
>   all the days of your life.
> [18] It will produce thorns and thistles for you,
>   and you will eat the plants of the field.
> [19] By the sweat of your brow
>   you will eat your food
> until you return to the ground,
>   since from it you were taken;
> for dust you are
>   and to dust you will return."[20]

The inevitability of death is only gently (and mercifully?) hinted at the end of this, and the new information is the curse on the ground, which we

19. Gen 3:16.
20. Gen 3:17–19.

are told will result in Adam's staying alive only by the sweat of his brow, against the obstacles of thorns and thistles, for the rest of his life.

From at least the time of Luther onwards this has been taken, for reasons that are exegetically obscure, to indicate a deterioration of the entire natural order, involving death, decay, disease, parasitism, meat-eating, extreme weather, and more.

But actually all it says is that, for Adam, the productiveness of the ground will be cursed—and that by greater *vigor* of the living order in the form of thorns. Much of that could, actually, be accounted for by his expulsion from the sacred garden, for he no longer has access to the fruit of the many trees growing there, and must farm the steppe. But there is more. Although few commentators actually seem to refer to it, the curse on the ground is said later to be *lifted*, in Genesis 8, as part of the "general amnesty" tied up in God's covenant with Noah after the flood:

> [20] Then Noah built an altar to the LORD and, taking some of all the clean animals and clean birds, he sacrificed burnt offerings on it. [21] The LORD smelled the pleasing aroma and said in his heart: "*Never again will I curse the ground because of humans,* even though every inclination of the human heart is evil from childhood. And never again will I destroy all living creatures, as I have done.
>
> [22] "As long as the earth endures,
> seedtime and harvest,
> cold and heat,
> summer and winter,
> day and night
> will never cease."[21] [my emphasis]

Note that the curse on the ground is treated in a separate sentence from the destruction of all living creatures, governed by a different verb— they do not clearly refer to the same thing. Now although the flood would obviously have disrupted at the very least that year's harvest, agricultural imagery is not used in the flood narrative at all, although other symbols of "de-creation" are. Neither is the word "curse" mentioned within the narrative about the flood, but the word instead harks directly back to what God says to Adam in chapter 3. If there was an existing curse on the ground (to warrant the words "never again,") it was that spoken to Adam, and in the light of Noah's sacrifice that curse has ever since been rescinded.

---

21. Gen 8:20–22.

This, at least, is the sense conveyed by virtually all the English translations of verse 21, and even by the Septuagint Greek, though not by all the commentators. Gordon Wenham,[22] for example, says that the word order implies that God will refrain from adding *further* curses to the soil, not rescind the old one. But one wonders whether such grammatical precision would govern the meaning so tightly if one were not already committed to the belief that the earth is still accursed through Adam's sin. For there is further evidence in the account of the birth of Noah, many years before the flood:

> [28] When Lamech had lived 182 years, he had a son. [29] He named
> him Noah and said, "He will comfort us in the labor and painful
> toil of our hands caused by the ground the LORD has cursed."[23]

I'm not sure how it could be clearer: the ground (but only the ground) in Lamech's time is already cursed by the Lord, causing labor and painful toil of their hands—much the same wording as in Genesis 3:18, and in 8:21, with no other such curses being mentioned in between. Noah is destined to provide comfort in that specific situation, although he is not usually regarded as a provider of comfort to anyone—just as a survivor of utter devastation. But in fact he does so, because by his intercession the original curse on the ground, which has lasted ten generations, is lifted.

There is, in fact, an interesting parallel in this with the Atrahasis flood myth of Mesopotamia, long noted to be have some relationship to the Genesis flood story, and probably dating ultimately from the third millennium BCE. Both may well reflect the historical memory of a time of famine before the flood.[24] Although the biblical story has a different purpose from its pagan parallels, and in some ways is an antidote to them, there nevertheless *are* parallels, which may sometimes aid our interpretation. In one passage, the gods are increasingly troubled by humankind's "noise" (which may well have moral connotations[25]) and they cut off nature's gifts of food:

> When the second year arrived
> They had depleted the storehouse.
> When the third year arrived
> The people's looks were changed by starvation.

22. Wenham, *Genesis 1–15*, 190.

23. Gen 5:28–29.

24. I take all the ANE flood narratives to refer, in all probability, to the inundation of the Euphrates involving Shuruppak, c. 2900 BCE. But in any case the texts have literary links to Genesis.

25. See Gen 18:20–21.

When the fourth year arrived

Their upstanding bearing bowed,

Their well-set shoulders slouched,

The people went out in public hunched over.

When the fifth year arrived,

A daughter would eye her mother coming in;

A mother would not even open her door to her daughter. . . .

When the sixth year arrived

They served up a daughter for a meal,

Served up a son for food. [26]

Because one of the gods breaks solidarity and supplies food, the flood is sent immediately after this instead. So as in Genesis, a period of famine in response to divine displeasure is followed by the flood. Incidentally, at this time the god Enlil also says "Let the womb be too tight to let the baby out." There are reminders of Eve's punishment there too, perhaps.

Once more, then, we can say that there is nothing whatsoever in God's words of condemnation in Genesis 3 that supports any change in the natural order: the snake is humbled, the woman has family problems, and the soil (and nothing more) is made unproductive for several generations until the curse is lifted for Noah. Natural evil has not had much of a look in so far.

The vegetarian earth

A third passage habitually brought to bear on the question of natural evil is the creation ordinance of Genesis 1, in which both animals and humanity are allocated vegetable food.

> [29] Then God said, "I give you every seed-bearing plant on the face of the whole earth and every tree that has fruit with seed in it. They will be yours for food. [30] And to all the beasts of the earth and all the birds in the sky and all the creatures that move along the ground—everything that has the breath of life in it—I give every green plant for food." And it was so.[27]

Let me first say that even if we took this as precluding non-vegetarian animals at the creation, it would have nothing to say about the absence of

26. Dalley, *Myths from Mesopotamia*, 26–27.

27. Gen 1:29–30.

animal *death*. Herbivores die from many causes other than being eaten by predators.

In point of fact, the idea that there was no animal death and no meat-eating renders the possibility of a harmonious creation as scientifically unrealistic as the idea that the vast majority of species were completely redesigned to be "red in tooth and claw" after the fall (without a scrap of evidence either from the Bible or science).

In the *Origin of Species* Charles Darwin spends several pages building his case for the innate overproduction of nature with examples of how quickly the earth would be overrun if all the offspring of even slow-breeding species like elephants survived:

> There is no exception to the rule that every organic being naturally increases at so high a rate, that if not destroyed, the earth would soon be covered by the progeny of a single pair.[28]

But even he was unaware of the vast biomass of the creatures at the base of the food chain—such as insects on land and plankton at sea—whose unchecked reproduction would make the earth uninhabitable within no more than a year or two. Such an Eden would be like the plagues of Egypt on steroids. Alfred Russel Wallace, the cofounder with Darwin of evolutionary theory, writing decades after Darwin's death, quotes a calculation by W. B. Hardy, FRS, that the offspring of the protozoon *Paramecium* alone would in 350 generations (that is about two years) occupy a sphere larger than the then-known universe.[29]

Burial under bugs would not be the worst of it, though. For taken literally the passage in Genesis does not *proscribe* meat at all, but *prescribes* green vegetables for all flesh (except humans, who also get to eat fruit). There are many animals that specialize in consuming dung, animal detritus like shed skin cells (if cells were allowed to die in this version of paradise!), non-green plants like fungi, honey, and so on. The text forbids all these. Perhaps the mountains of unprocessed feces would be the worst aspect.[30]

The committed Creationist might, perhaps, suggest that animals had a limited reproduction rate to prevent these evils. If so, he would be speculating on mere interpretive hints and inferences by denying outright what *is*, quite clearly, stated in the text—the command to go forth, multiply, and fill the earth. Fecundity is one of the key themes of the creation narrative.

28. Darwin, *Origin*, 588.

29. Wallace, *The World of Life*, 372.

30. Until the introduction of dung beetles, Australian fields remained permanently covered in cow-pats (https://en.wikipedia.org/wiki/Australian_Dung_Beetle_Project).

These excesses aside, it is quite impossible that any ecosystem could survive with just green plants as its food source, or that anteaters, chameleons, or swifts could even begin to survive on them. Fortunately, as Derek Kidner pointed out in his commentary on Genesis half a century ago:

> The assigning of every green plant for food (RSV) to all creatures must not be pressed to mean that all were once herbivorous, any more than to mean that all plants were equally edible to all. It is a generalization, that directly or indirectly all life depends on vegetation, and the concern of the verse is to show that we are all fed from God's hand.[31]

Two useful interpretive points may be added to this, based on the known structure and purposes of Genesis. The first is that one element of the creation narrative is a polemical contrast with the polytheistic creation myths of the surrounding nations. In the Babylonian myth *Enuma Elish*, for example, humankind was created in order to provide food for the gods (and to save them hard work). So for Genesis to stress that God himself feeds both his human and animal creation is not at all stating the obvious, but rather establishing a radically new theology.[32]

Secondly, it is a hermeneutical commonplace that Genesis 1's seven-stage creation consists of his making, in the first three days, "domains" (the heavens, the sea and the earth), and in the second three days "functionaries" for those domains (heavenly bodies, birds and fish, animals and humanity). Land vegetation is treated not as a functionary on day six, but as part of the environment on day three. So vv 29–30 are, in effect, about handing over the supportive environment to its inhabitants. In no way does that limit either humanity or animals to eating only vegetation.

Some interesting issues do remain, which may or may not be significant in what is admittedly not the most transparent of passages. We've already seen that only humanity is given access to trees bearing fruit with seeds, whereas both human and beast may eat green herbs. But one may also note that the third category of vegetation created on day three—grass—appears to have no consumers allocated to it. That seems a little hard on the cattle and sheep, but may in fact be a strong clue not to read the text too literalistically.

Another issue is that in Genesis 9:1–3, after the flood, the fear and dread of humanity falls on the animals, and humanity is given permission to eat them. Now there are some interesting nuances here. What humanity

---

31. Kidner, *Genesis*, 52.

32. "God's provision of food for newly created man stands in sharp contrast to Mesopotamian views which held than man was created to supply the gods with food." Wenham, *Genesis 1–15*, 33.

is given permission to eat is, in the NIV, "everything that lives and moves," but the Hebrew term is *remes*, which as John Walton again points out from a word study, seems to indicate a particular *category* of beast distinct from both "livestock" and "wild animals"; that is non-domesticated herd animals like wild cattle, antelope, deer, gazelle, and ibex—in other words, typical prey animals.[33] It looks, then, as if after the flood humanity is being given permission to hunt as well as keeping domestic animals (which it had done since at least the time of Cain, if not Adam), perhaps because of the food shortage already mentioned before the flood and, no doubt, worse after it.

Whatever the implications of the post-flood permission in Genesis 9, and indeed of the verse about vegetation in Genesis 1, we should note that it adds nothing to the case for an animal kingdom taking to bloody pursuits, because the later concession applies only to humankind, not animals. And even that happens not at the time of the fall but ten generations later. No description of any transition in the diet of the creatures, whether actual, permissive, or evil, is given in the text at all.

Careful attention to the Hebrew nouns, in fact, also helps clarify the creation of the animals themselves back in chapter 1. For the living creatures (*nepes* = "soul") brought forth "after their kinds" on day six are *behemah* (meaning domestic livestock), *remes* (which as we have already seen probably means "non-domesticated prey animals"), and *hayya* (which are the wild animals—the predators).[34] Incidentally, these three functional categories are the only three "kinds" mentioned in the text, as opposed to the multiple quasi-Linnaean "baramins" of creation science.

Genesis 1:30 says nothing at all about the diet of the sea creatures, either by way of permission or prohibition. I trust that nobody will suggest they ate green herbs, or the tree of life. The real reason for the omission, of course, is that the second day of creation is concerned with the separation of waters rather than anything else. On day five the water creatures are shown to occupy their environment by "teeming" there, as the land creatures occupy theirs by eating the vegetation.

The very vocabulary of the creation account, then, militates against an entirely vegetarian, predator-free world before the fall, and not just because wild beasts are mentioned in contrast to prey animals, but because domestic animals are mentioned too. What was Adam supposed to do with domestic sheep and cattle, if both milk and meat were forbidden, and clothes not yet required? Perhaps they'd help him plough the thorny

---

33. Walton, *Genesis*, 341.

34. Ibid., 125.

soil, but that would only be after the fall had excluded him from the freely available fruit of trees in the garden.

But to be honest, there is little point in marshalling further arguments *against* the idea that most of the creatures we have now actually received their present forms, habits, and mortality because Adam sinned, since there is, as we have seen, precious little in Genesis ever to suggest the idea in the first place. The whole theory is built on sand, or perhaps we should say, since it depends on an overblown emphasis on Adam's role in the world, the whole theory is built on the dust of the ground.

Good, very good, stupendous

To complete our look at key passages within the book of Genesis itself, we must deal with the argument that the repeated use of the phrase "God saw that it was good" cannot be truthfully applied to things as they are now, and must therefore mean that before the fall things were much better, if not perfect, and that this necessarily means there was no death, no decay, and no suffering.

In the first place, let us remember that what he had created was "good" in *God's* eyes, which may have no bearing whatsoever on what is good in *our* eyes. Ezekiel, after all, wrote:

> [29] Yet the Israelites say, "The way of the Lord is not just." Are my ways unjust, people of Israel? Is it not your ways that are unjust?[35]

Why should our opinions on God's ways be any more reliable than those of the Israelites?

The word "good" (*tob*) appears in chapter 1 of the light in v 1, of the land and sea (v 10), of vegetation (v 12), of the heavenly bodies (v 18), of the sea and sky creatures (v 21), of the animals (v 25), and finally, in v 31, of everything, which God calls "very good." It is no coincidence that the word appears seven times in the creation story (like other key words in Genesis; numerology is a sophisticated compositional feature of the whole Pentateuch).

Tob has as wide a semantic range as its equivalent English word "good," and may or may not carry moral connotations, being just as often applied to "usefulness" of function as to anything deeper. For example, in the context of the first chapters of Genesis it is used of the trees that are *good* for food (2:9, 3:6), of the tree of the knowledge of *good* and evil (2:9 *etc.*), of the

35. Ezek 18:29.

SCRIPTURE ON THE FALL

good gold mined in Havilah (2:12), and negatively, of the *not-good* lack of a companion for Adam (2:18).

Once more, John Walton's careful use of word study is helpful. He suggests that insight is gained into the meaning of "good" by asking what "not good" implies in 2:18. He takes into account the Israelites' experience of the works of creation being sometimes inauspicious to them, and concludes:

> As a king sets up an administration by which the state will operate, so God is setting up the administrative organs of the cosmos. Time, climate, and vegetation represent the tripart governing structure of the cosmos (as the executive, judiciary, and legislative branches constitute the means by which the American government operates). They were perfectly conceived and properly initiated in suitable functioning order, though they have now become agents that threaten survival and forces against which we struggle to no avail.[36]

Now, in the light of our study of God's use of the creation in chapter 1, I would quibble with Walton about whether God's "administration" has "become" anything at all, other than what it always was to begin with. A tool does not change by being put to a new use. If God sometimes uses these agents in judgement of humanity, it is because *humanity* has changed (which is not in dispute here), not because creation has changed. It is also doubtful if it is fair to say that God's creation *habitually* works against us. Our survey of the biblical material in the previous chapter suggested that, for the most part, creation is used to bless us. Jesus said:

> [44] But I tell you, love your enemies and pray for those who persecute you, [45] that you may be children of your Father in heaven. He causes his sun to rise on the evil and the good, and sends rain on the righteous and the unrighteous.[37]

But in any case, if the sense of *tob* in Genesis 1 has functional, rather than ethical, significance there is nothing that makes it *necessary* for creation to have been profoundly reworked to account for appearances today. We cannot look around, fail to see perfection, and conclude that the "goodness" has gone out of it. To do so is to accept Richard Dawkins assessment:

> The universe that we observe has precisely the properties we should expect if there is, at bottom, no design, no purpose, no evil, no good, nothing but pitiless indifference.[38]

36. Walton, *Genesis*, 115–16.
37. Matt 5:44–45.
38. Dawkins, "God's Utility Function," 85.

In fact, it is fairly self-evident that any such conclusion must be fatally subjective. Just how much "non-perfection" will we allow to be present before we decide (as if we were the ones to decide!) that it is too much? What in the world *can't* count as suffering or evil on somebody's reckoning? Make all the animals vegetarians, and their provision abundant, and our vegetarian animals might still get hungry on the way to the tree, or thirsty on the way to the waterhole—and it could be taken as evidence of a fallen world. If we can't have the deer fighting for mates, and if instead they are virtuously monogamous for life, they would still have to be born in *exactly* a 50:50 sex ratio lest the odd bachelor or spinster suffer loneliness. Is it an evil that our own cells are programmed to die to keep our bodies functioning at all? And so on.

In the human realm, I have just listened to a radio interview with a mountaineer speaking about the unique life-enhancing thrill of danger. Are we to conclude that he is out of step with God and that the earth was made only for the risk-averse? C. S. Lewis was quite justified biblically in having his fictional *hrossa* hunt and kill the fierce *hnakra* in the unfallen world of Malacandra in his partly allegorical *Out of the Silent Planet.*[39]

No, only God can decide what constitutes the goodness of his world. And since he has not told us in Scripture that he has altered his ideas and changed things around (either deliberately or by force of changed circumstances), then once again we simply have no justification for inventing a new universe out of thin air, or out of over-interpreted Bible verses, which amounts to the same thing.

The same is true when considering the views of old-earthers who believe "natural evil" stems from the processes inherent in creation itself, and especially evolution, and that God's aim is to overcome such evil. It's a question of accepting either the authority of God's word, which says that what he created was "very good," or that of contemporary people who say on their own authority that it wasn't.

Both groups of people, one presumes, in order to give "evil" anything more than a purely subjective meaning, must take into account something like Augustine's definition of evil: a privation of some good. The Creationist must account for the lack of any mention of such a privation in the biblical text, outside the boundaries of humankind, and the Evolutionist for such a privation being, apparently, built into the very fabric of creation by the God who is incapable of evil . . . but yet (apparently) speaks untruth in Genesis by pronouncing his work "very good."

---

39. Lewis, *Out of the Silent Planet.*

Geneticist and epidemiologist Seymour Garte has pointed out to me that Genesis 1, rather surprisingly, does not call the pinnacle of creation, humankind, "good," apart from the general summary of v 31. He suggests that this might be because the creation is directed *towards* and *for* humankind's good. This seems to me very reasonable, and underlines the point I have been making here—that "good" refers to "fitness for purpose." Humankind, in God's rational and spiritual image, is very much created as an end in itself, rather than "for a purpose," even though it is given the role of ruler of this world, under God. The rest of creation, at least as it is set forth in Genesis, functions on behalf of humankind—God's viceroy and priest in his cosmic temple—and its "goodness" is directed to that end. As Psalm 8 puts it:

¹ LORD, our Lord,
    how majestic is your name in all the earth!
You have set your glory
    in the heavens.
² Through the praise of children and infants
    you have established a stronghold against your enemies,
    to silence the foe and the avenger.
³ When I consider your heavens,
    the work of your fingers,
the moon and the stars,
    which you have set in place,
⁴ what is mankind that you are mindful of them,
    human beings that you care for them?
⁵ You have made them a little lower than the angels
    and crowned them with glory and honor.
⁶ You made them rulers over the works of your hands;
    you put everything under their feet:
⁷ all flocks and herds,
    and the animals of the wild,
⁸ the birds in the sky,
    and the fish in the sea,
    all that swim the paths of the seas.
⁹ LORD, our Lord,
    how majestic is your name in all the earth!

Chapter 3—Other Red Herrings

Your enjoyment of the world is never right, till every morning you awake in Heaven; see yourself in your Father's Palace; and look upon the skies, the earth, and the air as Celestial Joys: having such a reverent esteem of all, as if you were among the Angels. The bride of a monarch, in her husband's chamber, hath no such causes of delight as you.

—THOMAS TRAHERNE (1636–74)[1]

All flesh corrupt

IN THIS CHAPTER I will look at the main Scriptures outside the creation and garden narratives that are used to argue for a "fallen creation." The first passage is still in Genesis, and is occasionally used to support the corruption of the natural world. It is the preamble to the flood narrative in Genesis 6. As the KJV puts it:

> The earth also was corrupt before God, and the earth was filled with violence. And God looked upon the earth, and behold it was corrupt; for all flesh had corrupted his way upon the earth.
> And God said unto Noah, the end of all flesh is come before me; for the earth is filled with violence through them; and behold I will destroy them with the earth.[2]

The interpretation would be that not just humanity, but the whole of nature, has become wicked and violent, so that the animals, now addicted to hunting and killing, have to be destroyed too. There is already some sleight of hand going on in that, simply from ignoring the previous verses. To begin with, the cumulative narrative since the exile from the garden has been all

1. Traherne, *Centuries*, 1/7, 19.
2. Gen 6:11–13.

about the increase in *human* violence. Then chapter 6 begins with the mysterious episode of the marriage of the "sons of God" with "the daughters of men," and with the possibly linked stories of giants. Whatever this means, clearly God disapproves, because he first limits "the days" of humankind, probably by announcing the date for judgement rather than the reduced age of people, and then (in the same KJV version):

> And God saw that the wickedness of man was great in the earth, and that every imagination of the thoughts of his heart was only evil continually.
>
> And it repented the LORD that he had made man on the earth, and it grieved him at his heart.
>
> And the LORD said, I will destroy man whom I have created from the face of the earth; both man, and beast, and the creeping thing, and the fowls of the air; for it repenteth me that I have made them.
>
> But Noah found grace in the eyes of the LORD.[3]

So it is humanity's *present* wickedness that causes both the human and animal death in the flood, and the man Noah who is shown grace by being saved, and through him the others on the ark. In any case, a brief consideration of the story shows that an "evil natural world" cannot be the real issue. In the first place, the blame for the corruption is laid at the feet of "all flesh," which immediately excludes the inanimate world, not to mention the only thing that might be said to be altered in the text, the thorns and thistles of Genesis 3:18 (remember that vegetation, not "flesh", being part of the environment of day 3, not of the functionaries of day 6). Volcanoes and hurricanes are exempted from all blame! And so are sea creatures, which are, literally, in their element during the flood.

In the second place, if the "corruption" and "violence" referred to the proliferation of life-forms exhibiting adaptations for predation, parasitism, and so on, then it is immediately apparent that bringing a breeding colony of them into the ark would have no remedial effect whatsoever. Predators and parasites would simply emerge from the ark to breed true "after their kinds."

I don't want to attempt a complete commentary on the significance of the flood story here, but most of the problems it holds regarding "fallen creation" are solved once one follows the modern translations in interpreting "all flesh" as "all Adam's descendants" (e.g., NIV: "all people"). It is human sin that leads to human violence, and although a major point of the story is to show that even Noah remains tainted with sin (witness his

3. Gen 6:5–8.

later drunkenness), it is a lot more plausible for the narrative to suggest the possibility of purifying the race from evil, by preservation of a righteous man, than purification of creation from predation, through rescuing carnivores. In any case, it is not only carnivores, but gentle herbivores too, that were destroyed in the flood.

The question does indeed remain as to why God should wipe out the animals, and indeed the whole landscape, because of human sin, but it's a question that the idea of a fallen natural world does nothing to answer at all. The best explanation I have come across is the Hebrew concept of the land's being ritually polluted by the human blood shed upon it. This echoes the blood of Abel "crying from the ground" in chapter 4, explains the specific link to "violence" and also makes sense of the covenant God cuts in chapter 8, which is all about promising not to destroy the earth again, but demanding an individual accounting from both humans and animals that shed *human* blood, and so defile the image of God. In other words, Noah's covenant introduces the concept of individual judgement for human bloodshed, and of holding that judgement in store until the end of the age, setting the stage, incidentally, for the Bible's salvation history.

In a similar way Leviticus speaks of the corruption of Canaan by the detestable sexual sins of its inhabitants, and not by the actions of its animals:

> [25] Even the land was defiled; so I punished it for its sin, and the land vomited out its inhabitants.[4]

Even more germane is a passage in Numbers:

> [33] "Do not pollute the land where you are. Bloodshed pollutes the land, and atonement cannot be made for the land on which blood has been shed, except by the blood of the one who shed it. [34] Do not defile the land where you live and where I dwell, for I, the LORD, dwell among the Israelites."[5]

The flood itself, as virtually all commentators agree, is representative of an act of de-creation by God: he temporarily returns his world (or the polluted part of it if the flood is viewed as localized) to its original state of watery chaos before, as it were, re-creating it as the waters recede and the ark's inhabitants once more "go forth and multiply upon the earth."

4. Lev 18:25.
5. Num 35:33–34.

The satanic world

Although I've not seen it so used, this text from 1 John could be seen as a proof text that the whole nature was usurped by Satan after the fall:

> [19] We know that we are children of God, and that the whole world is under the control of the evil one.[6]

To interpret it thus would, of course, be to deny the whole theology of nature we have seen so far in the Old Testament. But the explanation, of course, lies in what John habitually means by "the world." In 2:15 he writes:

> [15] Do not love the world or anything in the world. If anyone loves the world, love for the Father is not in them.

A Platonic, or even Gnostic, dislike for the material realm could be understood here, were it not that John goes on to describe "everything in the world": the lust of the flesh, the lust of the eyes, and the pride of life. It is this world of idolatrous desires that will pass away, and consistent with John's habit, "the world" in chapter 5 represents the human world apart from God. It has no bearing whatsoever on created nature.

Bondage to decay

One major passage that seems on the face of things to overturn the conclusion that creation is still "as created" is the passage in Romans 8 which speaks of the creation itself being liberated from its bondage to decay. It deserves extended treatment:

> [18] I consider that our present sufferings are not worth comparing with the glory that will be revealed in us. [19] For the creation waits in eager expectation for the children of God to be revealed. [20] For the creation was subjected to frustration, not by its own choice, but by the will of the one who subjected it, in hope [21] that the creation itself will be liberated from its bondage to decay and brought into the freedom and glory of the children of God.
> [22] We know that the whole creation has been groaning as in the pains of childbirth right up to the present time.[7]

This would seem, on superficial reading, to refer to the curse on nature in Genesis 3 that led to death, and nature's subsequent liberation from death with the revelation of the glory of God's sons, presumably at Christ's second

6. 1 John 5:19.
7. Rom 8:18–22.

coming. Only we have already seen that Genesis 3 contains no such curse, making these five verses the first and only scriptural witness to such a radical degradation of nature.

There is a rather useful principle that if a doctrine is taught at only one place in Scripture, there is a pretty good chance you've misinterpreted the passage. That is certainly the case here. It has to be questioned if a "fallen creation" is really what Paul has in mind at all in this single instance of just five verses. There are many things within the text, in comparison with the Genesis account, which do not tie up, and which seem to point elsewhere, and particularly to Paul's innovative development of the theology of resurrection and the age to come.

The "fallen" understanding of Romans 8:21 has, in fact, conflated "decay" in the NIV with the quite separate notion of "death," and even more illegitimately, sometimes with "suffering," assuming that one means the other and that neither had any presence in creation before the fall. But whatever else one can surmise about the Edenic world, one can confidently say that decay occurred. If not, then where did plants obtain their nutrition, or where *would* they have obtained it as organic nutrients were depleted over time? What would happen to the banana skins Adam threw away, or the excrement of human and beast?

So if one attempts to relate Romans 8 to "fallen nature" in literal biological terms, one has to explain why those innocent life-forms that *depend* on decay for their livelihood (the earthworms, the fungi, the very green plants that depend on decayed humus for nutrients) would not be eagerly *dreading*, rather than hoping for, the abolition of decay. Those animals which had become subject to *death* through humanity's sin might desire a change, but death is not mentioned in the text, and it is rather tendentious to translate "the whole creation in bondage to decay" as "animals in bondage to death."

Let us instead look at the context of the passage. Having extolled human life in the Spirit over life in the flesh, Paul turns to Christian suffering in the flesh. Our passage leads on to (and paves the way for) the assurance that nothing can separate believers from Christ's love, and the whole context of this is that our sufferings and subsequent glory reflect those of Christ. Those sufferings cover hardship and persecution, bodily privation and violence, and the opposition of spiritual powers—in other words what we might call specifically *Christian* suffering. These are the substance of our "groaning" in the Spirit (v 23). There is no word there of the common problems of being mortal, except that the culmination of our hope is eternal life in Christ after physical resurrection from the dead, of which Christ himself is the forerunner.

Secondly, let us look at some key words in Paul's vocabulary.

Creation:

We cannot simply *assume* that Paul means "nature" by this word. The word *ktisis* certainly covers that, but elsewhere (e.g., Mark 16:15, Col 1:23) it means the human creation only. In the immediate context of the chapter, the features of creation to which Paul draws attention (vv 38–39) are death and life, angels and demons, present and future, all powers, height, and depth. Not only are none of these mentioned in the original Genesis account of creation, but not a single one of them is subject to biological death or decay. Conversely Paul omits any reference to the ordinary animal world, or to the inanimate elements we consider most disordered and chaotic, such as earth, water, and atmosphere.

Frustration:

The word is *mataiotes*, occurring only twice more in the NT where it means "sinful ignorance" or "empty boasting." However it also corresponds to the Hebrew *hebel*, which it represents in the Septuagint Greek Bible with which Paul would have been very familiar as a diaspora Jew. In most places in the OT it has the same connotation of moral emptiness and futility, but the majority of references occur in the book of Ecclesiastes. Here it refers to the futility of all human affairs, the overall message being that God has subjected humankind to such "vanity" in the hope he will seek his purpose in God alone. In fact, Ecclesiastes is fruitfully viewed as a commentary on the effects of the Genesis fall in the world of humanity. It could well be that Paul, in turn, is commenting on Ecclesiastes, in the light of the promised resurrection, by using the same keyword in Romans 8.

But in no case does the rest of Scripture use either the Greek or Hebrew words to refer to the natural world. If Paul is using it thus, he is using the word in a new way.

Hope:

The usual Greek word *elpis* is used here. But who is exercising hope? If the creation is meant, it is pertinent to ask in what sense the nonhuman creation could be said to "hope" at all. No animal is capable of either dread or hope for the future (other than the fear of imminent death)—those things are entirely human attributes. Even if "decay" *did* indicate "death," is it actually true to say that mortal animals, let alone the whole inanimate creation, are longing that death should cease? It would seem either that

Paul is not referring to the "natural" creation at all, or that he is personify-
ing it for some specific reason.

But it could equally be that the "hope" is actually being exercised by the
One whose will subjected it, that is God. The sense would be that it was for
some future purpose (the "hope") rather than for some past misdemeanor,
that God put creation in bondage. This is more rational, for even assuming
inanimate creation to be capable of hope, then from its viewpoint it would
not have been subjected, if it were corrupted by the fall, to frustration "in
hope," but to frustration as part of humanity's judgement. Creation might
have (figuratively speaking) *gained* hope from the plan of salvation later
revealed, but that is not what the passage says.

What is certainly clear is that the object of "this hope" in v 24 means
the redemption of our human bodies from sin and death, and this salvific
sense is its predominant meaning throughout the Old and New Testaments.

Liberated:

This word comes from the root *eleutheros*. In the NT its use is always either
of liberation from human slavery, or from sin, or (by the same token) from
the law. It is never used of the nonhuman realm, nor of death apart from
as the penalty for sin. So once more, if nature is referenced, it is in some
figurative personification, rather than literally.

Bondage:

Douleia similarly, though not a common word in the New Testament, can
also cover human slavery or, more commonly, bondage to the law (and
through it to sin), the sense Paul gives it in v 15 of this chapter. Again, it is
never used of death *per se*, nor of course to decay.

Decay:

Phthora, decay or corruption, is again not a hugely common word in
the New Testament. The New Testament uses it and its cognates both of
biological decay and of the result of sin, and in some cases both may be
meant. So in 1 Corinthians 9:25 athletes compete for a *corruptible* crown,
which is clearly a biological, or at least material, use. In Romans 1:23 "images like *corruptible* men" reflects principally the mortality of man too,
though perhaps hinting at moral weakness too. In 1 Corinthians 15:42 and

50 the corruption, again, is that of human mortality. Sometimes, but not in Paul, a purely moral/spiritual corruption is meant (Jude v 10; 1 Pet 3:4; 2 Pet 1:4; 2:12; 2:19). Paul's own use of the word, however, is always to do with mortality, not immorality.

Yet it is not without significance that this word is the one used in the Septuagint to render the Hebrew *shachath*, which as we saw earlier in this chapter carries the sense both of human sinful corruption and of *ritual pollution* of the land consequent to this. Most notably, this is its sense in Genesis where it occurs three times in 6:11–12 and nowhere else. This triple repetition emphasizes that the "whole land/earth" had become corrupt, and that "all flesh had corrupted his way" (KJV) upon the land/earth. As the NIV recognizes by translating this phrase "all the people," human sin and ritual pollution, rather than the presence of biological decay or natural evil, is meant in this passage. It would in any case be foolish for God to judge this latter sort of corruption if, indeed, he had deliberately subjected the earth to it according to Romans 8.

All these keywords, then, are used elsewhere often, and in some cases virtually exclusively, of the world of humanity, and particularly of the human moral and spiritual sphere. We ought certainly to be cautious of the assumption that in this passage alone they are used of the physical effects of the fall on nonhuman creation, especially when the surrounding context deals entirely with the realm of the Spirit and salvation from sin.

Before suggesting what I believe to be the true import of this passage, it may be useful to cover the various ways ancient theologians viewed the passage; not that they have a unified "orthodox" view, but that they provide useful insights and, almost to a person, do *not* interpret it as evidence of a corrupted natural world as moderns do.

The next chapter consists of a study of the ancient authors on the doctrine of "fallen creation" overall, but I think it convenient to deal with their views on this particular passage here.

Irenaeus quotes Romans 8:21 in a discussion of the resurrection of the dead.[8] Ever the conservative exegete, he gives no direct interpretation of "creature," but does go on to use the word "creature" ("creation" in modern versions of Romans) twice of human beings in the page or so of comment. It seems clear that he assumes the human creation is the subject of the passage.

Methodius, however, does seem to apply the term to the created order as a whole. He speaks of the whole world being ordained to continue rather than be destroyed (in contradiction of heretical teaching that the physical

8. Irenaeus, *Ad. Haer.* V. XXXVI.3. (Roberts and Donaldson, *Ante-Nicene Library*, Vol IX, 197).

world is temporary).[9] The verse appears in describing the created order's intrinsic material corruptibility and mortality, and its future transformation to incorruptibility. There is no reference to sin in his treatment.

Archelaus, also dealing with heretics, alludes to our passage in his fragmentary *Disputation with Manes* when he writes: "Then the universal creation will be moved and perturbed, uttering prayers and supplications, until he delivers it from its bondage."[10] By this he clearly implies the rational creation (capable of prayers and supplications), and probably the human rather than the angelic.

Origen is characteristically influenced by Platonic ideas of the inferiority of matter to spirit, and comes at the passage in a rather left-field way from our point of view, though striving, he says, to teach "what is in accordance to the creed of the church." Ours is actually quite a favorite text of his, quoted several times. In *De Principiis*[11] he is discussing rational beings, both corporeal and incorporeal. Largely this is to discountenance any pagan tendency to worship the heavenly bodies as gods, on the grounds that they too are created rational beings. He reasons that in Romans 8 "creature" signifies the sun, moon, and stars, because they are clothed with bodies, and set apart to the office of giving light to the human race. His point seems to be that Paul mentions them as the greatest of the nonhuman creation. The "vanity" to which they have been subjected, he suggests, is simply their corporeal nature "as a kind of burden which enfeebles the vigor of the soul."

In other words, his contrast (whilst couched in Platonic, anti-corporeal thought) is between the corruptible first creation and the transformed creation in Christ—not between a good creation corrupted by sin and then restored by Christ. The same emphasis occurs in his other uses of the text.[12]

John Chrysostom in his commentary on Romans, in contrast to the others, does suggest that the personification of creation in Romans 8 is a literary technique signifying the lower (irrational) creation's bondage to corruption because of humanity's sin. This he sees, however, as God's own work "intended for our correction." Questioning the unfairness of this apparently unjust action of God's, he argues that creation has had no wrong done to it for (a) it was made on our account anyway (b) there is no evil involved to a creation "void of soul and feeling" and (c) it will eventually become once

9. Methodius, *Discourse on the Resurrection* VIII. (Ibid., Vol XIV, 143).

10. Archelaus, *Disputation with Manes.* (Ibid., Vol XX, 358).

11. Origen, *De Principiis* 1,VII.5. (Ibid., Vol X, 63).

12. *De Principiis* II.IX.7 (ibid., 133); III.V.1 (ibid., 254); III.V.4 (ibid., 258); *Contra Celsum* V.XIII (ibid., Vol. XXIII 281); VII.LXVI (ibid., 486); VIII.5 (ibid., 495).

more incorruptible for our sake.[13] You'll note that even in Chrysostom the modern idea of the Devil's agency in nature's change is completely absent. Also note that the "corruptibility" of the whole created order rather than "animal death" is his concern, though that might well be included.

Augustine returns to the more common (in those days) interpretation of "creature" as the rational creation, and in his case he means the human creation in the sense of "the whole human being." One modern source summarizes his interpretation:

> Augustine understands this verse [8:22] to refer to the entire human being, which includes body, soul and mind and in this sense "all creation," on the grounds that the text says "omni creatura," not "tota creatura" (De diu.quaest.67,5). The former adjective is understood distributively, as applying to all created things which have body and soul and mind, and only human beings meet this definition; the latter adjective is understood collectively, as applying to all created things without restriction. According to this interpretation creation in its entirety is subjected to vanity, i.e., to earthly change and vulnerability, but in hope of resurrection (Exp. prop. Rom 53; De diu. quaest. 67).[14]

In summary, then, the early interpretation of Romans 8 is pretty varied, but refers in most cases (a) to some aspect of the rational creation, rather than to nature and (b) to the corruptibility inherent in our material condition rather than to the effects of the fall, Chrysostom being the only exception.

Martin Luther: taking one example only from a much later age (the age, as I shall argue, in which the "fallen creation" teaching first took hold) Luther has a rather ambiguous attitude to the question of a fallen creation, and his *Lectures on Romans* gives probably his most mixed message about it. Interestingly he starts by saying that most interpreters of the passage take it to refer to humanity (not nature) as the "creature." For himself, he prefers to see is as nature, subjected to vanity by humanity. Yet he mainly attributes this vanity not to a change of nature's character, but to the misuse of nature by humanity (in a rather novel understanding uncongenial to the "traditional view"), for he says:

> For all that God made "was very good" (Gen 1:31) and is good to this day.[15]

---

13. Chrysostom, *Homily 14.*
14. Patte and TeSelle, *Engaging Augustine,* 137.
15. Luther, *Romans,* 238.

Its redemption he takes to mean a restoration of its proper use by humanity, which is not inconsistent with the Patristic views we have seen. Yet he also condemns philosophers and theologians for talking of nature's felicity and not perceiving its mourning and sighing, and fields the idea (admitting it to be without scriptural proof) that the sun was brighter before the fall. Yet even this relatively late interpretation is a far cry from the almost universal assumption now that Paul teaches that nature has been rendered evil by the fall, and is groaning to be purified at the second coming of Christ.

What are we to conclude from all this? Certainly not that nature is corrupted by the fall, which is neither warranted by the text nor understood by all but a small minority of earlier interpreters. It seems to me that we should understand it in the context of Paul's understanding of the cosmic effect of Christ's resurrection, or in other words the "new heavens and new earth" first taught in Isaiah (but inherent in the Eden story—see chapter 4).

To Paul, the victory of Christ brings more than just a return to the innocence of the first creation. It replaces the kind of life that is of the earth with the life that is of heaven. This is most fully expounded in 1 Corinthians 15: Jesus was raised, in his human body, as the firstfruits of a new kind of life, the spiritual rather than the natural. Likewise, in the resurrection those in Christ become eternal and imperishable:

> [42] So will it be with the resurrection of the dead. The body that is sown is perishable, it is raised imperishable; [43] it is sown in dishonor, it is raised in glory; it is sown in weakness, it is raised in power; [44] it is sown a natural body, it is raised a spiritual body.
>
> If there is a natural body, there is also a spiritual body. [45] So it is written: "The first man Adam became a living being"; the last Adam, a life-giving spirit. [46] The spiritual did not come first, but the natural, and after that the spiritual. [47] The first man was of the dust of the earth; the second man is of heaven. [48] As was the earthly man, so are those who are of the earth; and as is the heavenly man, so also are those who are of heaven. [49] And just as we have borne the image of the earthly man, so shall we bear the image of the heavenly man.
>
> [50] I declare to you, brothers and sisters, that flesh and blood cannot inherit the kingdom of God, nor does the perishable inherit the imperishable.[16]

If the kingdom, to Paul, cannot be inherited by the perishable, it follows that the new heavens and the new earth, which constitute the "home

---

16. 1 Cor 15:42–50.

of righteousness,"[17] must also become imperishable downstream of the new creation in Christ.

And so, Paul is suggesting in Romans 8, the natural creation (which he has personified for literary purposes) has been, from its original foundation, tied to mortality but longing for immortality, to corruption but awaiting incorruption, to the naturally empowered (*psuchikos*) but destined for the spiritually empowered (*pneumatikos*).

If the fall affected this, we may surmise that it was only because the long winter of human history has delayed the spring of the world's transformation for so long. Had Adam not sinned, and had he stayed in the garden to learn wisdom ("the tree of good and evil") from God in the shelter of immortality ("the tree of life"), it would seem that his eventual role would have been, somehow, to spread the fruit of Yahweh's garden to the whole created order long ago as the ruler and subduer of creation, in the image of God. The garden would have been a bridgehead for imperishability to the whole world.

As it is, the salvation that God has now achieved by his own arm,[18] through the incarnation of Christ, is in the wisdom of God far more glorious, and perhaps even the final state more wonderful. But since what is to come is still unknown and indescribable, it is foolish to make the attempt. But what is certain is that it was not how Creation was in the first chapter of Genesis, and therefore the pre-fall state is not what is being described in Romans 8, but the result of new creation in Christ.

Wolves and lambs

This leads rather neatly to the last set of passages I will deal with, urged in support of the doctrine of a fallen natural world, which is in Isaiah. The first is in the context of a Messianic prophecy, in which the Branch of Jesse will defeat Israel's enemies and unite them, judging the wicked in favor of the righteous. It begins:

> [6] The wolf will live with the lamb,
>   the leopard will lie down with the goat,
> the calf and the lion and the yearling together;
>   and a little child will lead them.
> [7] The cow will feed with the bear,
>   their young will lie down together,
>   and the lion will eat straw like the ox.

17. 2 Pet 3:13.
18. Isa 59:16.

[8] The infant will play near the cobra's den,
    and the young child will put its hand into the viper's nest.
[9] They will neither harm nor destroy
    on all my holy mountain,
for the earth will be filled with the knowledge of the LORD
    as the waters cover the sea.[19]

Isaiah 65 has similar contents, in a passage announcing the new heavens and new earth. It clearly describes the same future situation, for

[25] The wolf and the lamb will feed together,
    and the lion will eat straw like the ox,
    and dust will be the serpent's food.
They will neither harm nor destroy
    on all my holy mountain,"
says the LORD.[20]

The argument from YECs (and admittedly, from one early commentator on the passage, Irenaeus, see chapter 6) is that these passages predict a return to the original state of Eden. I guess the Old Earth argument might be that they show God's dissatisfaction with his now fallen creation, and his desire to replace it. Yet this was never a universal understanding. Matthew Henry, writing in the era most concerned to seek the "plain meaning" of Scripture, seems to take the Isaiah 11 passage as purely metaphorical of mended *human* relationships in his commentary:

Unity or concord, which is intimated in these figurative promises, that even *the wolf shall dwell* peaceably *with the lamb;* men of the most fierce and furious dispositions, who used to bite and devour all about them, shall have their temper so strangely altered by the efficacy of the gospel and grace of Christ that they shall live in love even with the weakest and such as formerly they would have made an easy prey of . . . Christ, who is our peace, came to slay all enmities and to settle lasting friendships among his followers, particularly between Jews and Gentiles.[21]

Certainly both passages portray a contrast between the present age and the age of Messiah. The first comment to make on the text itself is that these passages are indeed prophetically symbolic rather than literal. This is abundantly clear from chapter 65:20, which pictures the new age as free of infant mortality, yet with people dying of old age at, usually, over a

19. Isa 11:6–9.
20. Isa 65:25.
21. Church, *Matthew Henry's Commentary*, 845.

hundred years old. This is pictured as an equivalent sign of blessing to the tameness of wolves. So Isaiah's vision of the future age still contains human death, giving no support at all for the fictional time of deathlessness for animals claimed for the beginning. When the New Testament picks up "new earth" language, it is clearly on the understanding of eternal life and the defeat of death in the light of the Resurrection: mere longevity must therefore be a metaphor.

But for *what* are these passages metaphors? Only of gospel fellowship, as Matthew Henry understood? It is very clear as we dig deeper that the picture in both is of "the Great Israelite Covenant Dream"—the ideal life of an independent farmer dwelling amongst his kinsmen and cultivating his allotted land inheritance on the slopes of Mount Zion, close to the king and to God's temple, "everyone under his own vine and under his own fig tree."[22]

The animal references must be understood in this context, rather than as a description of nature in the raw. In each case a wild animal is paired with the livestock to which, in this present age, the latter might fall prey, to the loss of the farmer. No wild herbivores are mentioned. It is more to do with the Israelite landholder dwelling in God's promised safety than the correction of a cruel natural order.

There *is* a hint of Edenic imagery in the mention of the snake, which in chapter 65 eats dust (a reminder of the effectiveness of God's curse in Genesis 3) and in chapter 11 is safe for a child to play with. This, I think, is intended as a *contrast* with the garden, not a return to it: in the old Eden you couldn't trust your wife with the snake, but in the new you can even let your baby play with it. But this imagery is used less in order to compare the new world with Eden than to emphasize God's new beginning: "Eden on steroids."

There is indeed a contrast, whatever the metaphorical context, between this present age and the age to come. But is there any implication that this is a contrast between a damaged creation and a repaired one? I would argue, rather, that it's a contrast between the first, good creation and a new, better creation. This is a progression that actually goes back to Genesis 1, and helps us understand not why the present creation is "naturally evil," because Scripture does not state that it is, but why it could be better than we find it. I will turn to examining that in the next chapter.

22. Mic 4:4.

Chapter 4—When "Very Good" Isn't Good Enough

How can I make you understand, when you do not understand the poets? The hnakra *is our enemy, but he is also our beloved. We feel in our hearts his joy as he looks down from the mountain of water in the north where he was born; we leap with him when he jumps the falls; and when winter comes, and the lake smokes higher than our heads, it is with his eyes that we see it and know that his roaming time is come. We hang images of him in our houses, and the sign of all the* hrossa *is a* hnakra. *In him the spirit of the valley lives; and our young play at being hneraki as soon as they can splash in the shallows. . . And I say also this. I do not think the forest would be so bright, nor the water so warm, nor love so sweet, if there were no danger in the lakes.*

—C. S. LEWIS (1898–1963)[1]

Disorder built into creation

IN THE LAST CHAPTER I made the argument that some of the passages often used to contrast the present age of evil with the coming age of restoration, particularly Romans 8 and the Messianic passages in Isaiah in which wild beasts become docile, are better understood as contrasting the first creation, *as it came from the hand of God*, with a new creation that was intended even before sin intervened. In this chapter I will look at some of the scriptural evidence for this, particularly from the Genesis 1 creation account itself.

1. Lewis, *Out of the Silent Planet* , 86–87.

Genesis 1:1—2:3 (which, remember, is a functional and anthropo-centric account, not a materialist cosmology) speaks of God systematically imposing order on chaos. But when he creates man, it is not only as his image on earth but in order to "rule" and "subdue" it. Necessarily, then, the world was not completely orderly or subdued already, and that is because some elements of "chaos" or "disorder" (but not evil) remained. I will return to that later after putting it in the context of the account.

The "chaos" or "disorder" in question is the Hebrew *tohu wabohu* ("formless and empty," NIV) in Genesis 1:2. Whether you take verse 1 as the first act of creation or as a summary heading (that question has been discussed since at least Basil of Caesarea in the fourth century!), this situa-tion is where God starts the creation process in earnest. As John Walton and others have pointed out, "chaos" is not necessarily the best translation to use, with its pagan connotations both of non-createdness and of evil.

Rather, the governing sense is that of *lack of utility*, and in an account focused on the role of humanity as the goal of the creation, it is lack of func-tion for *humankind* that is most in view. Elsewhere in Scripture, *tohu* indicates desert places where only screech owls and other marginal creatures live, and often it is used of situations where civilization has been destroyed in judge-ment and cities are deserted, as if returning to the earliest stage of creation.

In Genesis 1 *tohu wabohu* takes the form, particularly, of *darkness* and *the deep (tehom)*. The land, or earth, is useless and empty because it is dark and covered with water. The significant point is that God deals with this lack of order not by destroying it, but by pushing it aside and giving it function in relation to the order he creates.

And so when God creates light, he separates it from the darkness and alternates the two, so that the darkness becomes the night, with its regular appearance and its various valuable functions.

As for the deep, God's first act is to divide it in two, and to use the upper part of the waters (which in my view should be seen phenomeno-logically as "clouds" rather than as a theoretical or imaginary cosmic ocean) both to separate earth from heaven, concerning which see the next section, and to bless the earth with rain.

The remainder of the deep is pushed aside by the formation of the earth, or land, proper, to form the seas, which are kept within strict bounds. Both sets of waters receive their own inhabitants on the fifth day—the lower waters bring forth fish and other sea creatures, and the upper waters gener-ate birds, both of which are of clear benefit to humankind.

And yet, despite their integral role in the Genesis creation, throughout the rest of Scripture both these elements—the night and the sea—retain their aura of danger and disorder. For example, regarding darkness, the penultimate plague of the Exodus is darkness, and the death of the firstborn occurs at midnight. Night terrors are mentioned in Psalm 91, evil people make a covenant with the night in Jeremiah 33. And the New Testament contrasts the night of the present and the day of the coming kingdom in the light of Christ, as a recurrent theme.

Similarly, the waters return to de-create the world by covering the land in the flood. The sea is the barrier to Israel's escape from Egypt until God parts it, and returns to drown Pharaoh's troops—a victory which other passages describe in terms of the Canaanite myth of God's defeat of Rahab the chaos monster.[2] Jonah tries to escape God by going to sea,[3] which claims his life, and he, like the psalmist,[4] expresses wonder that God is present even in the depths of the ocean. In the New Testament, of course, we have Jesus's calming of the storm and the perhaps conscious echo of Jonah in Paul's shipwreck, in which the sea apparently seeks to oppose, yet actually facilitates, Paul's prophesied trip to Rome.

At this point let me refer you forward, to the last visions of John in Revelation 21, about the final age to come. In verse 1 we learn that in the new heaven and new earth "there was no longer any sea." In verse 25 we are told that there is no night in the new Jerusalem. These are clear references back to Genesis 1—but Genesis 1 is about the world *before* sin and its curse. What Revelation is saying, in symbolic terms, is that what God left of *tohu wabohu* in his original creation (for his own good purposes, of course), will not be present in the new creation.

And so what is being taught is not simply that God will remove what is evil, but rather that by removing what is evil (in the form of human and angelic wickedness), the way is cleared for a new creation better than the first ever was—a creation that was always in God's mind. Let us now turn to another strand of evidence in Genesis 1.

Separation from God built into creation

The temple imagery of Genesis 1 has been noted occasionally since Patristic times, but amongst modern evangelical scholars, has been recently and

2. For example, Ps 89:9–10, Isa 59:9–10.
3. Jonah 1:3.
4. Ps 139:8.

extensively discussed by John Walton,[5] Greg Beale,[6] and Richard Middleton,[7] and many others dating back to the early 1980s.[8]

Not to dwell on the detail, the major divisions of this "cosmic temple" correspond to the main divisions within the Hebrew tabernacle and temple (or at another level, to the increasingly holy space in the land of Israel itself). Perhaps this is best illustrated in a table:

Genesis Cosmic Temple	Hebrew Temple	Land of Israel
Heavens	Holy of Holies	Jerusalem Temple
Firmament	Curtain of the Temple	Wall of the Temple
Sky (and mountains)	Sanctuary of Priests	Jerusalem
Land	Court of Worshippers	Land of Israel
Sea	Outside World	Lands of the Gentiles

Now, the thing I wish to note in particular is that viewing the original Genesis creation in this way, one can see that the account sets up, *as part of creation itself*, a radical separation between God and his dwelling, the heavens, and humanity and its domain, the earth. The divisions are the same as in all versions of Israel's tabernacle or temple, the pattern "shown on the high mountain" to Moses having the same hierarchy of holiness: only Israelites have admission to the temple courts, priests to the sanctuary, and the high priest, once a year only, to the holy of holies.

This, of course, is a profound contrast to what is promised under the New Covenant, in which at the moment of Jesus's death, the temple curtain was torn in two; and the corresponding picture in Revelation chapter 21 is of the breaking down of all the temple barriers between humanity and God: in v 3, God dwells with humans, and even personally wipes all tears from their eyes. The breakdown of cosmic barriers is represented by the (continuous) descent of the Holy City, the new Jerusalem, from heaven to earth (v 2). Even the third column of the table is represented by the absence of any temple in the city (v 22).

5. Walton, *Genesis*.

6. Beale, *The Temple*.

7. Middleton, *A New Heaven and a New Earth*. His development of the observation that, unlike the earthly temple, the earth in Genesis 1 is not said to be filled with God's glory, is very relevant here.

8. Levenson, "The Temple and the World."

Before drawing conclusions from that, let me direct your attention to Genesis 2, and other passages in the Bible dependent on it. That chapter introduces something entirely new. The garden of Eden is widely recognized to represent a temple precinct in a number of ways.[9] Firstly, the ANE concept of a sacred garden sanctuary is not uncommon in literature. Then various biblical temple themes are introduced here, such as the tree of life that resembles the seven-branched *menorah*, with its almond buds and blossoms, the entrance on the east side, and the cherubim that come to guard access to it (but only after Adam and Eve are expelled). The river of Eden finds its echo in Ezekiel chapter 47 and Revelation chapter 22.[10] Furthermore, as Gordon Wenham points out, the verbs used for Adam's work in the garden, "work" and "take care" (NIV) are also, and only, used together in relation to the Levites' tabernacle ministry.[11]

Yet even apart from these, the very fact that Adam and Eve are clearly in intimate communion with God there shows it to be a sacred space.[12] It reads as if the garden is a kind of outpost of the heavens on earth. But one thing is notably missing from the imagery, and that is any indication of a separating curtain in the garden. Adam and Eve are forbidden to eat from the tree of knowledge "in the midst of the garden" (where God walks in 3:8), but they are not forbidden the tree of life, which also grows there. Indeed, they need to hide from God's view among the trees when they see their nakedness—there is no curtain, and no firmament to shield them from view.

Even those punitive cherubim with their flaming sword reinforce the message that this garden is a place of unlimited access to God, not of hierarchical grades of holiness, quite unlike the usual temple imagery. For they guard access to the entire garden after the fall in the way that the temple cherubim guard the holy of holies, not the temple perimeter. This is unlike the temple—but it is very like the imagery of the New Testament, and the visions of Revelation about the city of God, whose gates are always open.

9. Wenham, "Sanctuary Symbolism in the Garden of Eden Story."

10. See also Ps 36:8; Ps 46:4.

11. Num 3:7–8, 8:26, 18:5–6.

12. Inevitably, some scholars disagree that there is temple imagery in either Genesis 1 or 2, notably Daniel Block, who nevertheless recognizes he is swimming "against an overwhelming current of scholarly opinion" (Block, "Eden: A Temple?," 3). In that chapter even he agrees that Eden becomes *represented* in the later temple: "However, as noted above, the Edenic features of the tabernacle, the Jerusalem temple, and the temple envisioned by Ezekiel are obvious." To me the literary unity of the Pentateuch suggests a *mutual* use of imagery between Genesis 1 and the tabernacle in Exodus, at least. The ultimate problem, I think, is in failing to distinguish two distinct types of temple, as I discuss here.

This open access is also like some other strands in the Old Testament. John Sailhamer makes an extensive case in *The Meaning of the Pentateuch*[13] for saying that God intended, and invited, the newly freed nation of Israel to worship him "face to face" on Mount Sinai (just as Moses did). After three days preparation they were, at the blast of the trumpet, to come "up into the mountain" and he would speak with them. But lacking faith, when the trumpet blew they let fear overcome obedience and stood "at a distance," and the text graphically records the trumpet becoming louder and louder as if in frustration at their hesitation. In the end, they delegate Moses to do the work of mediation and, according to Sailhamer, end up with multitudes of laws added "because of transgressions,"[14] and a failed covenant that ends in exile from the land—just like Adam and Eve's banishment from the garden. Instead of becoming a kingdom of priests[15] to the world, they become a kingdom *with* priests, who alone may approach God on their behalf.

Moses himself, despite his failures, has access to Yahweh "face to face," as in the garden, resulting in the need for him to wear a veil in front of the people when he came down from the mountain, because his face shines from God's presence—an image Paul compares to our own direct access to the Father in Christ.[16]

My point in all this is to show that what is described in Genesis 2 is a new step beyond the "goodness" of the Genesis 1 creation. The latter left us with a human race (or perhaps Adam and Eve as a primordial couple, if the passage is taken that specifically) commissioned to subdue the still not fully tamed earth, but like the writer of Ecclesiastes, aware that God is in heaven, and they are on earth.[17]

But according to God's unfolding plan, in chapter 2 God himself breaks through that separation, and comes down to meet with Adam and Eve on earth, only to have that communion broken, for Adam and his race, by sin. Had the first sin not occurred, we may surmise that the spiritual bridgehead between heaven and earth would have remained open from then on, and that the face-to-face knowledge of God would, in some way, have spread through the whole earth.[18] As it is, Israel failed to achieve it at Mount Sinai, and it has only become possible because of the new, effective covenant of Christ.

---

13. Sailhamer, *The Meaning of the Pentateuch*.

14. Rom 5:20.

15. Exod 19:6.

16. 2 Cor 3:12–18.

17. Eccl 5:2.

18. Hab 2:14.

What this says about the creation

The implication of these two strands of teaching drawn from Genesis 1 and 2 is that there are identifiable differences between the first and second creations that are *not* attributable to the fall, but to the difference between the two creations themselves. The first was good, but the new would be better, and the changes were within God's plan even apart from sin, which was, in fact, an interruption to its inauguration, albeit within the secret counsel of God an interruption anticipated from eternity, which would bring greater glory to his Son.[19]

The first creation, though it included humanity without sin, also involved a holy separation between earth and heaven. Perhaps there were people who worshipped gods, or even one God, before Eden—but if so they worshipped him from afar, rather than in intimacy. Furthermore, for God's own purposes, the created order contained elements that were in some sense disorderly or dangerous to humanity (represented by the darkness and the deep), only to be removed finally, like the barrier between heaven and earth, in the new creation.

Therefore, although the creation was rightly called "very good" by its Maker, meaning good for the purposes for which he created it, it was not paradise on earth—for that was reserved for the *actual* paradise on earth of chapter 2.

This line of thought enables us to think more clearly about what we would expect to find both in God's good creation now, and what we might look for in exploring the distant past historically or scientifically. For example, consider that creation command to humankind to "rule and subdue the earth."

For those who accept an old earth, it is clear that the world had existed successfully without human intervention or government for billions of years, so what can this "rule" mean? The fact of the fall into sin prevents us from being able to answer this question completely from history—there is nothing with which to contrast it apart from humanity's corrupted world.

The workaday physical occupations of agriculture and civilization seem to be part of it, bringing the primeval world to order for human good. But could it not also be that part of humanity's intended "Edenic" role was to "tame" the wilder aspects of nature that were acceptable and even admirable in the prehuman world, but shown to be a less than perfect expression of God's loving nature, not to mention dangerous to humanity, once his viceroy appeared on the scene? Is not Genesis suggesting that God delegated the final

---

19. Eph 1:3–10; Col 1:15–20; Rev 13:8.

part of the ordering and subduing of his world to humankind, on the understanding that it would be achieved in a true faith relationship with God?

Humanity, though, failed to bring about any such transformation. The Bible teaches that this failure is to be remedied by the transforming work of Christ, the last Adam. He completes the work that humanity failed even to begin properly. So it is not that, through humanity's sin, nature became corrupt and needs to be restored to Eden, but that because of humanity's sin, the primeval world failed to be completed and needs the work of Christ to take it forward. Indeed, it would seem possible that in God's economy the work that Christ achieves in the creation though his passion is even beyond what humanity was originally commissioned to do, just as his salvation from sin takes us not back to Eden, but beyond that to the realm of the spirit where temptation can never again harm us.

Does that future include vegetarian lions? The absence of shadows? The abolition of seaside holidays? I think it is dangerous to conclude such things from what are, after all, prophetic metaphors. Even the New Testament is careful to employ veiled imagery in describing the age to come. But it is even more dangerous to conclude that the elements belong to Satan, or that carnivorous lions are in any sense "evil" or "fallen," especially when Psalm 104:20 presents them as so piously seeking their food from God.

Chapter 5—Powers and Principalities

> [4] *"Where were you when I laid the earth's foundation?*
>
> *Tell me, if you understand.*
>
> [5] *Who marked off its dimensions? Surely you know!*
>
> *Who stretched a measuring line across it?*
>
> [6] *On what were its footings set,*
>
> *or who laid its cornerstone—*
>
> [7] *while the morning stars sang together*
>
> *and all the angels shouted for joy?*

—JOB 38:4–7

Ubiquity in Scripture

To COMPLETE THE BIBLICAL picture of the nonhuman creation in the world since the fall, I want to make a brief examination of the "powers and principalities" that are mentioned at various points, and especially, often scarcely noticed, in the New Testament. The reason I consider them relevant here is because, as well as being indicated as personal angelic or demonic beings in the Bible, some references make them appear to be more akin to what we might call natural *forces* in the world, and so potentially part of the brief of this book.

But they are also relevant because the "traditional view" attributes satanic agency to the natural creation. Remember Spurgeon's words from the introduction: "the slime of the serpent is on it all . . ." Is there in fact any basis in Scripture for this demonization of nature?

Rather, I suggest that the existence of Satan and corrupt angels, rational agents having malign influences within the world of humanity, does not affect our subject, the supposed corruption of the natural world. As we

60

saw in chapter 1, there is just one direct reference to Satan's involvement in natural events in Job 1, but Satan as pictured there is a servant of Yahweh, if an ambivalent one, and the resources he uses to plague Job are God's, not his own, and they are used only with divine permission.

Yet one notes with some surprise that Paul, when talking about the creation, habitually says far more about apparently angelic powers and principalities than he does about what we would call the natural world. For example, in rejoicing in the impossibility that anything in all creation can separate believers from Christ, he says:

> [38] For I am convinced that neither death nor life, neither angels nor demons, neither the present nor the future, nor any powers,
> [39] neither height nor depth, nor anything else in all creation, will be able to separate us from the love of God that is in Christ Jesus our Lord.[1]

It is interesting that not one of these created things is mentioned in the Genesis creation account. Similarly, in expressing Christ's lordship over creation he writes:

> [15] The Son is the image of the invisible God, the firstborn over all creation. [16] For in him all things were created: things in heaven and on earth, visible and invisible, whether thrones or powers or rulers or authorities; all things have been created through him and for him.[2]

It would appear to be the same created authorities who are represented as Christ's enemies in 1 Corinthians 15:

> [24] Then the end will come, when he hands over the kingdom to God the Father after he has destroyed all dominion, authority and power. [25] For he must reign until he has put all his enemies under his feet.[3]

Beings or institutions?

Now, it is common in the NT to conceptualize the cross as a victory over Satan. In fact the earliest popular atonement theory of Patristic times was the "ransom theory," in which the life of Christ was paid to Satan as a ransom

1. Rom 8:38–39.
2. Col 1:15–16.
3. 1 Cor 15:24–25.

for souls he kept imprisoned by sin and death, only for Christ to outwit him by his resurrection. Yet there is more to powers and authorities than the devil himself. There must even be more to them than ontologically evil powers, or we would be opening the door to theological dualism. Whether or not they are involved now in moral evil, these are "powers" and "authorities" created by God and therefore, presumably, with some intended ongoing role for good in creation. Our task is to identify what those roles are.

In fact, Paul uses the same word "authorities" to commend Christian respect for earthly political authorities, and it is not obvious that he is referring to anything fundamentally different from the powers and authorities mentioned in the previous passages:

> 13 Let everyone be subject to the governing authorities, for there is no authority except that which God has established. The authorities that exist have been established by God. ² Consequently, whoever rebels against the authority is rebelling against what God has instituted, and those who do so will bring judgement on themselves.[4]

So it would appear that, in the political sphere, all God-given authority operates through these powers: if so, their created purpose is somehow to enable human government, whether good or even oppressive or unbelieving government, to function.

Belief in personal angels with a significant role in the affairs of the world is less common than it once was. The Enlightenment, of course, was suspicious of all things supernatural. But in academic interpretation of the Bible things have changed too. Since influential books by Hendrik Berkhof[5] and G. B. Caird[6] after World War II (years which concentrated many minds on the nature of evil) a prominent and actually quite useful stream of interpretation has viewed these powers not as "bad angels" but in terms exclusively of the political and other power structures of the world. In this view, to quote John Stott (who prefers to see them in personal terms):

> . . . it has been suggested that Paul himself had begun to "demythologize" the concept of angels and demons, and that he sees them rather as structures of earthly existence and power, especially the state, but also tradition, law, economics and even religion.[7]

---

4. Rom 13:1–2.
5. Berkhof, *Christ and the Powers*.
6. Caird, *Principalities and Powers*.
7. Stott, *The Cross of Christ*, 233 (footnote).

In other words, this view sees the "authorities" as the effects of "collective psyche" beyond the power or control of the individual. What induces mildly disgruntled citizens to end up in a mob committing atrocities? Why do some really bad ideas dominate cultures like a meme[8] pandemic? What is it about charismatic politicians from Adolf Hitler to John F. Kennedy that enables them to bend millions of ordinary people to their agendas? It surely doesn't happen to the rest of us. I think it is quite a useful concept to see power and authority as something more than simply good or bad people fortuitously gaining rational assent from others.

But Stott points out, I think rightly, that this impersonal interpretation does not do justice to the specific mention Paul makes of some of these powers being in "the heavenly realms," e.g., Ephesians 6:12:

> [12] For our struggle is not against flesh and blood, but against the rulers, against the authorities, against the powers of this dark world and against the spiritual forces of evil in the heavenly realms.

Neither does it do justice to the language of punishment associated with them that we saw above in 1 Corinthians 15:24. What is clear is that Paul is not simply tossing apocalyptic ideas about in the wind—that is not his style—but has developed some biblical ideas in a way that is coherent to him, though perhaps largely alien to our post-Enlightenment worldview.

It may well be that both the personal and the structural aspects are true, and that Paul is deliberately ambiguous in how he uses the term. Such "compound" views are propounded by D. E. H. Whiteley,[9] Michael Green,[10] Walter Wink,[11] and Markus Barth.[12] Nigel Goring Wright also writes:

> We are not obliged to agree with John Stott that the New Testament has nothing to say about social structures, or that the position outlined [in these writers] represents an "uneasy compromise." The point is precisely that the power structures of human life are vulnerable and open to invasion by the powers of darkness, or, indeed, that it is out of the powers of darkness

---

8. "Meme"—a really bad idea in its own right: a fanciful unit of ideas, equivalent to the gene, and popularized by Richard Dawkins largely as a way to discredit religion (but inconsistently, not atheism or science) as a dangerous contagion.

9. Whiteley, *The Theology of Paul.*

10. Green, *I Believe in Satan's Downfall.*

11. Wink, *Naming the Powers.*

12. Barth, *Ephesians 4–6.*

and the fallen human beings from whom they operate that a spiritual dynamic is generated.[13]

In other words, then, it may even be that it is human sin that in some way makes the powers, which God created for good, evil. One such idea is the theme found in Isaiah 24, where God's judgement on the earth (24:1) involves punishing "the powers in heavens above and the kings on the earth below."[14] This linkage clearly implies that whatever these powers are up to, it's not some distant and separate celestial rebellion but is intimately associated with what's gone wrong in the world of humans. That's why, whether you accept them as personal angelic agencies or "demythologized" human phenomena, they're important theologically, and are not to be quietly sidelined or left to Charismatics busily "binding territorial demons" to no obvious effect.

A very detailed study of these powers, as true spiritual entities, and of how the Old Testament describes their role in the world and in political government is given in Michael Heiser's study *The Unseen Realm*,[15] and I can't begin to explore the ramifications here fully.

But one way of understanding how our familiar political and social "powers" might relate to angelic agencies "in the heavens" is by employing the concept of "participation," or what we might call "correspondence," that is found in the work of Owen Barfield.[16] In some way, under this view, there is a spiritual *correlation* between power exerted by these supra-human forces, and the power exerted by, and the accountability of humans for, their own treatment of others. Pilate has power, but only because it is given from above,[17] and yet he is its accountable wielder, not merely its victim.

What convinces me of the importance of "the powers" is that they underpin a good part of Paul's theology of atonement, namely that associated with the concept of *Christus Victor*, which in slightly garbled form as the "ransom theory" was the main Patristic theory of salvation, and which is increasingly popular today. In the letter to the Colossians Paul writes:

> [9] For in Christ all the fullness of the Deity lives in bodily form,
> [10] and in Christ you have been brought to fullness. He is the head over every power and authority. . . .
> [13] When you were dead in your sins and in the uncircumcision of your flesh, God made you alive with Christ. He forgave

13. Wright, *A Theology of the Dark Side*, 144.

14. Isa 24:21.

15. Heiser, *The Unseen Realm*.

16. Barfield, *Saving the Appearances*.

17. John 19:11.

us all our sins, [14] having canceled the charge of our legal indebtedness, which stood against us and condemned us; he has taken it away, nailing it to the cross. [15] And having disarmed the powers and authorities, he made a public spectacle of them, triumphing over them by the cross.[18]

I would suggest that both key elements of the cross are here—by it Christ disarms and triumphs over these mysterious powers, but the means by which he does it is substitutionary atonement for human sins. It would appear that, whatever the powers are, they've "got something over us" which the selfless and sacrificial death of Christ "disarms," a power no doubt originating in the Eden narrative. For other Scriptures, referring to Satan as the accuser as well as the tempter, hint that the vicious circle is because our sin is justly accused by him, resulting in our death. Since Satan is referred to as "the Prince of this world," offering Jesus in the wilderness its power structures in return for worship, one supposes that he speaks on behalf of the authorities that Paul means here. Remove sin, and they no longer have us in their power.

A role in nature?

But why do they exist in the first place? It seems to me the popular assumption, insofar as one exists in popular Christianity now, rests on some Miltonian idea of a primordial rebellion in heaven leading to a bunch of wicked angels muscling in on human affairs by sheer main force, starting with a bit of agitprop in Eden involving a commandeered snake. But here, to me, is where it gets more interesting than that. In Colossians, Paul's first mention of the powers, as we saw above, is in 1:15–16:

[15] The Son is the image of the invisible God, the firstborn over all creation. [16] For in him all things were created: things in heaven and on earth, visible and invisible, whether thrones or powers or rulers or authorities; all things have been created through him and for him.

Paul is clearly conflating, as he habitually does, every source of authority that matters to us, whether "the rulers, the authorities, the powers of this dark world" or "the spiritual forces of evil in the heavenly realms." It would appear that the same phenomenological realities are involved, seen both from earthly and spiritual perspectives. And these authorities, all, were created as authorities under and for Christ—and presumably, since from

18. Col 2:9–15.

chapter 2 we see they have a say in our affairs, they were created for the benefit of humankind, but have somehow gone wrong.

This explains what, otherwise, seems Paul's (together with Peter's, actually) apparently odd attitude to governments. Both commend obedience to Caesar, and to any other authorities whatsoever, as being created by God for humanity's good, even though both Jewish and Gentile power structures were clearly antagonistic to the gospel and led to the death of both apostles. Paul is seeing authority itself as an actual "thing," an element of creation made for us, involving angelic powers with God-given dignity and hence worthy of respect, just like their human counterparts. In both Peter's[19] and Jude's[20] letters, concerning angelic powers, one finds the same sense of respect for what God has ordained, even though they have fallen into evil and although God—who alone has the right—will punish them in time.[21]

At this point, then, let me suggest (somewhat speculatively), the place of these powers in the business of the original creation, and how what God intended for good might have been perverted, not through a pre-creation war in heaven, but through the failure of humankind—the only creature, angels not excepted, made in God's image.

I suggest that in the original economy of creation the "powers and principalities" were created, like the other angelic beings, as servants for the people created in the image of God, that is in the image of the Son. "Are not all angels ministering spirits sent to serve those who will inherit salvation?"[22] That means that however personal their power, it was intended to be under the control of sinless humanity to assist in the government of the world, under God.

The image of God in humankind was intended to be shown partly in the social structures—we may even say political structures—built up as the population of the earth increased. It seems that arrangements for communal power and authority were built into that plan. What happens to that, then, in the eventuality of the reality of sin? Those heavenly/earthly powers were not withdrawn, any more than the ability to make fire or to throw rocks was withdrawn. They remained as invisible, but very powerful, forces.

19. 1 Pet 2:10–12.

20. Jude 8–10.

21. The link between political and spiritual "powers" as instituted by God is worthy of much more study. The moral ambivalence of both seems to be related to the inscrutability of God, for Scripture enjoins the same kind of respect for even harmful celestial beings as it does for corrupt human authorities as God's agents. See 2 Pet 2:10–12; Jude 8–10, where it may seem surprising that slandering devils is seen as a sin, rather than a virtue.

22. Heb 1:14.

Imagine that Bronze Age humanity had possessed the power of nuclear fission—the power of authority structures are on that kind of level of potency. Such an idea is consistent with the oldest mythologies of humanity—it is notable that in Mesopotamia, it was believed to be the descent of kingship (not kings) from heaven that began civilization.[23]

Only, with sinful persons taking the reins of power, one has what Nigel Goring Wright calls a "Sorcerer's Apprentice" situation. Give the powers distorted instructions, and it's the equivalent of a madman pressing the nuclear red button. Forget the need to give them guidance altogether, and like robots in a science fiction tale they are in danger of becoming autonomous and dangerous. And so in this scenario, our oppression by the powers—a very real theme in Scripture—is the direct result of our misuse of them. The angelic fall, if such it can be termed, might even then be the result, rather than the cause, of our own, at least in the sense that it was God's plan for humankind's glorification that was the occasion for Satan's envy and malice in the garden.

I have included this chapter on "the powers" because they are a genuine part of creation, and clearly of more importance to it, particularly in Paul's theology, than is often considered now. And yet the texts we have seen referring to them seem to relate their effects exclusively to the world of human beings, and particularly to the political realm. Do they also have any influence over the natural creation?

If we consider humankind's commission in Genesis 1, to rule and subdue the world, there would need to be political power structures in place for humanity to function in such a role. If we also consider the implicit theme in Genesis 2 (echoed through the Bible in new creation teaching) that Adam's race would be involved in the ultimate transformation of the cosmos which, in the event, is performed through Christ, then one might reasonably imagine "powers and authorities" to be involved at the natural level too, and so subject to the same perversion as in the political realm.

After all, when Christ comes as King to rule by the Spirit, it is at the expense of the failed and discredited heavenly powers. Since Christ also comes to transform the cosmos by the same Spirit, is it not similarly by overthrowing corrupted powers within nature?

Although this seems logical enough, the fact is that it does not appear that any role in the running of the natural world is attributed directly to such powers and authorities, either in New Testament in the Old, whereas God claims exactly such a role. It does seem that Paul's treatment of them,

---

23. "After the kingship descended from heaven, the kingship was in Eridu," begins the Sumerian king list.

by far the most developed in Scripture, views them as involved only in the human, and especially the political, sphere.

In the wilderness temptation, Satan promised Jesus the kingdoms of the world—but not the kingdoms of nature. This only tends to confirm what we discovered in chapter 1—that God remains solely in charge of the non-rational creation, and that there is therefore no justification for regarding it as fallen. The conclusion appears to be that neither the sin of humanity, nor the corruption of the angelic powers, is associated in Scripture with any major changes in nature.

This concludes our consideration of the biblical material.

Section 2—The Theologians

Chapter 6—When Life Was Good

[11] *"You are worthy, our Lord and God,*

   to receive glory and honor and power,

for you created all things,

   and by your will they were created

   and have their being."

—REV 4:11

A dubious theological history

MANY EVANGELICALS ARE ASTONISHED to hear it suggested that for three quarters of the church's history the doctrine of a fallen creation was either unknown, or very much a minority view. Yet during most of the centuries of Christianity the natural creation has been seen as fundamentally *good*, unchanged in essentials from how it was first created by God, and therefore to be understood as a demonstration of God's wisdom, goodness, and power, and as a stimulus to wholehearted praise and worship. Even the strand of early interpretation that does speak of changes because of the fall seldom equates this with nature actually becoming evil.

This high view of the natural creation was, in fact, one of the things that distinguished Christianity most markedly from popular paganism, in which nature was "a hostile force constantly threatening to overwhelm us."[1] Contrary to modern romanticized notions polytheistic religion was less about living in harmony with nature than trying to appease the right gods or goddesses to prevent disaster.

This chapter and the next will be a survey of that theological history, and I will then, in the following one, attempt some explanation, including

---

1. So writes Alister McGrath of the pagan influence on the Anglo-Saxon poem *Beowulf* (*The Re-enchantment of Nature*, 84).

a brief, new account of one historical reason for the change to today's more negative view. It will be seen that this began at the start of the early modern period, particularly within the Protestant movement, and escalated out of all proportion thereafter up to the present. I'll quote at some length to allow the authors to speak for themselves. The ancients may also supply some worthwhile concepts for rethinking our own assumptions about nature.

As we survey the material, one thing we should keep in mind is that before the nineteenth century, the effects of the fall on nature were inextricably tied to its effects on humankind. The universal assumption of young earth chronology explains that. Irenaeus, for example, assumed that animals were vegetarian before the fall, but he held that Adam sinned before the evening he, and the animals, were created[2]—any carnivores would scarcely have had time to catch one square meal.

Since James Hutton and Charles Darwin, though, it has been necessary to account for the state of the natural world before humankind—a matter of a mere five days in the old literal chronology, but billions of years in the new. The discussions of the old writers, then, did not need to consider these matters separately as we do. What is amazing is that this is not what makes a theodicy of nature unnecessary for them. It is the fact that they do not see that there is anything *wrong* with nature even in the present state of humanity's misery. That should surely give us pause for thought.

Pre-Christian Jewish sources

It has often been remarked how little any doctrine of the fall is alluded to either in the Old Testament or early Jewish thought in general. We can, however, point to a couple of disparate Jewish sources overlapping the Christian era for hints on any connection Jews perceived between the garden events and the present natural world, before proceeding to the Christian sources.

Philo of Alexandria

The great Jewish philosopher Philo (c. 25 BCE–c. 50 CE) wrote both an allegorical commentary on Genesis, and a more "popular" set of questions and answers on it.[3] In commenting on the judgements of God in Genesis 3 (Q48–Q50) he takes the curse on the serpent as grammatically plain

---

2. Irenaeus, *Against Heresies* V XXIII 2 (Roberts and Donaldson, *Ante-Nicene Library*, Vol. IX 117). His reasoning is recapitulation: that Christ died on the same day that Adam sinned, Friday.

3. Philo, *Questions on Genesis*.

(but then allegorizes the serpent as "human desire"), the punishment of the woman as the inevitable fruit of sinful people living together, and the curse on the soil as, principally, an allegory on cultivating vice (leading to "sorrow and other ills" and loss of rationality) as opposed to virtue (leading to health). No change to the natural world is mentioned. The expulsion from Eden (Q56) Philo takes entirely spiritually as an exclusion from wisdom into ignorance.

Flavius Josephus

The historian of the Jewish revolt (37–c. 100) apparently received training from Pharisees, but was no religious sage. He naturally commences his *Antiquities*, a Jewish history for a Roman readership, with Genesis. His "fall" is treated in a low-key and almost trivial manner: Adam and Eve eat the fruit of the tree of wisdom against God's command and find themselves naked. In punishment:

> God told Adam that the earth would no longer produce anything of itself except in return for grinding toil. He punished Eve through childbirth, and deprived the serpent of feet so that it would have to wiggle across the ground. Then God removed Adam and Eve from the garden to another place.[4]

Patristic to mediaeval periods

Theophilus

The first of the church fathers to write on the creation was Theophilus, who was seventh Bishop of Antioch from 169–183. Describing the days of creation, he writes:

> Moreover, the things proceeding from the waters were blessed by God, that this might also be a sign of men's being destined to receive repentance and remission of sins, through the water and laver of regeneration. . . . But the monsters of the deep and the birds of prey are a similitude of covetous men and transgressors. For as the fish and the fowls are of one nature—some indeed abide in their natural state, and do no harm to those weaker than themselves, but keep the law of God, and eat of the seeds of

---

4. Josephus, Flavius, *Antiquities Bk 1* (Maier, *Josephus*, 20).

the earth; others of them, again, transgress the law of God, and eat flesh, and injure those weaker than themselves.

. . . The quadrupeds, too, and wild beasts, were made for a type of some men, who neither know nor worship God, but mind earthly things, and repent not. . . . And the animals are named wild beasts from their being hunted, not as if they had been made evil or venomous from the first—for nothing was made evil by God, but all things good, yea, very good—but the sin in which men were concerned brought evil upon them. For when man transgressed, they also transgressed with him.[5]

At first sight this may seem to lend support to the "fallen nature" theme, but if so it deals solely with the existence of carnivores. Some (not all, notice) of the originally good animals "transgress" and eat meat. But note the allegorical treatment: the carnivores are a *type* ("similitude") of sinful humans, not an evil in themselves. Then, also, Theophilus makes no observations from nature itself, but infers the creatures' sinfulness from the fact that they have departed from the provision of plants for food in Genesis 1:30, which he takes as a command (a dubious conclusion, as we saw in chapter 2). Also note the quasi-rational way the animals follow the moral lead of their ruler, much as servants sin because of their master's example. The *Catholic Encyclopedia*[6] attributes this to "the anthropomorphic tendency of primitive minds which appears in the doctrine of metempsychosis." It is notable that Theophilus is the only ancient authority this encyclopedia article can cite for animal suffering (or actually, animal violence) being the result of the fall, for the doctrine doesn't appear again for several centuries.

Irenaeus

By contrast, Irenaeus, the only other second-century writer to deal at length with the creation (and, contrary to what is often claimed nowadays, with the fall of the race and original sin too), says nothing about it. His interpretation of Genesis 3 is straightforward, and hardly goes beyond the text itself.[7] The ground is cursed on man's behalf, and Eve is punished in childbirth and marriage, but the full curse is on the serpent, which Irenaeus takes to represent Satan. The exile from Eden accounts for thorns hindering cultivation,

5. Theophilus of Antioch, *Apology to Autolycus* Bk 2 chapter XVI–XVII (Roberts and Donaldson, *Ante-Nicene Library*, Vol. III, 82–84).

6. Sharpe, "Evil."

7. Irenaeus, *Against Heresies* III XXIII 3 (Roberts and Donaldson, *Ante-Nicene Library*, Vol. V, 365).

and they face death. Other passages speak of humanity's bondage to Satan through sin, but say nothing of the natural world's involvement.

However, it is true that Irenaeus, commenting on Isaiah 65:11, seems to assume that the prophecy about lions eating straw is a return to a vegetarian situation before the fall:

> And it is right that when the creation is restored, all the animals should obey and be in subjection to man, and revert to the food originally given by God (for they had originally been subjected in obedience to Adam), that is, the productions of the earth.[8]

Clement of Alexandria

Clement (150–215) was a professional theologian whose *Stromata* is a miscellany of teaching. In one passage he compares the creation allegorically with the Decalogue (perhaps, incidentally, the first oblique Christian reference to "natural law"):

> For by the "finger of God" is understood the power of God, by which the creation of heaven and earth is accomplished; of both of which the tables will be understood to be symbols. For the writing and handiwork of God put on the table is the creation of the world. . . .
>
> And the representation of the earth contains men, cattle, reptiles, wild beasts; and of the inhabitants of the water, fishes and whales; and again, of the winged tribes, those that are carnivorous, and those that use mild food; and of plants likewise, both fruit-bearing and barren.[9]

This writer's attitude to carnivores contradicts that of Theophilus: he says they were created that way by God's righteous "law." It is Clement's understanding that was to predominate in the church into the late middle ages, and in Roman Catholicism even longer.

Lactantius

Lucius Lactantius (240–320) was religious advisor to the Emperor Constantine. In *A Treatise on the Anger of God*, written against Stoic and Epicurean philosophers, he says:

8. Irenaeus, *Against Heresies* V XXXIII 4 (ibid., 366).
9. Clement of Alexandria, *Stromata* VI XIV (ibid., vol. XII, 383.)

> [W]e understand that even [dumb animals] in the same manner were made by God for the use of man, partly for food, partly for clothing, partly to assist him in his work; so that it is manifest that the divine providence wished to furnish and adorn the life of men with an abundance of objects and resources, and on this account He both filled the air with birds, and the sea with fishes, and the earth with quadrupeds.[10]

Having endorsed human meat-eating and possibly leatherwork in Eden, in the same chapter he argues that God necessarily included both "good and evil" (meaning here only dangerous or injurious) things in creation, or humans could not have been rational, choosing, beings; an early version of the free will defense. In another work, in describing how God is intelligence, perception, and reason, Lactantius writes how he provided for irrational beasts at the dawn of creation:

> For He clothed them all with their own natural hair, in order that they might more easily be able to endure the severity of frosts and colds. Moreover, He has appointed to every kind its own peculiar defense for the repelling of attacks from without; so that they may either oppose the stronger animals with natural weapons, or the feebler ones may withdraw themselves from danger by the swiftness of their flight, or those which require at once both strength and swiftness may protect themselves by craft, or guard themselves in hiding-places. And so others of them either poise themselves aloft with light plumage, or are supported by hoofs, or are furnished with horns; some have arms in their mouth—namely, their teeth—or hooked talons on their feet; and none of them is destitute of a defense for its own protection.
>
> For if you take from these the natural clothing of their body, or those things by which they are armed of themselves, they can be neither beautiful nor safe, so that they appear wonderfully furnished if you think of utility, and wonderfully adorned if you think of appearance: in such a wonderful manner is utility combined with beauty.[11]

God's wise creation here is described in terms both of beauty and utility, but clearly within the context of the world even as we now see it, with threats from both weather and other beasts.

> For what if you should say, that birds were not made to fly, nor wild beasts to rage, nor fishes to swim, nor men to be wise, when

10. Lactantius, *A Treatise on the Anger of God* XIII (ibid., vol. XXII, 26).

11. Lactantius, *On the Workmanship of God* II (ibid., vol. XXII, 52).

it is evident that living creatures are subject to that natural disposition and office to which each was created?

. . . But since all the races of animals, and all the limbs, observe their own laws and arrangements, and the uses assigned
to them, it is plain that nothing is made by chance, since a perpetual arrangement of the divine plan is preserved.[12]

Once more, it is the present creation that he describes as being "in
original condition." The realization that each creature has its own "law" from
God, rather than deviating from a moral law that applies to every creature as
well as humans made in God's image, is a useful insight for today's debates.

Athanasius

Athanasius of Alexandria (about 296–373) was the great hero of the Arian
controversy in the fourth century, who endured exile many times in defense
of apostolic truth. He was also a supreme theologian. He wrote:

Now, nothing in creation had gone astray with regard to their
notions of God, save man only. Why, neither sun, nor moon,
nor heaven, nor the stars, nor water, nor air had swerved from
their order; but knowing their Artificer and Sovereign, the
Word, they remain as they were made. But men alone, having
rejected what was good, then devised things of nought instead
of the truth, and have ascribed the honor due to God, and their
knowledge of Him, to demons and men in the shape of stones.[13]

Like Lactantius, he is clear that the natural realm remains now as it was
first created. So is his contemporary Cyril, Bishop of Jerusalem.

Cyril

In his *Catechal Lectures*—basic teaching for baptism candidates—Cyril
(313–386) writes:

God's command was but one, which said, Let the earth bring
forth wild beasts, and cattle, and creeping things, after their
kinds and from one earth, by one command, have sprung di-
verse natures, the gentle sheep and the carnivorous lion, and
various instincts of irrational animals, bearing resemblance to

12. Lactantius, *On the Workmanship of God* VI–VII (ibid., 63).
13. Athanasius, *On the Incarnation* XLIII III.

the various characters of men; the fox to manifest the craft that is in men, and the snake the venomous treachery of friends, and the neighing horse the wantonness of young men, and the laborious ant, to arouse the sluggish and the dull.[14]

Once more, the original creation is linked clearly to not only meat-eating, but to various traits which, in humankind, would be immoral but which, in God's economy, have their essential place:

If thou knowest not the nature of all things, do the things that have been made forthwith become useless? Canst thou know the efficacy of all herbs? Or canst thou learn all the benefit which proceeds from every animal? Ere now even from venomous adders have come antidotes for the preservation of men. But thou wilt say to me, "The snake is terrible." Fear thou the Lord, and it shall not be able to hurt thee. "A scorpion stings." Fear the Lord, and it shall not sting thee. "A lion is bloodthirsty." Fear thou the Lord, and he shall lie down beside thee, as by Daniel. But truly wonderful also is the action of the animals: how some, as the scorpion, have the sharpness in a sting; and others have their power in their teeth; and others do battle with their claws; while the basilisk's power is his gaze. So then from this varied workmanship understand the Creator's power.[15]

Note here how Cyril hints that nature's propensity to harm humankind stems from a change in humankind, not in nature, to be remedied by biblical faith. Thomas Aquinas will pick up this theme a millennium later, but we have already noted it in the biblical witness in chapter 1.

Basil

The Cappadocian Fathers were three of the most brilliant theologians the church has seen, developing teaching foundational for both east and west. Basil (330–379), bishop of Caesarea; his brother Gregory Bishop of Nyssa (c. 332–395), and Gregory of Nazianzus (329–389), Patriarch of Constantinople all held a high view of creation. Basil, also known as Basil the Great, was like Cyril not only a great theologian but a great advocate for the poor. He composed a number of homilies on creation. Speaking of birds:

14. Cyril, *Catechetical Lectures* 9 XIII–XIV.
15. Ibid.

But we have enough words of common usage to characterize each species and to mark the distinction which Scripture sets up between clean and unclean birds.

Thus the species of carnivora is of one sort and of one constitution which suits their manner of living, sharp talons, curved beak, swift wings, allowing them to swoop easily upon their prey and to tear it up after having seized it. The constitution of those who pick up seeds is different, and again that of those who live on all they come across. What a variety in all these creatures![16]

And on beasts:

"Let the earth bring forth the living creature." Thus when the soul of brutes appeared it was not concealed in the earth, but it was born by the command of God. Brutes have one and the same soul of which the common characteristic is absence of reason. But each animal is distinguished by peculiar qualities. The ox is steady, the ass is lazy, the horse has strong passions, the wolf cannot be tamed, the fox is deceitful, the stag timid, the ant industrious, the dog grateful and faithful in his friendships.

As each animal was created the distinctive character of his nature appeared in him in due measure; in the lion spirit, taste for solitary life, an unsociable character. True tyrant of animals, he, in his natural arrogance, admits but few to share his honors. He disdains his yesterday's food and never returns to the remains of the prey. Nature has provided his organs of voice with such great force that often much swifter animals are caught by his roaring alone. The panther, violent and impetuous in his leaps, has a body fitted for his activity and lightness, in accord with the movements of his soul. The bear has a sluggish nature, ways of its own, a sly character, and is very secret; therefore it has an analogous body, heavy, thick, without articulations such as are necessary for a cold dweller in dens.[17]

Most significantly, all these are not the result of human sin, but of divine wisdom:

What language can attain to the marvels of the Creator? What ear could understand them? And what time would be sufficient to relate them? Let us say, then, with the prophet, "O

16. Basil, *Homilies on Creation* VIII III.
17. Ibid., IX III.

Lord, how manifold are thy works! In wisdom hast thou made them all."[18]

Thus in nature all has been foreseen, all is the object of continual care. If you examine the members even of animals, you will find that the Creator has given them nothing superfluous, that He has omitted nothing that is necessary. To carnivorous animals He has given pointed teeth which their nature requires for their support.[19]

This comports with Basil's assumption that death was part of the natural creation from the beginning:

So nature, being put in motion by the one command, passes equally through birth and death in a creature, while it keeps up the succession of kinds through resemblance, to the end. Because it is so that a horse succeed to a horse, a lion to a lion, an eagle to an eagle. And while every one of the living beings is preserved by these uninterrupted successions, she directs them to the end of it all.[20]

Gregory of Nazianzus

Another of the Cappadocian Fathers, Gregory has in one of his theological orations a long passage on creation, in discussing the nature of God. It actually begins with a theology that would have pleased the natural theologian William Paley (or the founder of the intelligent design movement Phillip E. Johnson), but introduces the main discussion on the created order thus:

[Paul] confesses the unsearchableness of the judgements of God, in almost the very words of David, who at one time calls God's judgements the great deep whose foundations cannot be reached by measure or sense; and at another says that His knowledge of him and of his own constitution was marvelous, and had attained greater strength than was in his own power or grasp.[21]

We are to expect, then, some things that seem morally ambiguous to us, but not to God, in nature. After a chapter on the wonder of humankind,

---

18. Ibid.
19. Ibid.
20. Ibid., IX II.
21. Gregory of Nazianzus, *Second Theological Oration* XXI.

he further establishes God's wisdom by observations on the natural world, for which there is space only for a few extracts:

> Shall I reckon up for you the differences of the other animals, both from us and from each other . . . ? How is it that some are gregarious and others solitary, some herbivorous and others carnivorous, some fierce and others tame, some fond of man and domesticated, others untamable and free? And some we might call bordering on reason and power of learning, while others are altogether destitute of reason, and incapable of being taught. . . . [H]ow is it that some . . . delight in beauty and others are unadorned; some are married and some single; some temperate and others intemperate; some have numerous offspring and others not; some are long-lived and others have but short lives?[22]

And not only in their forms, but their predatory skills, is God's hand seen:

> . . . Now Holy Scripture admires the cleverness in weaving even of women, saying, Who gave to woman skill in weaving and cleverness in the art of embroidery? This belongeth to a living creature that hath reason, and exceedeth in wisdom and maketh way even as far as the things of heaven.
>
> But I would have you marvel at the natural knowledge even of irrational creatures, and if you can, explain its cause. Whence do bees and spiders get their love of work and art, by which the former plan their honeycombs . . . and the latter weave their intricate webs by such light and almost airy threads stretched in divers ways, and this from almost invisible beginnings, to be at once a precious dwelling, and a trap for weaker creatures with a view to enjoyment of food?[23]

Gregory proceeds to eulogize the plant kingdom and inanimate nature, saying of the sea:

> Have your natural philosophers with their knowledge of useless details anything to tell us, those men I mean who are really endeavoring to measure the sea with a wineglass, and such mighty works by their own conceptions? Or shall I give the really scientific explanation of it from Scripture concisely, and yet more

22. Ibid., XXIII.
23. Ibid., XXIV–XXV.

satisfactorily and truly than by the longest arguments? "He hath fenced the face of the water with His command."[24]

If the wisdom and goodness seen in "secondary natures," he concludes, is so great, how much more the wisdom of God himself? Of "evils" in creation he says not one word.

John Chrysostom

John, also an Archbishop of Constantinople (347–407), was named "Golden-mouth" for his preaching style, which comes across even in his preserved and translated sermons. He too accepts the fierceness of the very nature of animals as God's wise purpose in creation—which is remarkable considering how much more experience than us the ancients had of their power to destroy their livestock or even their families:

> Again, the irrational animals have their weapons in their own body; thus, the ox has his horns; the wild boar his tusks; the lion his claws. But God hath not furnished the nature of my body with weapons, but hath made these to be extraneous to it, for the purpose of showing that man is a gentle animal. . . . For it is not only in our possessing a rational nature that we surpass the brutes, but we also excel them in body.[25]

It should be noted that his homily on Genesis 3, like that of Irenaeus, is a straight exposition of the text, with no mention of natural evil. He adds that human death was an act of God's mercy as well as of judgement, in limiting the extent of a sinful life.

Chrysostom does take a different view in his interpretation of Romans 8, which I addressed in chapter 3. However, this should be assessed in the light of Chrysostom's clear avowal of God's governance of "natural evil":

> Hold fast this argument then with me, and let it ever be fixed and immoveable in your minds, that not only when he confers benefits but even when he chastises God is good and loving. For even his chastisements and his punishments are the greatest part of his beneficence, the greatest form of his providence. Whenever therefore you see that famines have taken place, and pestilences, and drought and immoderate rains, and irregularities in the atmosphere, or any other of the things which chasten human nature, be not distressed, nor be despondent, but

24. Ibid., XXVII.
25. John Chrysostom, *Homily 11 on the Statues.*

worship Him who caused them, marvel at Him for His tender care. For He who does these things is such that He even chastens the body that the soul may become sound.

Then does God these things saith one? God does these things, and even if the whole city, nay even if the whole universe were here I will not shrink from saying this. Would that my voice were clearer than a trumpet, and that it were possible to stand in a lofty place, and to cry aloud to all men, and to testify that God does these things. I do not say these things in arrogance but I have the prophet standing at my side, crying and saying, *"There is no evil in the city which the Lord has not done"* [Amos 3:6]—now evil is an ambiguous term; and I wish that you shall learn the exact meaning of each expression, in order that on account of ambiguity you may not confound the nature of the things, and fall into blasphemy.[26]

Augustine

Augustine of Hippo (354–430) is one of the most influential theologians in the church's history. Since John Hick wrote *Evil and the God of Love*[27] his theodicy has frequently been cited, and almost equally frequently deemed inadequate to account for natural evil. This is not surprising as Augustine did not intend it to deal with the natural world, but "for the spiritually damaged subject."[28] Since Augustine is such an important figure, and his teaching on nature is scattered widely and extensively in his work, I will give a number of quotes. First, let's address how he deals with Genesis 3 itself:

The very fact, after all, that everyone born in this life finds the search for truth impeded by the perishable body is what is meant by the toil and grief which the man gets from the earth; and the thorns and thistles are the pricks and scratches of tortuous, intractable problems, or else the anxious thoughts about providing for this life, which frequently choke the word and stop it bearing any fruit in man. . . .[29]

Note that his treatment is allegorical and spiritual: the thorns and thistles of life are "really" that which stops the word bearing fruit in our perishable lives, as in the parable of the sower. Nature he handles from other

26. John Chrysostom, *Three Homilies on the Devil* I IV.

27. Hick, *Evil and the God of Love*.

28. Surin, *Theology and the Problem of Evil*, 12.

29. Augustine, *On Genesis Against the Manichees* II 20. 30. (91).

angles. In his autobiographical *Confessions* he *prays* his theology as it affects him practically from day to day:

> To you nothing at all is evil, not only to you but to your creation at large, because there is nothing outside to break in and upset the order you have imposed on it. But in parts of it some things do not harmonize with other parts, and are considered evil for that reason. But with other parts they do harmonize and are good, good in themselves. . . . Let it be far from me to say: "These things should not be," for if these were the only things I could see, I should still long for the better, and should be bound to praise you for these alone. [But when I understood from Scripture the praise arising from all things both in earth and heaven] I did not now long for better things because I considered everything.[30]

Here we see the core of his thinking—that we see evil in creation only because we lack the big picture both of God's purposes, and of creation's functioning. He goes into more detail in *The City of God*:

> This cause, however, of a good creation, namely, the goodness of God—this cause, I say, so just and fit, which, when piously and carefully weighed, terminates all the controversies of those who inquire into the origin of the world, has not been recognized by some heretics, because there are, forsooth, many things, such as fire, frost, wild beasts, and so forth, which do not suit but injure this thin blooded and frail mortality of our flesh, which is at present under just punishment.
>
> They do not consider how admirable these things are in their own places, how excellent in their own natures, how beautifully adjusted to the rest of creation, and how much grace they contribute to the universe by their own contributions as to a commonwealth; and how serviceable they are even to ourselves, if we use them with a knowledge of their fit adaptations,—so that even poisons, which are destructive when used injudiciously, become wholesome and medicinal when used in conformity with their qualities and design; just as, on the other hand, those things which give us pleasure, such as food, drink, and the light of the sun, are found to be hurtful when immoderately or unseasonably used. . . .
>
> But we do not greatly wonder that persons, who suppose that some evil nature has been generated and propagated by a kind of opposing principle proper to it, refuse to admit that the

---

30. Augustine, *Confessions* VII [XIII] 19.

cause of the creation was this, that the good God produced a good creation.[31]

The same idea of the "big picture" is here, but there are several new things to note too. First is that he only considers "harm" in relation to *humanity*. Though he must have been as aware of nature's harshness to its own as we are, he simply saw no theological problem to address there, and no "privation of good." Secondly we find the biblical idea that some things may harm us because we deserve punishment: yet the things that execute such punishment are not in themselves evil, but good. The third is that he regards those who see evil in God's present creation as heretics. It is hard to see that he would not apply his final sentence to those who see either Satan or evolution as an "opposing principle" in nature, responsible for its "evils" independent of God's determining will. In this, of course, he is following in direct line from Irenaeus and his condemnation of the Gnostics—who were almost the only people attached to the early church talking about evil in the natural creation.

Later, Augustine justifies the goodness even of animal death, which must surely be instructive if we seek to understand evolution as a work of God:

> But it is ridiculous to condemn the faults of beasts and trees, and other such mortal and mutable things as are void of intelligence, sensation, or life, even though these faults should destroy their corruptible nature; for these creatures received, at their Creator's will, an existence fitting them, by passing away and giving place to others, to secure that lowest form of beauty, the beauty of seasons, which in its own place is a requisite part of this world. For things earthly were neither to be made equal to things heavenly, nor were they, though inferior, to be quite omitted from the universe.
>
> Since, then, in those situations where such things are appropriate, some perish to make way for others that are born in their room, and the less succumb to the greater, and the things that are overcome are transformed into the quality of those that have the mastery, this is the appointed order of things transitory. Of this order the beauty does not strike us, because by our mortal frailty we are so involved in a part of it, that we cannot perceive the whole, in which these fragments that offend us are harmonized with the most accurate fitness and beauty.
>
> And therefore, where we are not so well able to perceive the wisdom of the Creator, we are very properly enjoined to believe

31. Augustine, *City of God* XI 22.

it, lest in the vanity of human rashness we presume to find any fault with the work of so great an Artificer.... Therefore it is not with respect to our convenience or discomfort, but with respect to their own nature, that the creatures are glorifying to their Artificer. Thus even the nature of the eternal fire, penal though it be to the condemned sinners, is most assuredly worthy of praise.[32]

Augustine even doubts the commonly understood implication of Genesis 3:18:

Concerning thorns and thistles, we can give a more definite answer, because after the fall of man God said to him, speaking of the earth, Thorns and thistles shall it bring forth to you. But we should not jump to the conclusion that it was only then that these plants came forth from the earth. For it could be that, in view of the many advantages found in different kinds of seeds, these plants had a place on earth without afflicting man in any way. But since they were growing in the fields in which man was now laboring in punishment for his sin, it is reasonable to suppose that they became one of the means of punishing him. For they might have grown elsewhere, for the nourishment of birds and beasts, or even for the use of man.[33]

This recalls God's use of nature for blessing and cursing in the Mosaic covenant (see chapter 1). Finally, a word from Augustine's work on original sin, which may serve to hinder us from being too ready to compare animal behaviors with human immorality, and so draw the conclusion that "original sin" is in fact an evolutionary phenomenon with natural evil simply merging into moral evil:

God's work continues still good, however evil be the deeds of the impious. For although "man being placed in honour abides not; and being without understanding, is compared with the beasts, and is like them," yet the resemblance is not so absolute that he becomes a beast. There is a comparison, no doubt, between the two; but it is not by reason of nature, but through vice—not vice in the beast, but in nature [i.e. the difference between animal and human nature]. For so excellent is a man in comparison with a beast, that man's vice is beast's nature; . . .[34]

32. Ibid., XII 4.

33. Augustine, *On the Literal Meaning of Genesis,* 18:28 (93).

34. Augustine, *On the Grace of Christ and Original Sin* II 46.

John of Damascus

We move forward now to the seventh century. John (679–749), a monk and polymath, like his predecessors, seems unaware that the creation story is supposed to teach vegetarianism, for human or beast, before the fall:

> Moreover, at the bidding of the Creator it produced also all manner of kinds of living creatures, creeping things, and wild beasts, and cattle. All, indeed, are for the seasonable use of man: but of them some are for food, such as stags, sheep, deer, and such like: others for service such as camels, oxen, horses, asses, and such like: and others for enjoyment, such as apes, and among birds, jays and parrots, and such like. Again, among plants and herbs some are fruit bearing, others edible, others fragrant and flowery, given to us for our enjoyment, for example, the rose and such like, and others for the healing of disease.[35]

But as Greek Orthodox creationist Fr. Seraphim Rose[36] points out, and as I noted in the introduction, John's concept is actually more complex than the simple beneficence of nature. He in fact sees these provisions as created in anticipation of the needs of *fallen* humankind:

> God knew all things before they were made and He saw that man in his freedom would fall and be given over to corruption; yet for man's suitable use He made all the things that are in the sky and on the earth and in the water.[37]

If this were so it would be a remedy for evil, not an evil *per se*, a nature created to encompass the eventuality of evil; not a fall as the "traditional view" assumes. And hence the next paragraph suggests nature rising in justified rebellion against humanity after the fall, including some changes in its character:

> [T]he earth of its own accord used to yield fruits, for the benefit of the animals that were obedient to man, and there was neither rain nor tempest on the earth. But after the transgression, when he was compared with the unintelligent cattle and became like to them, after he had contrived that in him irrational desire should have rule over reasoning mind and had become disobedient to the Master's command, the subject creation rose up against him whom the Creator had appointed to be ruler: and it was

35. John of Damascus, *Exposition of the Orthodox Faith* II X.
36. Rose, "Genesis and Early Man."
37. John of Damascus, *Exposition of the Orthodox Faith* II X.

appointed for him that he should till with sweat the earth from which he had been taken.[38]

However, one must question the coherence of John's concept of *anticipated* utility for a fallen world: logically if God were to create animals that would become useful for food, plants that might become treatments for disease and even wild beasts to be "not without their uses, for, by the terror they cause, they bring man to the knowledge of his Creator," their fundamental natures *cannot* have been changed. And it is in this initial state of (according to John) "preparation for evil" that Genesis actually describes them as "very good."

Anselm

Moving forward to the eleventh century, Anselm (1033–1109) was possibly the greatest thinker ever to occupy the See of Canterbury. He wrote extensively on the nature of evil, but notably little (or actually, nothing) on natural evil, and so nothing on the effect of the fall upon it. The reason for this is simple: evil, to him, was *by definition* a product of free wills negating their original goodness. His profound philosophy of being saw what we call "evils" in nature simply as lower degrees of good, consistent with what Augustine had taught:

> Rather, it must be the case that every created thing both exists and is excellent in proportion to its likeness to what exists supremely and is supremely great. For this reason, perhaps—or, rather, not perhaps but certainly—every intellect judges that natures which are in any way alive excel non-living [natures], and that sentient natures excel non-sentient [natures], and that rational natures excel non-rational [ones].[39]

Thomas Aquinas

The importance of Thomas (1225–1275) cannot be overstated. His synthesis of Christian doctrine with the newly recovered teaching of Aristotle provided, quite simply, the intellectual underpinning of the entire late mediaeval period. Both his philosophy and theology still have many, possibly even an increasing number of, admirers today. The "Angelic Doctor's" perennial

---

38. Ibid.
39. Anselm, *Monologion*, 31.

influence lies partly in that he and the other scholastics sought not to re-define church doctrine, but to ground it intellectually and to develop its implications exhaustively. Accordingly we may assume his teaching on this matter to embody the doctrinal mainstream. And he says this:

> In the opinion of some, those animals which now are fierce and kill others, would, in that state [before the fall], have been tame, not only in regard to man, but also in regard to other animals. But this is quite unreasonable. For the nature of animals was not changed by man's sin, as if those whose nature now it is to devour the flesh of others, would then have lived on herbs, as the lion and falcon. Nor does Bede's gloss on Genesis 1:30, say that trees and herbs were given as food to all animals and birds, but to some. Thus there would have been a natural antipathy between some animals.[40]

Aquinas admits there are those against his view—but he names none and he may only allude to outliers like Theophilus. Note that he also cites the seventh-century Saxon monk Bede's commentary to show that Genesis 1:29–30 had not been taken as a universal command to vegetarianism by his orthodox predecessors either. As to how this "wild" version of creation was compatible with humanity's happiness before the fall, Aquinas argues that the God-given spiritual nature, the rational soul ruling the body, made humans essentially invulnerable before they sinned—what cannot hurt you cannot be regarded as an evil. In this he echoes the universal sense of human exceptionalism in early theology, which is sometimes missing today:

> Hence, according to the teaching of faith, we affirm that man was, from the beginning, so fashioned that as long as his reason was subject to God, not only would his lower powers serve him without hindrance; but there would be nothing in his body to lessen its subjection; since whatever was lacking in nature to bring this about God by His grace would supply.[41]

The later scholastics appear to add little to this definitive mediaeval teaching on the (lack of) effects of the fall on nature, though writers from Duns Scotus to Suarez have plenty to say on the question of evil (as sin) in relation to God's will. This appears to be because they, like their predecessors, simply recognized no problem of natural evil as such:

> Whether cast as a logical difficulty, or as an evidential one, the problem arises from conflict between belief in an omnipotent,

40. Aquinas, *Summa Theologiae*, Part 1:96:A1.
41. Aquinas, *Summa Contra Gentiles*, Book IV, 52.

all-good God, on the one hand, and the existence of pointless suffering, on the other. Medieval philosophers of all faiths regard this as a less pressing issue than moderns do, for few, if any, believe that there actually is any pointless suffering.[42]

But the early modern period, for the first time, begins to display a different humor. To this we now turn.

---

42. Kent, "Evil in Later Medieval Philosophy."

Chapter 7—Creation Fell in 1517

⁹ About noon the following day as they were on their journey and approaching the city, Peter went up on the roof to pray. ¹⁰ He became hungry and wanted something to eat, and while the meal was being prepared, he fell into a trance. ¹¹ He saw heaven opened and something like a large sheet being let down to earth by its four corners. ¹² It contained all kinds of four-footed animals, as well as reptiles and birds. ¹³ Then a voice told him, "Get up, Peter. Kill and eat."

¹⁴ "Surely not, Lord!" Peter replied. "I have never eaten anything impure or unclean."

¹⁵ The voice spoke to him a second time, "Do not call anything impure that God has made clean."

—ACTS 10:9–15

Early modern to modern periods

A PROFOUND REVERSAL IN the theological picture appears, surprisingly, as we come to the writings of the Reformers.

John Calvin

I cite Calvin (1509–1564) first, because his usually careful exegesis of Scripture provides a link with the older views. Thus in his commentary on Psalm 104:

> Although lions, if hunger compels them, go forth from their dens and roar even at noon-day, yet the prophet describes what is most usually the case. He therefore says, that lions do

not venture to go abroad during the daytime, but that, trusting to the darkness of the night, they then sally forth in quest of their prey. Herein is manifested the wonderful providence of God, that a beast so dreadful confines itself within its den, that men may walk abroad with the greater freedom. And if lions sometimes range with greater liberty, this is to be imputed to the fall of Adam, which has deprived men of their dominion over the wild beasts.[1]

Here we see, on careful reading, that like his predecessors Calvin assumes lions ate prey, though not people, before the fall. This accords with the idea of nature as God's obedient instrument for blessing or punishment, as described in chapter 1. Calvin's Genesis commentary on 1:28 mentions that some believe it teaches human vegetarianism, but he argues against this from other verses in Genesis. Animal predation he doesn't mention, but treats the whole command not as a prohibition, but as a declaration of God's abundant provision for all.

But in contrast his commentary on Genesis 3:18 goes against nearly everything we have read so far:

Therefore we may know, that whatsoever unwholesome things may be produced, are not natural fruits of the earth, but are corruptions which originate from sin. Yet it is not our part to expostulate with the earth for not answering to our wishes, and to the labors of its cultivators as if it were maliciously frustrating our purpose; but in its sterility let us mark the anger of God and mourn over our own sins. . . .

Moreover, Moses does not enumerate all the disadvantages in which man, by sin, has involved himself; for it appears that all the evils of the present life, which experience proves to be innumerable, have proceeded from the same fountain. The inclemency of the air, frost, thunders, unseasonable rains, drought, hail, and whatever is disorderly in the world, are the fruits of sin. Nor is there any other primary cause of diseases.[2]

Our former writers have sometimes suggested natural (good) creation being used in punishment. But here Calvin appears to suggest a wholesale corruption of nature, albeit still mainly as a judgement, and is apparently the first to suggest that Genesis's sparse reference to soil, thorns, and thistles was adopting "a brevity adapted to the capacity of the common people, . . . content to touch upon what was most apparent, in order that, from one example, we

---

1. Calvin, *Psalms*, Ps 104.

2. Calvin, *Genesis*, Gen 3:18.

may learn that the whole order of nature was subverted by the sin of man."[3] This appears to be a case of "It's right there, between the lines."

This is, on consideration, quite a dramatic theological departure, which has also been noted by authors like Alister McGrath and Robert J. Schneider, but without an attempt at an explanation:

> In this respect Calvin departed from the view of Aquinas and the Catholic tradition generally, which understands nature as showing the signs of imperfection that need to be brought to perfection by grace. Calvin went much further: creation has been corrupted by sin, suffers along with humankind disorder and death, and awaits its final restoration by the redemptive activity of Christ, the savior as well as the creator (McGrath 174–175).[4]

Such novelty and stepping beyond the biblical witness is rather uncharacteristic of Calvin, who was keen to preserve what had gone before except where it deviated from Scripture. We must therefore ask its origin.

Martin Luther

Luther (1483–1546), although the earlier Reformer, goes even further in his pessimism about nature than Calvin, though his starting point is still the existing teaching. So in his dispute with Erasmus on free will he writes:

> This must be said: if you want the words "they were very good" to be understood of God's works after the fall, you will notice that the words were spoken with reference, not to us, but to God. It does not say: "Man saw what God had made, and it was very good." Many things seem, and are, very good to God which seem, and are, very bad to us. Thus, afflictions, sorrows, errors, hell, and all God's best works are in the world's eyes very bad, and damnable.[5]

But a remark in his *Table Talk* resembles Calvin's position, if in muted form:

> Though by reason of original sin many wild beasts hurt mankind, as lions, wolves, bears, snakes, adders, etc., yet the merciful God has in such manner mitigated our well-deserved punishments

---

3. Ibid.

4. Schneider, *Theology of Creation*. His citation refers to McGrath, Alister E., *A Scientific Theology. Vol. 1: Nature*, Grand Rapids: Eerdmans, 2001, 174–175.

5. Luther, *Bondage of the Will*, 203.

that there are many more beasts that serve us for our good and profit, than of those which do us hurt . . . in all creatures more good than evil, more benefit than hurts and hindrances.[6]

See how he has transitioned from the concept of "good things that God might use for our punishment" to "more good than evil." "Natural evil" has seemingly made its first major appearance in Christian thought since the Gnostics refuted by Irenaeus, and in the mouth of its chief Reformer too. Luther's own commentary on Genesis 3 goes well beyond Calvin's, and light years beyond the older writers:

> . . . because [the earth] does bear many hurtful things, which but for man's sin she would not have borne, such as the destructive weeds, darnel, tares, nettles, thorns, thistles, etc., to which may be added, poison, noxious reptiles and other like hurtful things, brought into the creation by sin.
>
> For my own part I entertain no doubt that before the sin of the fall the air was more pure and healthful, the water more wholesome and fructifying, and the light of the sun more bright and beautiful. So that the whole creation as it now is reminds us in every part of the curse inflicted on it, on account of the sin of the fall.[7]

Note that none of this may be found in Scripture, as Luther himself admitted elsewhere,[8] with the exception, on one interpretation, of the advent of "thorns and thistles." His imagination is equally employed with the aftermath of the flood:

> This original curse moreover was afterwards greatly increased by the Deluge, when all the good trees were rooted up and destroyed, barren sands accumulated and both noxious herbs and beasts multiplied. . . . The earth herself indeed is innocent and would of its own free nature bring forth all things which are the best and most excellent. But she is prevented from doing so by the curse inflicted on man for his sin.[9]

Luther invokes absence of evidence for evidence of absence in the brief early chapters of Genesis:

6. Luther, *Table Talk*, 46 CIII.

7. Luther, *Genesis* 3:17, 314.

8. In his Romans commentary he says of the dimming of the sun, "This opinion cannot be proved from Scripture."

9. Luther, *Genesis* 3:17, 316.

... In the antediluvian state of the curse no other mention is made than of thorns, and thistles, and labor, and sweat; but now we experience numberless other additional evils. How many diseases and pestilential injuries are inflicted on the standing corn, on the plants of pulse, on trees, and finally on all the productions of the earth? How many evils are wrought by destructive birds and noxious caterpillars?

Add to these evils, extremes of cold and frost, thunderings, lightnings, excessive wet, winds, rivers bursting their banks, fissures of the earth, earthquakes, etc. Of none of these is any mention made in the state of things under the curse before the Deluge. My firm belief is therefore that as the sins of men increased the punishments of those sins increased also; and that all such punishments and evils were added to the original curse of the earth. . . .

In the same manner, as in the present day, we experience more frequent calamities befalling the fruits of the earth than in former times. For the world degenerates and grows worse and worse every day.[10]

Whence does Luther get this progressive destruction of the natural order up to, and after the flood, and even now "growing worse and worse every day"? Certainly not from Genesis, which says that in the covenant God makes with Noah after the flood he promises, "Never again will I curse the ground because of man," (Genesis 8:21). If anything, Scripture *rescinds* the curse, rather than increasing it (see chapter 2). In fact, even Gordon Wenham's strict grammatical interpretation of that verse[11] *excludes* any extension of the existing curse after the flood.

English Puritanism

I'll propose an explanation for this new pessimism in the next chapter, but whatever its reason it is clearly a radical departure from the old doctrine. And it is teaching that becomes progressively more negative, if that were possible, down the years. I've quoted at length from Luther, so I'll just give two brief citations of how things continued in this vein at the height of the Reformation. The *Westminster Greater Catechism* of the 1640s, answering its question on earthly punishments, says:

10. Ibid.
11. See chapter 2, and Wenham, *Genesis*, 190.

Q28: The punishments of sin in this world, are either inward
. . . or outward, as the curse of God upon the creatures for our
sakes.[12]

And that other monument to English Puritanism, *Matthew Henry's
Commentary*, says on Romans 8:20–21:

When man sinned, the ground was cursed for man's sake, and
with it all the creatures, . . . The creation is sullied and stained,
much of the beauty of the world gone. And it is not the least part
of their bondage that they are used, or abused rather, by men as
instruments of sin.[13]

The thorns and thistles of Genesis have now become "all the creatures,"
and their goodness (even to those who perceived their being used in judgement) has become "sullied and stained." Yet even Henry, commenting on
Isaiah 11:6–9, regards the vegetarian habit of animals before the fall as a
minority opinion:

The lion shall cease to be ravenous and shall eat straw like the
ox, as some think all the beasts of prey did before the fall.[14]

The older teaching did not disappear quickly, even amongst the
Reformed. The Puritan poet, John Milton (1608–1674), in describing the
days of creation in *Paradise Lost*, seems sometimes to glory in the wilder
products of God's hand. On the fifth day of creation God names leviathan,
and the eagle as well as the stork, nightingale, swan, and cock. His sixth
day has the lion "pawing to get free," the lynx, the leopard, the tiger, the
stag, the behemoth (like leviathan, from Job), before moving to serpents
and invertebrates.[15] In Book X Milton has Adam submit himself and Eve
penitently to the kindness of judgement—death (with hints of mercy),
pains in childbearing (recompensed with the fruit of the womb), laboring for sustenance (better than idleness!)—and adds "inclement seasons,"
mitigated by possessing fire.[16] This matches the old, gentler, view of nature
as well as the actual words of Genesis.

Similarly the metaphysical poet Thomas Traherne (1636–74) retains a
refreshingly high vision of nature. He writes:

---

12. Westminster Assembly, *Westminster Confession*, 85.

13. Church, *Matthew Henry's Commentary*, 570.

14. Ibid., 845.

15. Milton, *Paradise Lost* VII.387–503, 167–170.

16. Ibid., X.1010–1104, 252–255.

To contemn the world and to enjoy the world are things contrary to each other. How, then can we contemn the world,
which we are born to enjoy? Truly there are two worlds. One
was made by God, the other by men. That made by God was
great and beautiful. Before the Fall it was Adam's joy and the
Temple of his Glory. That made by men is a Babel of Confu-
sions: Invented Riches, Pomps and Vanities, brought in by Sin:
Give all (saith Thomas à Kempis) for all. Leave the one that you
may enjoy the other.[17]

This "other" can clearly only be enjoyed if it still exists.

Jacobus Arminius

Surprising support for the older view also comes from the Dutch theologian, Arminius (1560–1609), frequently seen as the supporter of free will
and therefore (obliquely and quite wrongly) of the independence of nature
from God. Instead his somewhat scholastic approach to theology follows the
ancient tradition on creation. A dense passage on the creation includes:

This world is an entire something, which is perfect and complete, having no defect of any form, that can bear relation to the
whole or to its parts; nor is redundant in any form which has
no relation to the whole and its parts. . . . This was necessary,
not only to adumbrate, in some measure, the perfection of God
in variety and multitude, but also to demonstrate that the Lord
omnipotent did not create the world by a natural necessity, but
by the freedom of his will.

This creation is the foundation of that right by which God
can require religion from man, which is a matter that will be
more certainly and fully understood, when we come more
specially to treat on the primeval creation of man; for he who
is not the creator of all things, and who, therefore, has not all
things under his command, cannot be believed, neither can any
sure hope and confidence be placed in him, nor can he alone be
feared. Yet all these are acts which belong to religion.[18]

An important (though not unique) observation here is that it is the in-
tegrity and goodness of a creation entirely under God's command that is the
very *foundation* of religion. There is no room here for the random, or partly
"free," evolution acting as a *Demiurge*, the exaggeration of his position on

17. Traherne, *Centuries* 1/7, 6.
18. Arminius, *Disputation*.

free will now seen in the open theism that has influenced many theistic evolutionists, for it would be the Demiurge, not God, who earned our worship. This total control of nature, in the present age, is even clearer in Arminius's teaching on providence regarding nature:

> My sentiments respecting the providence of God are these: It is present with, and presides over, all things; and all things, according to their essences, quantities, qualities, relations, actions, passions, places, times, stations and habits, are subject to its governance, conservation, and direction.[19]

I want to end this theological survey, at least of Protestant voices, with one more significant and influential name: John Wesley.

John Wesley

Wesley (1703–1791) takes the doctrine of fallen creation to new heights (or depths) of lurid description, achieving at last the kind of teaching frequently seen today. Extracts from just one sermon are sufficient to show the complete change from the teaching of the church fathers, from joy in God's creation to utter pessimism:

> As all the blessings of God in paradise flowed through man to the inferior creatures; as man was the great channel of communication, between the Creator and the whole brute creation; so when man made himself incapable of transmitting those blessings, that communication was necessarily cut off. The intercourse between God and the inferior creatures being stopped, those blessings could no longer flow in upon them. And then it was that "the creature," every creature, "was subjected to vanity," to sorrow, to pain of every kind, to all manner of evils.[20]

In fact, Scripture suggests that God still communicates with the lower creatures rather well, as I showed in chapter 1. But Wesley pictures all kinds of deprivations arising from this for the creatures:

> But in what respect was "the creature," every creature, then "made subject to vanity?" What did the meaner creatures suffer, when man rebelled against God? It is probable they sustained much loss, even in the lower faculties; their vigor, strength, and swiftness. But undoubtedly they suffered far more in their

19. Arminius, *The Providence of God.*
20. Wesley, *The General Deliverance.*

understanding; more than we can easily conceive. Perhaps insects and worms had then as much understanding as the most
intelligent brutes have now: Whereas millions of creatures have,
at present, little more understanding than the earth on which
they crawl, or the rock to which they adhere.

They suffered still more in their will, in their passions;
which were then variously distorted, and frequently set in flat
opposition to the little understanding that was left them. Their
liberty, likewise, was greatly impaired; yea, in many cases, totally
destroyed. They are still utterly enslaved to irrational appetites,
which have the full dominion over them. The very foundations
of their nature are out of course; are turned upside down.

As man is deprived of his perfection, his loving obedience
to God; so brutes are deprived of their perfection, their loving
obedience to man. The far greater part of them flee from him;
studiously avoid his hated presence. The most of the rest set him
at open defiance; yea, destroy him, if it be in their power. A few
only, those we commonly term domestic animals, retain more
or less of their original disposition, (through the mercy of God)
love him still, and pay obedience to him.[21]

But beyond their deficiencies, Wesley proceeds to attribute to animals
a host of positive vices:

Setting these few aside, how little shadow of good, of gratitude,
of benevolence, of any right temper, is now to be found in
any part of the brute creation! On the contrary, what savage
fierceness, what unrelenting cruelty; are invariably observed in
thousands of creatures; yea, is inseparable from their natures!
Is it only the lion, the tiger, the wolf, among the inhabitants
of the forest and plains—the shark, and a few more voracious
monsters, among the inhabitants of the waters,—or the eagle,
among birds,—that tears the flesh, sucks the blood, and crushes
the bones of their helpless fellow-creatures?

Nay; the harmless fly, the laborious ant, the painted but-
terfly, are treated in the same merciless manner, even by the innocent songsters of the grove! The innumerable tribes of poor
insects are continually devoured by them. And whereas there
is but a small number, comparatively, of beasts of prey on the
earth, it is quite otherwise in the liquid element. There are but
few inhabitants of the waters, whether of the sea, or of the rivers, which do not devour whatsoever they can master: Yea, they
exceed herein all the beasts of the forest, and all the birds of prey.

21. Ibid.

> For none of these have been ever observed to prey upon their
> own species: "*Saevis inter se convenit ursis*: Even savage bears
> will not each other tear."
>
> But the water-savages swallow up all, even of their own
> kind, that are smaller and weaker than themselves. Yea, such, at
> present, is the miserable constitution of the world, to such van-
> ity is it now subjected, that an immense majority of creatures,
> perhaps a million to one, can no otherwise preserve their own
> lives, than by destroying their fellow-creatures![22]

As if nature's disposition were not enough, Wesley denies even its aesthetic beauties:

> And is not the very form, the outward appearance, of many
> of the creatures, as horrid as their dispositions? Where is the
> beauty which was stamped upon them when they came first out
> of the hands of their Creator? There is not the least trace of it
> left: So far from it, that they are shocking to behold! Nay, they
> are not only terrible and grisly to look upon, but deformed, and
> that to a high degree. Yet their features, ugly as they are at best,
> are frequently made more deformed than usual, when they are
> distorted by pain; which they cannot avoid, any more than the
> wretched sons of men. Pain of various kinds, weakness, sickness,
> diseases innumerable, come upon them; perhaps from within;
> perhaps from one another; perhaps from the inclemency of sea-
> sons; from fire, hail, snow, or storm; or from a thousand causes
> which they cannot foresee or prevent.[23]

We're on familiar territory now. Wesley's eloquent sermon might
largely have been ghosted by Richard Dawkins (or even the former Catholic
priest, theistic evolutionist Francisco Ayala). And that is no coincidence, for
Wesley reflected the way ideas were developing throughout Enlightenment
Europe, but especially in Protestant territories. Furthermore, his influence
on popular Christianity, not only through the Methodist Awakening but
through the Pietist movement's predominance within US and European
evangelicalism, probably ensured the spread of this brand of imaginative
Bible interpretation to this day.

However, the quotation from the Calvinist Baptist Charles Haddon
Spurgeon in the introduction serves to show that thoroughly negative attitudes towards the natural creation came to predominate throughout the
evangelical world by the nineteenth century.

22. Ibid.

23. Ibid.

Secular trends

It is noteworthy how this progressively growing fear and even dread[24] of the natural creation was paralleled outside the theological world. I'll cite just one example, since it is the actual source of the slogan "red in tooth and claw" (used by Dawkins in *The Selfish Gene*). Canto 55–56 of Alfred Lord Tennyson's 1850 poem *In Memoriam A. H. H.*:

> Who trusted God was love indeed
>
> And love Creation's final law—
>
> Tho' Nature, red in tooth and claw
>
> With ravine, shriek'd against his creed.[25]

The subject was the deceased Arthur Henry Hallam, a friend who agonized with Tennyson about the conflict between God's love and nature's cruelty, purposelessness and heartlessness. If this sounds familiar, it is because the poem became a player in the debate surrounding natural selection after the publication of Darwin's *Origin of Species* a few years later.

Literary critic Holly Furneax writes in an essay on the *British Library* website:

> In the central lyrics of 55 and 56, Tennyson considers the theory of natural selection long before Darwin made it famous in On the Origin of Species (1859) . . . . The poet considers Nature to be *'so careful of the type . . . So careless of the single life'* (55, stanza 2), reflecting on the impersonal, amoral processes of the natural world in which types of species evolve without heed of the individuals who are extinguished along the way. This wanton waste of potential life—*'of fifty seeds'* Nature often allows only one to bear fruit—offers an allegorical expression of the waste of potential in the early death of Hallam. This seemingly senseless loss leads him to *'falter where I firmly trod'* on the *'world's altar stairs/That slope thro' darkness up to God'*.
>
> At the close of this lyric he has recourse to feelings which are posited against scientific discoveries, and he *'faintly'* reasserts his trust that at length the human race will be spiritually redeemed. In section 56, even that faint hope is crushed as Nature is personified as, famously, *'red in tooth and claw'*. The savage voice of Nature avers that thousands of species have been

---

24. The reverse, ironically, of what Scripture says happened after the flood (Gen 9:2), where the natural creation comes to fear and dread humanity.

25. Tennyson, *Works*, 314–16.

wiped out; the holy spirit is reduced to *mere 'breath'*, and man to *'desert dust'*.[26]

The poem as a whole became for Tennyson himself, according to many, an attempted theodicy in response to Darwin, and anticipates the anxious doubt expressed in most modern approaches to theodicy.

I close this chapter with a comment of Rev. Charles Kingsley from 1871 on the "state of play" he found, and lamented as unscriptural, within the Christian culture he knew:

> We have only, if we need proof, to look at the hymns—many of them very pure, pious, and beautiful—which are used at this day in churches and chapels by persons of every shade of opinion. How often is the tone in which they speak of the natural world one of dissatisfaction, distrust, almost contempt. "Disease, decay, and death around I see," is their key-note, rather than "O all ye works of the Lord, bless Him, praise Him, and magnify Him together." There lingers about them a savor of the old monastic theory, that this earth is the devil's planet, fallen, accursed, goblin-haunted, needing to be exorcised at every turn before it is useful or even safe for man.[27]

But of course, as we have seen the underlying assumptions about "the nature of nature" do not reflect at all the viewpoint of Christians in the first fifteen hundred years of the church, including those monks. What, then, actually led to the change?

---

26. Furneaux, *Introduction to In Memoriam*.

27. Kingsley, *Natural Theology*.

Chapter 8—Tracking the Fall of Creation

The myth of Prometheus means that all the sorrows
of the world have their seat in the liver. But it needs
a brave man to face so humble a truth.

—FRANÇOIS MAURIAC[1]

The Reformers' biblical literalism?

IT IS RATHER STRANGE, is it not, that a natural creation that the Bible and most of the church until late mediaeval times called "good" is now usually viewed as thoroughly tainted by evil? The creation hasn't changed, so what has reversed our worldview so diametrically? The answer, as I will try to show, may not be completely divorced from the fact that secularists also see nature as fundamentally flawed—the same mind-set, and essential elements of the same worldview, govern both viewpoints.

Was the negative view of nature that gained strength over five centuries and that now predominates in popular theology, in evolutionary biology and in theistic evolution, a correct or even an inevitable step? If we take a biblical view, the answer must be no, as we saw in chapters 1–5. Although the first significant manifestations of it that we have seen in the sources are in connection with the Reformation, with its motto *Sola Scriptura*, the teaching goes far beyond, even against, Scripture in a way that the earlier "good creation" teaching did not. That makes it potentially heterodox (as indeed we saw Augustine believed it to be in the chapter 6).

Does nature itself demand such a pessimistic view? Apparently so, if judged by the passionate way that people express doubts over God's goodness in creation from within or without the community of faith. But evidently *not* to the millions of earlier Christians who lived far closer to early death, plague, natural disaster, and the ravages of the wild beasts we have put safely in zoos or rendered extinct. They praised God for all creation.

---

1. Mauriac, *Le Nœud de vipères* (1932), in *Oeuvres Romanesques*, 151.

Nature has not changed—our attitudes have. Why? And why should that have been associated with the time of the Reformation?

As we have seen we cannot find the answer in the great majority of the early church fathers, or amongst the Scholastics, whom both Luther and Calvin studied at University in Germany and France respectively. Neither can we trace it to contemporaneous movements like the devotionally minded Brethren of the Common Life, who were responsible for Luther's early schooling. Their Thomas à Kempis wrote: "If your heart were right, then every created thing would a mirror to life and a book of holy doctrine, for no creature is so small and mean that it cannot display God's goodness."[2] And it certainly cannot be attributed to the Reformers' personal psychology, unless they started an epidemic of infective melancholy.

It has been proposed to me that it was the Reformers' emphasis on the literal interpretation of Scripture that is the key issue. That they took the literal meaning more seriously than even their immediate predecessors is undoubted. Just a generation before, earlier humanists like John Colet (a friend and influence of Erasmus), though eager to reform the purity of the church and to preach from Scripture, nevertheless still depended heavily on allegorical interpretation, and Colet was only feeling his way with the literal sense. In fact, Colet did not see his role as an expositor at all (which was fortunate as he had little grounding in the original languages), but as a mover of hearts.[3] His interpretations generally followed established precedent. In contrast the Reformers, like the humanist Erasmus as far as he accompanied them, treated discovering the primary, literal,[4] meaning of the Scriptures as the key task.

But though they broke new ground in literal understanding, we have seen in the first three chapters that the texts do not actually take us to a fallen creation unless we're already committed to going there. Furthermore

2. A Kempis, *Imitation of Christ* II 4, 88–89.

3. Gleason, *John Colet*, 117–18.

4. One must always remember that, to the Reformers, the "literal" did not mean "literalistic." The Bible translator William Tyndale perhaps expressed the position best in his *Obedience of the Christian Man* (175): we borrow words and sentences from one thing, and apply them to another, and give them new meanings. "We say, 'Let the sea swell and rise as high as he will, yet God has appointed how far he shall go'—meaning that the tyrants shall not do what they would, but only what God has appointed them to do. 'Look before you leap:' whose literal sense is, 'Do nothing suddenly, or without advisement.' 'Do not cut the bough that you stand on:' whose literal sense is, 'Do not oppress the commoners;' and is borrowed from hewers. . . . Nevertheless, the Scripture uses proverbs, similitudes, riddles, or allegories, as all other speeches do; but what the proverb, similitude, riddle, or allegory signifies, is always the literal sense, which you must seek out diligently."

we've seen in chapter 6 that those earlier writers who deal with the texts literally, such as Josephus and Irenaeus, and even John Chrysostom when he comments on Genesis 3, do not end up in that place. A respect for the literal meaning of Scripture is therefore clearly an insufficient explanation. One must question if it is a factor at all when it requires such a profound misreading of that literal meaning. The Reformers were generally better expositors than that.

Meanwhile, in Rome

At the same time, it is clear that only those taking the literal meaning of Scripture seriously *can* fall into error about that meaning. At the time of the Reformation the Catholic Church as a whole had only a limited interest in Scripture, and a predominantly allegorical understanding of it at that. Luther's opponent Cardinal Cajetan actually made himself somewhat unpopular amongst conservative Catholics by recognizing, in the light of the Reformers, the need to tackle the literal meaning in his commentaries. His Genesis commentary was appreciated and even used by Calvin when writing his own. But it was only after the Council of Trent that far more attention was paid, once more, to interpretation of Scripture by Catholics, and by that time, of course, the Reformers' work was itself at least an unconscious influence on it. A little later, Enlightenment thinking will also have influenced Protestant and Catholic thinking alike.

It is therefore difficult to completely disentangle who influenced whom, and how much. Nevertheless it still appears to be the case that teaching on the corruption of nature has, even until now, remained much less prevalent in Catholicism. Unlike the Westminster Catechism, quoted in the last chapter, the catechism of the Council of Trent doesn't mention it, though that may reflect its structure, "creation" coming under the heading of the Creed, "God the Father, maker of heaven and earth."

But the modern Catholic *Catechism*, approved by Pope John Paul in 1997 and the first such general doctrinal statement since that of Trent, says a lot about creation. It states that "physical evil" exists only because creation has not yet reached perfection (rather than having fallen from it):

> But why did God not create a world so perfect that no evil could exist in it? With infinite power God could always create something better. But with infinite wisdom and goodness God freely willed to create a world "in a state of journeying" towards its ultimate perfection. In God's plan this process of becoming involves the appearance of certain beings and the disappearance

of others, the existence of the more perfect alongside the less perfect, both constructive and destructive forces of nature. With physical good there exists also physical evil as long as creation has not reached perfection.[5]

It insists that each creature retains its creational goodness:

Each creature possesses its own particular goodness and perfection. For each one of the works of the "six days" it is said: "And God saw that it was good." "By the very nature of creation, material being is endowed with its own stability, truth, and excellence, its own order and laws." Each of the various creatures, willed in its own being, reflects in its own way a ray of God's infinite wisdom and goodness. Man must therefore respect the particular goodness of every creature.[6]

And it states that predation should be seen in terms of the order and harmony of God's will, not of evil:

God wills the interdependence of creatures. The sun and the moon, the cedar and the little flower, the eagle and the sparrow: the spectacle of their countless diversities and inequalities tells us that no creature is self-sufficient. Creatures exist only in dependence on each other, to complete each other, in the service of each other.

The beauty of the universe: The order and harmony of the created world results from the diversity of beings and from the relationships which exist among them. Man discovers them progressively as the laws of nature. They call forth the admiration of scholars. The beauty of creation reflects the infinite beauty of the Creator and ought to inspire the respect and submission of man's intellect and will.[7]

A similar positive approach was taken in the Encyclical of Pope Francis in 2015 called *Laudato Si'*. This comprehensive statement of Roman Catholic creation teaching cites the *Catechism* extensively. Typical statements include:

"By the word of the Lord the heavens were made." (Ps 33:6). This tells us that the world came about as the result of a decision, not from chaos or chance, and this exalts it all the more. The creating word expresses a free choice. The universe did not emerge as the

5. Catholic Church, *Catechism*, #310.

6. Ibid., #339.

7. Ibid., #340–341.

result of arbitrary omnipotence, a show of force or a desire for self-assertion. Creation is of the order of love. God's love is the fundamental moving force in all created things: "For you love all things that exist, and detest none of the things that you have made; for you would not have made anything if you had hated it" (Wis. 11:24). Every creature is thus the object of the Father's tenderness, who gives it its place in the world. Even the fleeting life of the least of beings is the object of his love, and in its few seconds of existence, God enfolds it with his affection.[8]

We understand better the importance and meaning of each creature if we contemplate it within the entirety of God's plan. As the Catechism teaches: "God wills the interdependence of creatures. The sun and the moon, the cedar and the little flower, the eagle and the sparrow: the spectacle of their countless diversities and inequalities tells us that no creature is self-sufficient. Creatures exist only in dependence on each other, to complete each other, in the service of each other."[9]

Fraternal love can only be gratuitous; it can never be a means of repaying others for what they have done or will do for us. That is why it is possible to love our enemies. This same gratuitousness inspires us to love and accept the wind, the sun and the clouds, even though we cannot control them. In this sense, we can speak of a "universal fraternity."[10]

There is nothing in this authoritative document about anything in nature being unplanned, or evil—or fallen. There seems, therefore, to be a degree of contingency in the way that Protestant creation theology has apparently diverged quite widely from the official teaching within Catholicism.

Prometheus unbound

The main explanation for this lies, I propose, in *sociological* forces, at the broadest level of historical cultural change. Specifically, I suggest it originated in an anomaly of the rise of Renaissance humanism (as it is now called) whose agenda forged the prevailing worldview of our own culture. The Renaissance is noted for recovering the knowledge of the ancient classical texts (and of the Greek church fathers too, incidentally). The Augustinian monk Luther was deeply influenced by it,[11] and Calvin is best described, intel-

8. Pope Francis, *Laudato Si'*, III.77.

9. Ibid., IV.86.

10. Ibid., V.228.

11. "While the Lutheran movement seems unimaginable without the preexistent

lectually, as a humanist. But humanism from its inception encompassed the idea that "Man is the measure of all things."[12] Rudolf Bultmann compares its viewpoint with the kind of Christian faith it began to replace:

> [Classical humanism] expresses the conviction that man by virtue of his spirit is able to shape his life in freedom and to subject to himself the world in which he has to live his life. The Christian faith expresses the conviction that man is not his own master, that the world is an alien country to him, and that he can gain his freedom from the world only with the help of divine grace which is freely given to the world from beyond.[13]

Cameron Wybrow, referring to a set of texts popular during the Renaissance, the *Hermetica*, writes (and provides extensive evidence) that:

> The themes in the . . . passage—likeness to God, immortality, nothing being impossible for man, the mastery of all arts and sciences, the comprehension of all nature by the human mind— are themes which were eventually linked with Genesis 1:26 and carried through the Renaissance into the modern age.[14]

In the early Renaissance classically informed humanists embraced the new anthropocentrism whilst seeking to retain their Christian identity, by seeing Adam as embodying this divine humanity's autonomous freedom and creativity, whilst playing down or denying its corruption. The fall therefore came to be seen, at least in part, as a good thing in enabling humanity's development.

But from the late fourteenth century, a more suitable hero was found in the classical Prometheus, the Titan who created humankind but then gave fire to them and was punished by the gods. Boccaccio's influential *Decameron*, for example, is arguably built around various retellings of the Prometheus story.[15] The image continued in use for centuries—for example Mary Shelley's *Frankenstein* was, rather ironically, subtitled *The Modern Prometheus*. Her husband's *Prometheus Unbound* employed the

German nationalist humanism, the Reformer himself remains equally unimaginable without the preexistent Biblical humanism, and for that matter without humanist modes of appeal to the layman." Dickens, *The German Nation and Martin Luther*, 51–52.

12. Protagoras, 490–420 BCE, as quoted by Plato, *Protagoras*.

13. Bultmann, "Humanism and Christianity," cited by Shinn, *Man: The New Humanism*, 174. I'd dispute that Christianity implies escape from the world, though, but redemption together with the world.

14. Wybrow, *The Bible, Baconianism, and Mastery*, 168.

15. Barcella, "The Myth of Prometheus."

myth to glorify revolution. Even in the last century Franz Kafka used it in a short story, "Prometheus," to express existentialist angst. In his version even the gods had forgotten the point of the argument—perhaps a reflection on the foundational status the myth had acquired for western society. For as Ernst Cassirer describes:

> [W]e have reached the point at which the Adam motif undergoes the inner transformation that enables it to merge with the Prometheus motif. No change in the content of the thought is necessary to complete this transition; a slight shift of the accent suffices. . . . If we compare Boccaccio's euhemeristic interpretation of the Prometheus legend with the medieval interpretation, we shall see that a change in basic attitude has taken place. In his Genealogia deorum, he distinguishes between two creations; the one called man into existence, and the other conferred upon this existence an intellectual content. The rough and ignorant man that came forth from the hands of nature could only be perfected by another act of creation. The first gave him his physical reality; the second gave his specific form. Here, Prometheus is a human hero of culture, the bringer of wisdom and of political and moral order.[16]

Cassirer later says:

> For the Renaissance, this image is evidently more than a mere allegory; it becomes the symbol of what the Renaissance is and is striving for as a total intellectual movement.[17]

Alister McGrath agrees with this assessment of the centrality of the Prometheus myth from Bacon through to the Enlightenment, particularly in relation to attitudes to nature:

> The rise of technology was seen as paralleling Prometheus' theft of fire from the gods. Defining limits were removed. Prometheus was now unbound, and humanity poised to enter a new era of autonomy and progress. The rise of technology was seen as a tool that would allow humanity to control and shape its environment, without the need to respect natural limitations.[18]

However, the appeal of the Prometheus myth was not universal. The same enduring spirituality that called forth the Reformation, probably not divorced from the kind of self-denying spiritual influence seen in the

16. Cassirer and Domandi, *The Individual and the Cosmos*, 95.
17. Ibid., 166.
18. McGrath, *Re-enchantment of Nature*, 78.

Brethren of the Common Life, meant that the aggressive secularism of Italy was diluted in the more restrained humanism of the northern Europe of Luther and Calvin. To some extent the Reformation was a reaction to Renaissance ideology, at least as it became embodied in the political and moral corruptions of the Roman Catholic Church.

But the prevalence of the myth could not leave the Reformers unaffected. Luther certainly read the *Decameron*, since he adapted one of its tales himself in his *Table Talk*.[19] The humanist Erasmus, who influenced both Luther and Calvin, admired Prometheus as a rational man:

> Prometheus means in Greek a man who takes counsel before acting, and Epimetheus one who acts first, and only then does common sense enter his head. To act like Prometheus, *prometheusthai*, is to meet misfortunes when they threaten by taking thought.[20]

As Joseph C. McLelland explains:

> Erasmus uses the myth in various ways, chiefly as symbol for his view of that virtù that is the hope of the human condition. Prometheus is an example for our imitation, that we should endeavor by human craft to strive after what is best and highest. It is noteworthy that we have now passed into the familiar Promethean vocabulary of human striving, human potential, human artifice: *Prometheus est nobis imitandus . . . humano artificio praestari.*[21]

Reformation religion was, in part then, a conscious revolt against this vaunting of human autonomy. One can surmise that this would include the Reformers' theological reaction against the humanists' sanitized Prometheus/Adam, who brings only wisdom and blessing, and their desire to reemphasize the downside of the myth—the judgement of Zeus and the despoiling of nature. Raised in and influenced, as they were, by a worldview that had elevated humanity so far above its scriptural station, an equally global judgement might seem to be what Scripture necessarily, though not overtly, implied, rather than the more exclusively human fall it actually describes.

But there is a more specific element, too. The Greek Prometheus cycle goes on to describe how part of Zeus's judgement on man was to create a woman, Pandora. The earliest version is a rather misogynist anticipation of Popeye the Sailor's "Wimmin is Jinx":

19. Luther, *Table Talk*, 353 DCCCLXIX.
20. Erasmus, *Adages* 1 i 31.
21. McLelland, *Prometheus Rebound*, 66.

From her is the race of women and female kind: of her is the
deadly race and tribe of women who live amongst mortal men
to their great trouble, no helpmates in hateful poverty, but only
in wealth.[22]

There was already an inviting parallel here with Eve for those already
seeing Prometheus as Adam. But later tellings recount the famous story of
the jar from which Pandora unwittingly, by foolish curiosity, released all the
evils in the world:

> For ere this the tribes of men lived on earth remote and free
> from ills and hard toil and heavy sickness which bring the Fates
> upon men; for in misery men grow old quickly. But the woman
> took off the great lid of the jar with her hands and scattered
> all these and her thought caused sorrow and mischief to men.
> Only Hope remained there in an unbreakable home within
> under the rim of the great jar, and did not fly out at the door;
> for ere that, the lid of the jar stopped her, by the will of Aegis-
> holding Zeus who gathers the clouds. But the rest, countless
> plagues, wander amongst men; for earth is full of evils and the
> sea is full. Of themselves diseases come upon men continually
> by day and by night, bringing mischief to mortals silently; for
> wise Zeus took away speech from them. So is there no way to
> escape the will of Zeus.[23]

It was actually Erasmus himself who first translated the Pandora
myth (and, by a mistranslation, introduced "Pandora's Box" into the culture). Given this extensive background, stretching across Europe and back
in time into the fourteenth century, it is hard to imagine how the Reformers could have *resisted* reading these classical accounts back into their understanding of the fall in some way. The bare account of Genesis seems not
to do justice to the gravity of humanity's fall from such an exalted role as
the humanist Adam/Prometheus ideal. Indeed, Calvin's commentary on
Genesis 3:18, to which I referred earlier, appears to confirm the associa-
tion directly by quoting an ode by Horace:

> When from Heaven's fane the furtive hand
>
> Of man the sacred fire withdrew,
>
> A countless host—at God's command —
>
> To earth of fierce diseases flew;

22. Hesiod, *Theogony*, 590–593.
23. Hesiod, *Works and Days*, II.90–105.

And death—till now kept far away

Hastened his step to seize his prey.[24]

The line prior to the quotation reveals the owner of "the furtive hand." He is the "son of Iapetus"—none other than Prometheus himself! The ode refers both to him and to the resulting curses of Pandora's box.

Now clearly it would be simplistic to suggest that Calvin took his doctrine from the Greeks (or their pagan Roman interpreters). Rather I am suggesting that the narrative of humanity that developed through the Renaissance, and that is so aptly summed up in the Prometheus myth, had by Calvin's time thoroughly colored humanist thinking about humanity, and hence the way that he read the text of Genesis. Or to put it another way, it is doubtful that Horace's quotation would have seemed fully appropriate to the interpretation of Genesis 3:18 from within a different cultural context.

So natural evil, we now find, flew out of a jar in a Greek myth, and not primarily from Christian Scripture at all.[25]

The ratcheting up of the description of evil and the increasing involvement of Satan, until it reached the level we have seen in Wesley's time, could be seen either as embellishment over the years, or perhaps as an unconscious reaction to the ever more autonomous and divinized self-image of humanity, and the deliberate exclusion of God, as the Renaissance became the Enlightenment and the Enlightenment our own self-obsessed age. In either case the doctrine of the fallenness of creation turns out, to our surprise, to be an unintended by-product of the very same human-centered ideology that brought our secularist and materialist culture into existence.

Theodicies and anti-theodicies

A related factor in the growth of the concern about "natural evil," to which I alluded in the introduction of the book, was the development of theodicy in the form pioneered by Gottfried Leibniz in his book *Theodicy* of 1709. If theodicy had ever been a question for mediaeval minds, it had taken the form of how God could be holy given the existence of evil ("evil" always meaning, as we have seen already, the wickedness of rational beings).

24. Horace, *Carmina* I.3.

25. One can perhaps trace the influence of John Chrysostom too, who sees natural evil in Romans 8, but why Calvin should prefer his (minority) view over his usual mentor Augustine still requires explanation. In any case, Chrysostom taught the subjection of creation to corruption for humanity's correction, not the escape of uncontrolled evil outside its control.

Leibniz, however, also began to tackle what is now sometimes called the "atheist problem of evil," or in other words, how God can even *exist* if evil of any sort exists. In this, given that atheism was so rare in his time, he may have been opposing the Socinian heresy, whose proponents, like the open theists, claimed that evil challenged God's omniscience (for he would not, they said, have created the world knowing that evil would arise).

As time went by, and the Enlightenment produced an atmosphere countenancing for the first-time rejection of the very existence of God, a truly atheistic form of the "problem of evil" was taken up by those like David Hume:

> Is he willing to prevent evil, but not able? Then is he impotent.
> Is he able, but not willing? Then is he malevolent. Is he both able
> and willing? Whence then is evil?[26]

This form of presentation should be familiar from anyone who has encountered the New Atheists. In the empirical atmosphere of Hume's times, and with theodicy being no longer a so much a matter of God's holiness but of his competence, it would have seemed grist to the mill to bring in evidence from the natural world to support the case. With God now placed in the dock, a natural creation corrupted apart from its own choice made a far better charge for believers to answer than the voluntary wickedness of rational souls.

Nature, remember, was already coming to be seen as fallen and therefore in part evil. As Josef Goebbels found, a lie repeated often enough comes to be seen as incontrovertible truth. If you're always arguing about *why* God allowed nature to be evil, you will soon forget that the first proposition (that it *is* evil) is open to question.

I suggest, however, that even this strand of the development owes its origin to the Prometheus myth—or at least to the view of humanity as autonomous that made the Prometheus story so congenial to the western mind. It both expressed and helped to form the worldview of human independence from God, and was also a factor in reinforcing it. People were no longer attempting to understand God's ways in theodicy, but to submit them to human criticism.

As far as our own subject goes, the Prometheus myth helped to seal the image of nature as cursed by an oppressive God to become humankind's enemy, and even its own. Pushed further, nature could even be seen as a fellow victim of the injustice at the heart of things, a conclusion encouraged by the Darwinian picture of a cosmos founded on constant deadly struggle,

---

26. Hume, *Dialogues Concerning Natural Religion,* 186.

and effectively abandoned to its own devices by a deist God (whether or not one believed in him).

The questions about God's moral responsibility seem pressing and inevitable—and perhaps unanswerable—because they are implicit in the Western worldview, which is like worldviews in general quite invisible to those who hold it. See from outside that worldview, by an Augustine or an Aquinas, for example, the questions are more likely to seem meaningless. That is likely to be the reason we simply do not see them addressed in the earlier periods.

Some implications

The Prometheus myth is very potent, both in itself and as an incredibly apt summary of the whole humanist project. In that sense it is the foundation myth of our present civilization, replacing the mediaeval Christian archetype, Adam, with a pagan fiction, the Titan Prometheus, autonomous and wise—and unjustly punished by Zeus. Once one is alerted to this motif, it turns up everywhere you look in the modern world, which is not surprising since cultures mold themselves by their myths, even when the origins have been largely forgotten.

For example, Adam's morality was based on God's command—Prometheus's on autonomy in despite of the gods' authority. Which is closer to the basis of modern morality? Adam lived in obedience to God apart from one sin—to Prometheus self-determination is above all things. Adam was wise and righteous, but became corrupt—Prometheus brought refinement and progress to an originally rough-hewn and restrictive creation. God was the great Artificer of everything, and Adam his imitator and assistant—Prometheus is now the artificer, and a Designer is denied any place in the closed system of nature. Adam's work was to tend and keep the creation—Prometheus's, in Baconian fashion, to torture it for its secrets and bend it to his will. Adam knew that every creature must give an account to God—Prometheus expects God to give an account of his treatment of every creature. Prometheus is Nietzsche's Übermensch, Galileo the mythic martyr of science to religion, the indomitable will of the people, and the improver of a bodged creation through genetic modification or transhumanism.

Somewhere in amongst those, in theological terms he is also the Microcosm whose fall was so calamitous that it inevitably took out the whole of nature with him. Adam's recourse, after the sin that affected only his seed, was repentance and faith. Prometheus's perceived destiny is to put things right himself—and to transfer the blame for the "mess" to God, author of a wayward evolutionary process (or for some Creationists, to Satan, elevated to the role of Demiurge of a secondary, corrupted, creation).

But what if my thesis is correct, and the whole concept of natural evil is no more than a re-imposition of ancient pagan pessimism over the innovative Christian view of a creation marred only by what sinful humanity itself does to it? What if the harm that nature causes us is, as the Fathers taught, the result of God's righteous judgement rather than of nature's participation in evil?

In that case, we have distorted Christian doctrine very badly to accommodate it to a worldview that is, in fact, diametrically opposed to the Christian worldview. It was the desire for autonomy that led humankind into exile from the garden. If, directly or indirectly, the quest for that autonomy has led us to doubt or deny the goodness of God's creation, then there must be serious consequences.

I will look at some of those, but also at the more positive effects of correcting them, in chapter 13. Before that, though, I want to take a look at nature itself, through the eyes of science, and show that accounts of its delinquency have been, to say the least, somewhat exaggerated.

Section 3—The Science

Chapter 9—Bogeys in the Evolutionary Coal-Cellar

I now suspect that just as a deer herd lives in mortal fear of its wolves, so does a mountain live in mortal fear of its deer. And perhaps with better cause, for while a buck pulled down by wolves can be replaced in two or three years, a range pulled down by too many deer may fail of replacement in as many decades. So also with cows. The cowman who cleans his range of wolves does not realize that he is taking over the wolf's job of trimming the herd to fit the range. He has not learned to think like a mountain. Hence we have dustbowls, and rivers washing the future into the sea.

—Leopold Aldo (1887–1948)[1]

Horror shows and window tests

IF THE WOES OF creation have long been given full expression by eminent Christian preachers such as Wesley and Spurgeon, whom I quoted earlier in this book, they have been raised to new levels in discussions of evolution. You may be familiar with this famous quote by Richard Dawkins, part of his argument against purpose in the universe:

> The total amount of suffering per year in the natural world is beyond all decent contemplation. During the minute that it takes me to compose this sentence, thousands of animals are being eaten alive, many others are running for their lives, whimpering with fear, others are slowly being devoured from within by

1. Aldo, "Thinking Like a Mountain."

rasping parasites, thousands of all kinds are dying of starvation, thirst, and disease.[2]

But theistic evolutionists, in significant numbers, are no less forceful in their desire to emphasize nature's darkness. Physicist and theologian Robert J. Russell writes:

> . . . it is hard to deny that nature "red in tooth and claw" is a suffering nature, full of agony, of pitiful and often senseless death, blind alleys, merciless waste, brute force. Is it entirely anthropomorphic to recognize in pre-human nature something which eventually becomes that which in that which in the human realm is evil?[3]

Karl Giberson, cofounder with Francis Collins of the evolutionary creation organization *BioLogos*, blogged in support of another BioLogian, Darrel Falk, about his contention that the design of mice-eating cats and bubonic plague should under no circumstances be attributed to God:

> The natural world has some terrible creatures in it, and it is hard to imagine God intentionally designing such nasty things. In 1860 Darwin even raised this in a letter to the American biologist Asa Gray:
> "I cannot persuade myself that a beneficent & omnipotent God would have designedly created the Ichneumonidae (wasp) with the express intention of their feeding within the living bodies of caterpillars, or that a cat should play with mice."
> Creationists have long tried to wriggle off this particular hook by arguing that the nasty features of the world are the consequences of human sin—by-products of the curse. But the truly nasty stuff precedes the appearance of humans, which makes this argument suspect at best.[4]

It would be interesting to know how Asa Gray, who unlike Giberson and so many present-day theistic evolutionists believed that evolution was directed to specific goals by God's providence, replied to Darwin's letter—that would surely be illuminating. But we do know his settled views on creation from his review of the *Origin of Species*, which shows that he, at least, had no problem imagining that God *did*, as a matter of fact, intentionally design such "nasty things":

2. Dawkins, "God's Utility Function," 85.
3. Russell, *Cosmology*, 242.
4. Giberson, *Evolution and the Problem of Evil.*

At least, Mr. Darwin uses expressions which seem to imply that the natural forms which surround us, because they have a history or natural sequence, could have been only generally, but not particularly designed, a view at once superficial and contradictory; whereas his true line should be, that his hypothesis concerns the order and not the cause, the how and not the why of the phenomenon, and so leaves the question of design just where it was before.[5]

The Catholic scientist Franciso Ayala, writing a review for *BioLogos* in 2011, aligns more with Giberson and Falk than with Gray:

But humans are chock-full of design defects. We have a jaw that is not sufficiently large to accommodate all of our teeth, so that wisdom teeth have to be removed and other teeth straightened by an orthodontist. Our backbone is less than well designed for our bipedal gait, resulting in back pain and other problems in late life. The birth canal is too narrow for the head of the newborn to pass easily through it, so that millions of innocent babies—and their mothers—have died in childbirth throughout human history.[6]

Another claim that God sits at arm's length from a morally dubious evolutionary process (which is also the sole means of biological creation) comes from theologian Keith Ward:

If natural science shows that many genetic mutations are fatally harmful to organisms, that is a strong indication that any theory of creation that attributes every event to the directly intended action of a good and omnipotent God is mistaken.[7]

There really doesn't seem much of creation left to God after all this. My intention here is not to press the case, already made over several chapters, that these sentiments ignore the clear teaching of Scripture and historic

---

5. Gray, "Darwin and his Reviewers."

6. Ayala, *On Reading the Cell's Signature*. In Dembski and Ruse, eds., *Debating Design*, 78, Ayala cites, with approval, this passage by atheist David Hull: "The evolutionary process is rife with happenstance, contingency, incredible waste, pain, death and horror. . . . Whatever the God implied by evolutionary theory and the data of natural selection may be like, he is not the Protestant God of waste not, want not. He is also not the loving God who cares about his productions. He is not even the awful God pictured in the Book of Job. The God of the Galapagos is careless, wasteful, indifferent, almost diabolical. He is certainly not the sort of God to whom anyone would be inclined to pray."

7. Ward, *Theistic Evolution*, in Dembski and Ruse, eds., *Debating Design*, 262.

theology (not to mention its being an axiom of monotheism) that God is the sole Creator and sustainer of everything that is in the world, even of those things that might appear wild or even harmful to us. Neither do I intend to dwell on the parochial subjectivity of theological arguments taking the form "I would not have created things that way if I were God."

Instead I will attempt the more restricted task of showing how hyperbolic these arguments are with respect to the real world. If you are committed to a belief that the existence of *anything* harmful in nature cannot be consistent with God's existence or with his love, then you will not be impressed. But others may find it helpful to look at some evidence that our world, even granted the existence of evolution, is not quite such a hellhole as many people, including Christians, seem overly eager to claim.

I concede that there is a place for the discussion of suffering in death and nature. But is the kind of language seen in the quotations above really conducive to a sufficiently nuanced consideration of the matter? In other words, is the picture of the universe given there truly representative of reality? Or is it, perhaps, so wildly polemic as to be a calumny on our Creator, and shoddy science to boot? To begin in a general way I invite you to consider the last time you stepped into the world of nature—or better still, to take ten minutes out to do so now, outside your own door.

What was it like for you? How many agonized animal screams did you hear? How much sheer horror did you see? Animals being eaten alive, maybe? How did the implacable malevolence of the world feel to you, not to mention the overwhelming indifference and hostility of the universe? I'm writing this in Devonshire, England, but the collective experience of all who read this should provide some kind of representative experience of the world.

My chickens are well, thanks, but then they do have a protected environment. One died, peacefully, earlier this year. There was a pair of wagtails darting around the pony's feet; after tasty insects, I guess. I was privileged to see their elaborate courtship dance last spring. A wren has been patrolling the bank by our bedroom window daily for a couple of years now. Our regular swallows are wintering in South Africa, after producing three successful broods in the stable this summer. There's a fox we often see sitting on our hill apparently just enjoying the sunshine and the rolling view in his vulpine way. A mole has excavated a veritable metropolis in an unused part of the meadow. We have also had a trio of carrion crows resident in our field for several years. In the past they've stolen a few eggs, until they were outwitted by rubber substitutes.

There are also rather too many rabbits in the field. I'll dwell on them a little, partly because they're well down the food chain and partly because I know a bit about them. Many rabbits obviously don't survive long, or there'd be far more. Foxes get a few—though the rabbits tend to outrun them. The buzzards have a go at them, but if the bunnies weigh above 500g it's really just target practice—and it's not unlikely that both parties enjoy the adrenaline rush. The tawny owls probably do better at serious hunting, but at night, when we can only hear them converse.

Rabbits in Britain suffer endemic myxomatosis, which probably makes them feel pretty ropy until a predator knocks them off. As it happens I actually saw the first case in the years I've lived here this week. I noticed a sick rabbit the evening before last, and yesterday morning I spotted that our three crows (Eeny, Meeny and Miny—pardon the familiarity) were dispatching it. Later it became a welcome winter meal for a buzzard. Today it's been completely recycled.

I learned how to diagnose myxomatosis in my gap year job at a government pest control laboratory. There I also learned that your average rabbit has several score of fleas and an average of about five tapeworms. Yet for all that, the rabbits seem pretty contented most of the time—they're not being eaten, painfully parasitized or agonized, often for years at a time. They're just munching our herb garden. When they do get predated, it's normally when they're getting old and slow or sick, and it's usually by something keen to finish the job quickly and have supper.

In other words, it's the natural world that the ancient Bible writers knew well—full of variety, fecundity, and exuberance as well as the occasional violence—for all of which they offered unstinted praise to its Creator. If the world really was implacably malevolent it would hardly be as richly populated as this after four billion years, would it?

As for that overwhelmingly hostile universe, what has it ever done to you? Admittedly there are few places in it where you'd feel comfortable, but nobody's asking you to step outside your tailor-made Eden, are they? And though Jupiter may throw occasional asteroids at us, more often than not it soaks them up itself to protect us, for the solar system, like the universe itself, is extremely finely tuned in our favor. Fine tuning is the opposite of indifference, it seems to me. And anyway, how many people do you know who have actually been lost to asteroid strikes? As for the dinosaurs, maybe it was God's decision how their reign should end, since they all had to die at some stage anyway.

Catholic intelligent design writer Vincent Torley proposed a similar simple exercise for assessing the world's fallenness:

> I'd like to propose a test which I'll call Torley's Window Test.
> It's very simple. Wherever you are on planet Earth, I invite you

to have a look out your window and tell me: what do you see? No matter where you live, you will probably see a scene of great beauty—whether it be the natural beauty of the countryside, or the man-made beauty of cities.

In neither case, if you look out your window, are you likely to see any evil. You almost certainly will not see animals (or people) suffering excruciating pain, or dying a slow and agonizing death. And you probably won't see human beings performing depraved acts of wickedness, either. Which prompts me to ask: where is all the evil? Why is it almost nowhere to be seen? And why is beauty to be found everywhere?[8]

In fact one of the best scientific treatments of this subject I have come across was by the co-describer of the theory of evolution by natural selection, Alfred Russel Wallace. He wrote a whole chapter entitled "Is Nature Cruel?" in his final book, *The World of Life*. I'll draw on this work later, but at this stage will just point out his observation that the exaggerated rhetoric about the world's malevolence was around in his own time, amongst others in the antireligious work of Thomas Huxley, "Darwin's Bulldog," who saw fit to quote Dante's *Inferno*:

From the point of view of the moralist the animal world is on about the same level as a gladiator's show. The creatures are fairly well treated, and set to fight—whereby the strongest, the swiftest, and the cunningest live to fight another day. The spectator has no need to turn his thumbs down, as no quarter is given. He must admit that the skill and training displayed are wonderful. But he must shut his eyes if he would not see that more or less enduring suffering is the meed of both vanquished and victor. And since the great game is going on in every corner of the world, thousands of times a minute; since, were our ears sharp enough, we need not descend to the gates of hell to hear—

Sospiri, pianti, ed alti guai, (Here sighs, with lamentations and loud moans,)

. . .

Voci alte e floche, e suon di man con elle (Voices deep and hoarse, with hands together smote that swell'd the sounds)

8. Torley, *God: Lawgiver or Hypocrite?*

—it seems to follow that, if the world is governed by benevolence, it must be a different sort of benevolence from that of John Howard.[9]

It is noteworthy that despite Wallace's expert debunking of the horror stories, backed by a lifetime as a field naturalist and scientist, they are still standard fare in both secular and religious writing. Why? Perhaps Wallace had it right:

> We have here presented one of the strangest phenomena of the human mind—that numbers of intelligent men are more attracted by a belief which makes the amount of pain which they think does exist on the earth last for all eternity ... without any permanent and good result whatever, than by another belief, which admits the same amount of pain into one world only, and for a limited period, while whatever pain there is only exists for the grand purpose of developing a race of spiritual beings, who may thereafter live without physical pain—for all eternity![10]

It seems a shame that the spiritualist Wallace had a better handle on Christian theology than many Christians. It may not just be "attraction to a belief," though, that concentrates so myopically on pain, but the inertia of worldviews. Despite well-documented limitations to the idea, perception is nevertheless highly theory-laden, and worldviews are, in effect, unconsciously held theories. If, as I suggested in the last chapter, nature came over several centuries to be understood as inimical and violent, then it will tend to be seen that way unless the worldview is consciously challenged (perhaps by Torley's Window Test, or even by imbibing the Bible's worldview through that old evangelical habit, devotional Bible reading).

As an illustration, consider in how many different ways wild landscapes have been viewed over the last millennium. In mediaeval times, a rugged mountain was, literally, a wasteland of no use to human or beast, except perhaps when fleeing from invading armies. You would not take time out to walk up Snowdon. Nobody except a fisherman or sailor would take much pleasure from being on a beach, and an artist would rather paint a city than a natural landscape.

With romanticism came the idea of "sublimity" in nature, "nature" meaning essentially "free of people." That sublimity, though, was closely akin to dread. Mountains were described by words like "terrible," "awful" or "ghastly." Wordsworth walked up Snowdon by moonlight, to write about it.

9. Huxley, *The Struggle for Existence*, 163. John Howard was a prominent prison reformer.

10. Wallace, *The World of Life*, 371.

Romantic landscapes always heightened the dramatic and the intimidating, whilst seascapes were invariably stormy and usually involved shipwrecks.

Yet we come to the present time, and "wilderness" is seen as a form of domesticated beauty, a place to retire and be comfortably free of traffic noise, for public recreation rather than solitary spirituality. You climb mountains for the thrill, or microlight over them taking selfies. Snowdon has a railway ending at a summit café. Beaches require cocktail bars and windsurfing in order to become sublime.

So do you look at a wilderness and see uselessness, or sublimity, or amenity? It depends on which theory of nature you've unconsciously adopted. In all probability, it will be the same viewpoint as most of your contemporaries. The same is, to a great extent, true of the evils in nature.

Before looking in more detail at the general issues surrounding pain and suffering, I want to spend the rest of this chapter dealing with some of the specifically "evolutionary" problems brought up by pessimists about the creation. These include extinctions, evolutionary "blind alleys," merciless waste, arms races, and "evil" design. The next chapter I'll devote to the myth of "selfish" evolution.

Extinctions

Extinction is often presented as if it's a self-evident source of suffering, and the alleged millions of extinctions in earth's history seem to mean unimaginable amounts of suffering. But to become extinct just means to die without offspring—which many people, and many more animals, experience every day, often quite painlessly.

For most species extinction is not even sudden. Should the giant panda become extinct, it would be because its habitat shrunk too much to sustain a breeding population. That's a shame for panda-loving people, but to pandas, without a thought for the future, it's no big deal. They are slow breeders and solitary livers anyway. Even in more rapid extinctions, there is little drama. Do you really suppose that Martha, the last passenger pigeon, who died in the Cincinnati Zoo in 1914, was even aware of the predicament of her species?

Mass extinctions, like the K-T extinction event,[11] appear to be more gradual than usually supposed—the asteroid seems to have started a prolonged period of change. Still, what it was like to be killed by the Chicxulub

---

11. Known to the well-informed as the Cretaceous–Paleogene (K–Pg) extinction event.

asteroid strike is hard to imagine, but was surely no worse than being struck into oblivion by a large Tyrannosaur about its daily business.

But for the sake of accuracy alone, it's reasonable to challenge the huge numbers assumed for extinctions anyway. It's usually claimed that 99.9 percent of species are now extinct. Even if that were true, it wouldn't (as I have already shown) add one jot to the sufferings in nature.

It is routinely said to be wasteful for God to create so many now departed species, but that is meaningless. God can create things for their own sake, to last for a season—and the average life of a species, estimated as upwards of a million years, is 150 times longer than the age granted to the whole earth by young-earth creationists. And he can justly create them for a temporary role, such as the species believed to have "terraformed" the earth's atmosphere with oxygen in the Precambrian era. He can even create them for humankind now, or in the age to come, to discover and use as a motivation for praise (how often do you praise God for dinosaurs or ammonites?)—hundreds of former worlds are present in one as fossils! What richness!

In earlier centuries, when a different philosophy reigned, such vast numbers of species would be seen as an outworking of the "principle of plenitude," derived from Plato—that God creates every possible kind of being:

> *How many* kinds of temporal and imperfect beings must this world contain?—the answer follows by the same dialectic: *all* possible kinds. The "best soul" could begrudge existence to nothing that could conceivably possess it.[12]

Philosophers then might, perhaps, even have been persuaded that extinction was one good way of making room for all of them in the world.

But let's return to that 99.9 percent figure: it depends entirely on the *assumption* that Darwin's theory of "phyletic gradualism" is true—that species change infinitesimally in all directions, with selection preserving just a lucky few. But gradualism almost certainly *isn't* true, according to modern evolutionary theory. There are perhaps 10 million living species, and the best estimate of named fossil species is that of paleontologist Donald Prothero—approximately 250,000.[13]

That low figure is no longer thought to be entirely because the fossil record is impossibly poor. A paper by Michael Benton[14] shows, using three separate measures, that the fossil record is broadly reliable: we don't have all

12. Lovejoy, *The Great Chain of Being*, 50.
13. Prothero, "Fossil Record," 491.
14. Benton, "The quality of the fossil record."

the species that have been preserved, of course, and probably many were not fossilized at all, but we can now justly claim to have a representative proportion. There may well even be more living species than extinct ones—how would one possibly know?

Furthermore, that quarter of a million fossil species is distributed across maybe 200 million or more catalogued fossils in museums around the world—making an average of eighty-plus specimens of each species. That doesn't fit a pattern of predominantly gradual change with multiple extinctions, but one of stasis and relatively sudden and successful transformation—the very pattern suggested by the now well-accepted theory of punctuated equilibria.[15]

Very crudely, this theory suggests that small populations of a species become isolated and evolve quicker than the "resolution level" of the geological record can reveal—up to a million years or so. It's just not possible to observe if speciation takes place over the whole million years or just a generation or two. But the net result is that when the population reappears in the fossils, it's a new species, which then continues in the fossils much the same for as long as it exists at all. If, let us suppose, the original species then becomes extinct, the picture is closer to one new type replacing one old type, than to evolution wildly flailing around producing hundreds of "failures." That brings us to the emotive, but misleading, term of "evolutionary blind alleys."

Blind alleys

The picture (deliberately) conjured up by this term, and the related one of "failed experiments," is of ill-starred creatures stumbling about in anguish like misshapen Frankenstein's monsters until, inevitably and mercifully, they succumb in the bloody struggle for existence (only after a lot more agony, of course). This is tommyrot.

Like so many of these concepts it's a mainly theological idea with no real scientific value—"Look at all the waste in evolution, with all those failures littering the field. Would a Creator God really have shown such incompetence, especially given the suffering of all those badly designed unfortunates?"

Evolutionary "blind alleys" and "failures," it is held, demonstrate the existence of purposeless evolution. But the *real* question is, what evidence demonstrates the existence of such dead ends and failures? In fact, they are

15. Eldredge and Gould, "Punctuated Equilibria," 82–115.

circularly *assumed* to have existed from the predictions of the Darwinian gradualist model of evolution.

Extinctions are often cited as direct evidence of these "evolutionary dead ends" as if the connection were self-evident. But extinctions do not demonstrate failed directions of evolution, any more than the death of soldiers in battle necessarily demonstrates failed strategies. Rather they show changes of conditions that eventually exceed that type of organism's potential for adaptation. Steam engines were not dead-end technologies because they were eventually replaced with diesels. It only becomes a "failed experiment" if you make the continuance of a particular line the sole criterion of success, rather than (say) the health of the whole biosphere—which is more likely to be God's concern.

It only becomes a *tragic* failure if you weave some fanciful image of a last fish dying slowly in a desert with gasping regrets that she'll never see her grandchildren—a scenario that in real life would be the same as the millions of other similar fish that died in deserts fortuitously during the millions of years it was a flourishing species. Why is extinction any more wasteful and tragic than death itself? Both bequeath the earth to other living individuals, which is perhaps inevitable in any world constituted on change.

So extinctions as such count for nothing as evolutionary mistakes. What we're looking for are the abject failures: not the steam engines that gave way to diesels, but the steam toasters or steam battery packs that some moron patented before they sank into welcome oblivion. And those are much harder to come by in the biological world.

The fossil record, as I stated above, shows an overwhelming predominance of apparent stasis and sudden changes of successful forms (hence punctuated equilibria). Gradual transitions, even in the more rapid time scales of punctuated equilibria, are in nearly all cases postulates of the assumption that they "must" have existed, but not fossilized. The same is true of "evolutionary failures"—they *may* have occurred during times of speciation, or even as isolated lineages during stasis—but they don't actually manifest as fossils. They are a pure hypothesis.

How would we even recognize such a "failed experiment" if we did find a fossil? It would represent some species that once lived, and a live species is, by definition, more or less successful. Stillborn monsters seldom fossilize—and never take part in evolutionary experiments because they don't reproduce after their kinds. Low or declining numbers might be because a species is a failure—but more likely because the species occupies a specialized niche that is disappearing. Or a species may even just lose out in exceptional circumstances (like introduced grey squirrels ousting reds in the UK, global warming leaving nowhere for cold-loving species to go, and so on).

Some have said the giant panda ought to be quietly left to go extinct because it is so poorly adapted. But it has actually been around successfully since the Pleistocene, just as long as we have. If its habitat or other environmental factors are no longer conducive to its survival, then that's another matter—but it's not a blind alley.

How would one tell that any fossil is a "dead end"? Extreme body plans are no guide. We can have little idea of the entire world a strange fossil creature lived in, so it's impossible to say how well suited it was. It's even impossible to be sure how rare it was, because all agree the fossil record is at least somewhat patchy. Plenty of today's common plants and animals are weird, but highly successful.

For example, commonly it was said (and still is, in popular science texts) that the Irish elk became extinct because its increasingly disproportionate antlers, assumed to be sexually selected, eventually made the whole creature maladaptive—a blind alley. But all we really *know* is that it had big antlers and went extinct.

That redoubtable iconoclast, paleontologist Stephen J. Gould, drew attention[16] to findings that as deer species increase in size, their antlers *habitually* enlarge disproportionately. The giant elk, being the largest deer found, had antlers that followed this rule. This suggests that some kind of developmental constraint, or structuralist "law," was probably at work in the elk, rather than any evolutionary "experiment," whether that experiment was entirely directionless, an attempt to adapt to some supposed need that failed, or even the inexplicable love of the elk ladies for grotesque headgear.

But we don't really need Gould's excellent analysis to show the vacuity of the "dead end" hypothesis. For in fact *Megaloceros giganteus* (the giant elk's respectable name) shows in the fossil record from around 400,000 BP to 8,000 BP. That longevity in itself undermines any idea of a failed experiment. More significantly still, there seems to be no actual *evidence* that their antlers really did increase in size over that time. The whole argument, it seems, was simply, "Those antlers look too big to work. And the elk's extinct. They must have evolved gradually because everything does. Therefore they just got too large and the experiment failed."

But in fact, it looks as if giant elks died out because of the usual issues of lack of the right food when the ice age ended, perhaps aided by human spears and arrows. It was just another example of the common mortality of the created realm.

16. Gould, "The origin and function of 'bizarre' structures."

Merciless waste

Critics point to the vast reproductive rates, and almost equally vast mortalities, of certain species as evidence of criminal waste in the world. Examples might be the immense numbers of mosquitoes devoured annually by migrant birds in Siberia; or the huge clouds of plankton consumed by shoals of billions of sardines that, in turn, largely succumb to predators like dolphins, sharks, and gannets; or of course the prodigality of seed production in many plants. This is said to be a "merciless" waste (and, of course, agonizing all round).

Needless to say, this is pure anthropomorphism. We humans produce a few children—each a rational soul—and hope all will live long and prosper to change the world, and perhaps even to gain eternal life. These other species were created, and/or evolved, as the basis of the food chain. If they expect anything in life, it would be that most of their offspring will be food, except for those few destined to propagate the race.

As an analogy, imagine that I produce a thousand advertising handbills for this book to hand out in the street, in the expectation of maybe one profitable sale. I budget for the fact that 999 bills will become shopping lists or packing materials—partly because I use everybody else's useful handbills that way myself.

The idea of "waste" is plausible only because of the biologist's artificial focus on the individual struggle to survive. But ecologically nothing whatsoever is wasted, since everything depends on everything else (including plankton species recycling dolphin and shark waste). Even the profligate "waste" of seed production is the reason for beautiful finches. God's perspective likewise is to provide for his whole *oikonomos*, not just to maximize individual survival. As for the prey species, we have no evidence that they prefer the biologist's perspective to God's or the ecologist's.

It is only humans who leave behind mountains of waste to pollute the earth, and shoals of plastic bags to choke turtles. Nature has successfully recycled everything for four billion years.

Arms races

An evolutionary "arms race" is seen as the progressive mutual adaption of a predator and its prey, and therefore as textbook evidence for adaptive evolution. With respect to creation, it's almost enough simply to hint at such an image of the eastern and western blocs developing mutually assured nuclear destruction to set theodical pulses racing.

A common example is the cheetah and Thompson's gazelle, whose evolution has increased the speed and agility of both, it is said. This process is, somehow, seen as evidence against God as Creator:

> The cheetah, if we are going to talk design at all, is superbly designed for killing gazelles. But the very same designer has equally evidently strained every nerve to design a gazelle that is superbly equipped to escape from those very same cheetahs. For heaven's sake, whose side is the designer on?[17]

The first thing to say is that evolution adds absolutely nothing to what common knowledge from observing the created order itself shows: you can go out to Africa and see a fast cheetah hunt a fast gazelle. Each wins about 50 percent of the time. It's not controversial that slow individuals on either side will probably do less well.

We have also seen previously that the biblical God claims actually to find prey for the lions, so presumably for cheetahs too; and in the same passage he plays midwife to the mountain goats, so presumably to the gazelle as well.[18] The "designer" is therefore on the side of both species, for the good of all—and that has been known from antiquity—and if that troubles our human sensibilities that is our problem. One might as well worry whether God is on the side of both squirrels and nuts, giving one teeth and the other a shell.

If science could validly study design motives (as Dawkins seems to assume by the very act of dismissing design) we might well suggest that God used the speed of the gazelle to *limit* its predation to cheetahs alone (good for everybody), except that the evidence is more complicated than that. The existence of the arms race would seem to provide evidence for adaptive evolution, but once more, what evidence exists for the arms race itself? In fact it stands on pretty speculative ground. Cheetahs don't have an intimate predator relationship with one species at all (clearly a necessity for an arms race), but they hunt getting on for thirty species, based mainly on size rather than agility. They even occasionally hunt ostriches.

It's also a matter of dispute whether the cheetah evolved in America or East Asia, but one thing is sure from genetics: it faced two population bottlenecks at around 100,000 and 10–20,000 years ago that left it with such low genetic variability that skin grafts "take" on unrelated cheetahs as if they were identical twins. There *can* have been no arms race since the ice age, because they remain the same species, and entirely lack the necessary variation.

17. Dawkins, *The Greatest Show on Earth*, 384.
18. Job 38.

Furthermore, if they came from America, they can't have hunted gazelles, because there weren't any there, nor even antelope apart from the saiga, which they don't hunt now. In fact, the fossils suggest that cheetahs haven't changed appreciably since they first appeared in the fossil record.[19] The facts surely need to be true before we worry about the theodicy.

"Evil" design

In even attempting to answer the question of the "wicked" behavior of many creatures, I'm aware of being vigorously opposed not only by atheists and theistic evolutionists like those quoted above, but by Creationists who believe they see the effects of sin in nature. Carnivores are bad enough, but parasites are worse, as are spiders eating their mates or lions their rivals' cubs, bonobos being promiscuous, chimps waging war, and (I suppose) Venus fly traps utterly perverting the Genesis 1:18 command by eating animals.

But beauty is in the eye of the beholder. I saw a film documentary on tapeworms once, in which an expert was asked if she did not find studying such horrible parasites distasteful. She was genuinely hurt, and replied, "But they're wonderful creatures!" And so they are, especially if one believes that God made them for a purpose. One such purpose, only recently fully recognized, is that such parasites play the same role as top-level predators in many ecosystems, keeping their numbers in balance. Parasites are not optional to this created order.

A noted theistic evolutionist once dared me to claim that the exquisite design of pathological viruses was God's work, rather than that of a fallen evolutionary process (a second demiurgic Creator, in other words!). That seems unanswerable, until one notes the increasing evidence that viruses may be one of the major sources of genetic innovation in nature:

> [M]any important genes and regulatory elements and other things in cellular life forms have been borrowed from viruses. There is no question about that.[20]

Just as the rain may be used by God to bless or harm us, as we saw in the chapter 1, so may viruses. Both, indeed, may strengthen us spiritually through hardship.

---

19. *Cheetah*, Wikipedia. https://en.wikipedia.org/wiki/Cheetah.

20. Evolutionary and computational biologist Eugene Koonin in Mazur, *The Paradigm Shifters*, 68–69. Leading researchers interviewed in several chapters of that book echo the assertion.

We also often exhibit a double standard based on mere prejudice. If I describe a creature that fools the mother of another species into feeding it instead of her own young, whilst the interloper callously disposes of the real offspring, I may be describing the European cuckoo, *Cuculus canorus*. New Atheist evolutionary biologist Jerry Coyne holds this species up to his shocked students (along with the cheetah/gazelle arms race, in fact) as an example "showing nature in all its red toothiness and clawdom."[21] His squeamish biology students clearly never read nature books in kindergarten.

But *exactly* the same description applies equally well to dairy farmers (like righteous Abel?) who routinely kill male calves and submit their mothers to a lifetime of feeding their milk to humans like you and me. Only *we* have a choice, and the cuckoo doesn't. The dairy farmer along our lane is, nevertheless, a very friendly and upright chap—I don't know any cuckoos personally to compare.

Theologically, the key to all this is to understand what theologians like Augustine knew long ago, that the moral law given to us by God was just that—given to *us*. It was the law suited specifically to our *human* nature, which had we not sinned would have been natural to us still, as those made after the image and likeness of Christ, and which will again become natural once our salvation is complete. It is the law of human nature, as that nature was created to be.

But though it expresses, in human terms, God's love and righteousness (and so was seen to be completely fulfilled in the true man, Jesus Christ), it is not the law *of* God, in the sense that God should be bound by it. How could he be? We must honor our father and mother, but he has no parents. We are forbidden to take human life—but "our times are in his hands."[22] We must not steal, whereas "the LORD gives, and the LORD takes away."[23] We must not covet—but he *cannot*, for all things are his anyway.[24]

And if he is so much higher than us that the law of our lowly nature does not reach up to him, why should we expect our moral law to apply to lower natures? We saw in chapter 1 that all creatures obey God, and they obey him through the sometimes strange and exotic natures he has given them, be they the natures of sloths, parasitic wasps, squid, cats, or *Yersinia pestis* (*contra* Falk and Giberson[25]) each with its own unique law. In that restricted sense the creatures are literally "autonomous," that is, governed by

21. Coyne, *Mimicry*.

22. Ps 31:15.

23. Job 1:21.

24. Deut 10:14.

25. See *Horror shows and window tests* above.

their "own law" from God. The church fathers and Thomas Aquinas taught that each creature reflects some aspect of God's mystery and glory; and we saw in chapter 1 to what unexpected creatures the Lord compares himself, from the hen to the lion.

There is something of this sense inherent in Paul's teaching on the resurrection body in 1 Cor 15:

> [39] Not all flesh is the same: People have one kind of flesh, animals have another, birds another and fish another. [40] There are also heavenly bodies and there are earthly bodies; but the splendor of the heavenly bodies is one kind, and the splendor of the earthly bodies is another. [41] The sun has one kind of splendor, the moon another and the stars another; and star differs from star in splendor.[26]

"Flesh" surely means more than simply the flavor (or genetics) of meat, but rather the varying characteristics God has given to all mortal creatures. As N. T. Wright comments on this passage:

> Just because it is part of the "glory" of a star that it shines, that does not mean that everything else must have "glory" of that sort. It is no shame to a dog that it does not shine, or to a star that it does not bark.[27]

Yet it is highly significant that in this passage the creatures of the present age are not referred to in terms of shame at all, but in terms of their own individual kinds of *glory* from God. It may not even be coincidental that the passage goes on, in talking about human resurrection, to speak of our present bodies in terms *other* than glory:

> [42] So will it be with the resurrection of the dead. The body that is sown is perishable, it is raised imperishable; [43] it is sown in dishonor, it is raised in glory; it is sown in weakness, it is raised in power; [44] it is sown a natural body, it is raised a spiritual body.[28]

Human glory was always intended to coincide with immortality through the Spirit, and the presence of sin and death *in us* means dishonor, the opposite of glory. The glory of the earthly and heavenly creatures was never comparable to that God purposed for humankind—but in Paul's cosmology it appears to remain undiminished by our sad failure. How it will be transformed to greater glory in the light of our own final transformation

26. 1 Cor 15:39–41.

27. Wright, *The Resurrection of the Son of God*, 345–46.

28. 1 Cor 15:42–44.

remains to be seen—Romans 8, which we examined in chapter 3, might indicate that this, too, was always God's intention. Meanwhile, however, beasts are still mortal, and are still beasts.

We do not, of course, have to imitate the example of the beasts—their law is not our law. We may even, like some Bible writers and many mediaevals, use them proverbially as examples to emulate or avoid.[29] But "evil"? In God's good creation? Perhaps we should remember the words of God to Peter: "Do not call anything impure that God has made clean."[30] Especially when he long ago pronounced it "very good."[31]

29. The mediaeval bestiaries make an interesting study on how one can study nature in a manner conceptually far removed from modern science, thus revealing the parochial nature of our whole worldview.

30. Acts 10:13–15.

31. Gen 1:31.

Chapter 10—The Non-Presentation of Self in Everyday Life

Far overhead from beyond the veil of blue sky which hid them the stars sang again; a pure, cold, difficult music. Then there came a swift flash like fire (but it burnt nobody) either from the sky or from the Lion itself, and every drop of blood tingled in the children's bodies, and the deepest, wildest voice they had ever heard was saying: "Narnia, Narnia, Narnia, awake. Love. Think. Speak. Be walking trees. Be talking beasts. Be divine waters."

—C. S. LEWIS (1898–1963)[1]

Selfish evolution?

THE TITLE OF THIS chapter is based on a once influential social psychology book by Erving Goffman, *The Presentation of Self in Everyday Life*.[2] In around 250 pages, the author fully covers the ground of his subject, just like it says on the cover, writing (as one reviewer said on the cover) not only about

> Vogue models, clergymen and the dead, but also about Shetland crofters, Canadian Army dentists, dukes, beauticians, rajahs and a range of characters.

But one area is notably absent from Goffman's analysis of the self, and that is the entire nonhuman world. Given how much emphasis is often placed on the selfishness of the entire process of evolution that brought us into being, that might be seen as a surprising omission. Yet its absence is inevitable and correct, when one remembers that the concept of "self" is an

1. Lewis, *The Magician's Nephew*, 108.
2. Goffman, *The Presentation of Self.*

entirely human, even a social human, one. The self, and selfishness, fit neatly into the field of social psychology, but stop making much sense outside it. To speak of other animals as possessing a self is contentious. To speak of plants or bacteria or viruses possessing one is absurd. And to speak of an inanimate *process* like evolution being selfish is simply incoherent.

Let's look for that selfishness in our closest relatives on the evolutionary tree. As experimental psychologists David and Ann Premack write in their study of human intelligence:

> Although a chimpanzee passes the mirror test [touching its own face when viewing itself in a mirror], there is no evidence that it engages in either self- or social approval.
>
> The concept of self presupposes causal reasoning, the ability to reason: "Men pay attention to me because I am attractive." As we have seen, this kind of reasoning is not available to the chimpanzee.[3]

The chimpanzee, then, does not possess a self that could enable it to be selfish. The writers are confirming experimentally only what every thinking person has known for millennia—that there is a vast gulf fixed between us and the animals. If there is only a small difference between our genome and the chimpanzee's (1.6 percent is the figure the Premacks use) it tells us not that we've been wrong about the gulf, but that DNA coding is not the place to look for an explanation.[4]

If "self" is an inappropriate term when applied even to our nearest relative, how much more so when applied to a natural process of evolution of which its objects—unselfconscious organisms from bacteria to baboons—are completely unaware?

Yet the idea is as old as Darwin—or rather Malthus, whose work gave him the idea—that evolution is an entirely selfish process of struggling to survive, whether one views the selfish agent as the organism, falling over itself and treading on everything else in order to reproduce, or as Richard Dawkins's "selfish genes," cynically puppeteering our bodies and minds to reproduce themselves at our expense.

The reasons it matters, outside of science, are legion. The "struggle for survival" directly justified eugenic theory, two World Wars, and the

3. Premack and Premack, *Original Intelligence*, 215.

4. Biological anthropologist Jonathan Marks writes, on this: "Does it not stand to reason that if you essentially cannot tell human haemoglobin from gorilla haemoglobin, the sensible thing to do is look at something else? In other words, if you cannot tell a human from a gorilla, you really should not be in biology." (Marks, "What is the viewpoint of haemoglobin?," 245.)

Holocaust. It is held up as a natural law in economics and commerce. Accepted comprehensively, it nullifies the very existence of all that is human, by subordinating all human values to varieties of evolutionary self-promotion. And specifically it fundamentally undermines the Christian teaching that creation is good, leading amongst other things to an evolutionary theology in which creation means very little:

$$\text{God created autonomous Nature} \rightarrow \text{selfish evolution}$$
$$\rightarrow \text{selfish species} \rightarrow \text{aboriginal sin}$$

This is expressed by Karl Giberson in a recent book:

> Selfishness, in fact, drives the evolutionary process. Unselfish creatures died, and their unselfish genes perished with them. Selfish creatures, who attended to their own needs for food, power, and sex, flourished and passed on these genes to their offspring. After many generations selfishness was so fully programmed in our genomes that it was a significant part of what we now call human nature.[5]

But Darwin's "struggle for existence" was never anything more than a colorful metaphor for what, when expressed in more sober and accurate scientific terminology, is simply "differential reproduction." His "competitive warfare" model was very much a product of his English sociopolitical background, though it has far outlived Victorian social inequalities and colonial empire-building.

It is not, in fact, selfish to attend to ones needs for food or sex. A plant or animal not doing so is not being selfless, but dead. "Power" is rather more dubious a concept biologically—an instinct to fight is not at all the same thing as the human will to power, besides being anything but a universal trait in nature.

But let's give a not untypical example of how the "struggle for life" might play out in a real, adaptive, situation. Imagine a very docile, even community-spirited, small rodent whose life is marked by cooperative food-gathering activities and which mates for life in an uncompetitive way, the sexes being pretty equal in numbers. Unfortunately, their main predator is a small weasel that can get into their burrows. Or into most of them— smaller rodents with smaller burrows are not easily reached by weasels, especially once the latter have got fat by eating the bigger rodents. Accordingly, the smaller rodents, though identical in behavior to the bigger ones,

---

5. Giberson, "Living with Darwin's Dangerous Idea," 168–69.

will nevertheless tend to contribute more to the gene pool, leading over time to the evolution of a smaller variety.

Just who is being selfish here? Is it selfish to be slim? Alternatively, if instead we take a large and colorful bird with an elaborate courtship ritual, the more demonstrative variants of which get the girl, then what is being selected for is creativity, not selfishness. *All* the birds dance their hearts out with the same gusto—some are just born more beautiful.

When I was working in a pest control laboratory, captured wild rabbits were used (sadly for them fatally) in the research. Most of them, when their cage was approached, would tear round and round making shrill cries—except for one, which presumably because of some rare genetic variation would come amicably to the door of his cage and put his paw up to be stroked. The animal keepers refused point blank to allow the researchers to take him away. Friendliness was an absolute selective advantage in that situation over self-defense. There can be no universal principle that is guaranteed to provide evolutionary advantage—especially a pseudo-moral quality like "selfishness" in creatures without selves.

The trigger to Darwin's idea of the struggle for life was, as I have already noted, the work of Thomas Malthus on human populations (1798),[6] in which the same idea, that high rates of reproduction amongst the poor inevitably outstrip resources and so lead to differential survival, was the central thesis. He wrote at a time when the Industrial Revolution was producing unprecedented levels of abject poverty, and it was certainly true (metaphorically) to say that life, for millions, was a life-and-death struggle.

But was it a *selfish* struggle? There's no doubt that dehumanizing conditions often lead to dehumanized behavior—criminality, wife battering, child abuse, and so on. But even in such cases, sheer desperation rather than selfishness might be more to blame: drowning hopelessness in gin-soaked oblivion does nothing to aid survival. And as sympathetic and observant writers like Charles Dickens were at pains to point out, poverty was as likely to lead to acts of self-sacrifice actually aiding survival, or to examples of thrift or enterprise improving the lot both of the subject and of others.

As in Darwinian evolution, survival (and therefore offspring) in industrial Britain came by many different means that happened to work to resolve the "struggle." Selfishness might be involved in some of those means, but by no means inevitably—the cooperative temperance and trades union movements, born out of those times, were its very antithesis. The fundamental difference from evolution is that humans exercised

---

6. Malthus, *An Essay on Population.*

choices, for good or ill, and those choices were based on some kind of moral, or immoral, motivation.

All Darwinian evolution, on the other hand, is entirely divorced from any motivations at all,[7] other than those common to all life (to eat if hungry, for example). One is born with some pattern of variations, and it may or may not result in ones breeding somewhat better and so contributing more to the gene pool.

That even applies to human evolution. It is well known, for example, that genes for lactose tolerance in adults, once uncommon, have been gradually spreading through the human race since dairy farming was invented 10,000 years ago. You feed your kids milk, and some get sickness and diarrhea from it, but some do not. That perhaps only matters much if times are hard and there is nothing else for the children to eat, but it affects reproductive success, probably through simple survival to adulthood in those hard times. But anyone who says that *selfishness* has anything to do with it at all is crazy—being able to drink milk does not make you selfish. Nobody was even aware that the evolution of lactose tolerance was going on, for several thousand years.

Selfish genes?

Since Richard Dawkins reconceptualized adaptive evolution in 1976 with an even worse metaphor than "the struggle to survive"—the "selfish gene"—people who should know better have been taking it literally to mean that evolution itself is selfish. Of course, even if genes had discrete identities (which it's increasingly clear they do not—it is whole networks of DNA segments that cooperate to produce phenotypic effects), and even if those identities were rational and morally selfish, it wouldn't at all follow that they would lead to selfish organisms or people.

What I said about the survival of individuals would still apply to a gene selfishly determined to stick around for eternity: if generosity or friendliness were survival traits, genes would use them as readily as a good set of offensive or defensive weaponry. Even amongst people, hypocrisy can be a successful strategy to gain ascendancy. Or perhaps it would be more accurate to say that a gene for selflessness would compete just as hard to survive as a gene for selfishness—if it were true to say that genes "compete" at all,

---

7. Though it is looking increasingly likely that teleology—that is, intention—is very much a factor in real evolution.

which they don't. They just survive if they happen to code for advantageous traits, or disappear quietly if they are not.[8]

The "selfish gene" is still a more than bad analogy after all the years since Dawkins's eponymous book. Conor Cunningham, in *Darwin's Pious Idea*,[9] comprehensively demolishes the concept intellectually by showing it is philosophically meaningless. Even the existence of genes as such is increasingly questionable, or at least fights shy of a simple definition. Incidentally Cunningham adds the reminder that any theology wedded to a consensus scientific theory is destined soon to be widowed—would that more theistic evolutionists would appreciate that with regard to crude 1930s Neo-Darwinism and its selfish progeny.

Cunningham brings to light work based on wider biological principles than genetics alone, demonstrating that it is cooperation that is global and essential to life, and that selfishness (if even that could be a coherent concept in irrational beings with no sense of self) is always merely local and relative. Space forbids entering into that here, but examples would include the fact that both mitochondria and chloroplasts originated as symbiotic organs between different kingdoms of life, that vertebrate digestion depends on bacteria (which in turn depend on digestion), and so on into the mutual interdependence of entire ecosystems. It is a sobering thought that in the human body, microbial cells, from 500–1,000 species, outnumber human cells by ten to one (according to the *Human Microbiome Project*). We are in our very selves a model of interdependence!

Selfish altruism?

One issue that has challenged evolution since Darwin is that of "altruism," of creatures sacrificing their lives for others. It has usually been explained in terms of "kin selection" in various forms, i.e., that giving my life for a relative will help preserve at least some of my genes. In this way all altruistic behavior can be reduced to disguised selfishness. This cynical view reached its peak in sociobiology, where all human moral values were denied in Michael Ghiselin's quote:

> Scratch an altruist and watch a hypocrite bleed.[10]

or if you prefer, in J. B. S. Haldane's calculation:

8. I ignore here the fact that far more neutral or slightly disadvantageous genes get fixed in the population by drift than are selected adaptively. Current theory puts the survival of genes down to sheer luck, not selfishness.

9. Cunningham, *Darwin's Pious Idea*, chapter 2.

10. Ghiselin, *The Economy of Nature*, 247.

"I will die for two brothers or eight cousins"[11]

But for all the speculative genetic mathematics, kin selection and its kindred theories dilute the simplistic idea that each organism is pursuing a struggle for its own survival. If the self-sacrifice we see in animals and experience in ourselves "emerged" from such a struggle, it makes the virtue no more or less real than the practice of a science using a faculty of reason that "emerged" from the same struggle. If evolutionary altruism is illusory, then so is the biology that studies it. And if intellectual enterprise can, as we daily see, be pursued without any reference to reproductive success (by elderly bachelors like Alfred Russel Wallace, for example), then so can virtue be its own reward, and attributing everything to self-interest becomes meaningless.

The very fact that the same "selfish" motivations can produce such different outcomes in nature makes it a misleadingly crude way of seeing the world. Consider the European robin redbreast, icon of English Christmas cards and the subject of much folklore because of its friendliness to humans. Few other birds will perch on ones foot, as happened to me as I relaxed in a pub beer garden this year.

But a small part of that folklore has to do with their distinct *lack* of friendliness to other robins. Andrea Alciato's *Emblemata*, published in Paris in 1584, contains the proverb: *Unum arbustum non alit duos erithacos* (You won't find two robins in one bush). It's estimated that 10 percent of adult robin deaths result from territorial disputes. How selfish can you get? Well, I'm not so sure—last year near our stable I found a pair of dead robins, perhaps a foot apart, that had evidently *both* died disputing the ownership of a nearby nest box. Red in tooth and claw it may be, but as a selfish survival strategy it failed miserably. God, or perhaps neutral evolution *under* God, seems to have simply given robins a fighting spirit—and it works for them because, high mortality or not, they are pretty common.

Contrast them to another British passerine bird, the long-tailed tit. Selfish nature appears not only to have taught them to live in cheerful flocks which flit from tree to tree, but to have decreed that, if a pair loses their brood to predation (as happens to 10 percent of pairs despite possessing one of the most carefully woven nests of all British birds), they will find someone else's brood and help feed it. Why is that not as illustrative of nature's ways as "red in tooth and claw" is held to be?

Another case of the selective use of evidence for selfishness is the familiar one of humanity and the apes. Presumably the immediate context for Karl Giberson's quote earlier in this chapter[12] is the genetic similarity between

---

11. Quoted in McElreath and Boyd, *Mathematical Models*, 82.

12. See "selfish evolution" above.

us and chimpanzees, and the violence that has long been noted in the latters' behavior. Apart from domestic aggression, much has been made of primatologist Jane Goodall's observations of chimps in the wild organizing raiding parties on other troops, and even killing and cannibalizing their young.

When we see chimps as beasts in their own right, with natures of their own, rather than as funny little people, this poses no great moral issue. There is even an ongoing controversy amongst anthropologists over whether human incursions on chimp habitats produce, or increase, such aggression—which would be a true case of the fall affecting nature. But the popular idea is that it casts light on a probably evolutionary origin of human warfare in the common ancestor of chimps and humans five to seven million years ago.

But in this, the very different behavior of bonobos from chimpanzees is somehow neglected. They are commonly known as "chimps' peaceful cousins," their social harmony being attributed to a variety of surprising sexual activities. They are famous for making love, not war.

What is forgotten is that they are not only the chimpanzee's peaceful cousin—they are our own. Genomic studies show that we are just as closely related to bonobos as to chimps, and parts of their genome are far more similar to ours than to chimpanzees'.

The obvious conclusion ought to be that one cannot draw clear evolutionary links between behaviors in different species, however closely related. We humans might just as easily have inherited our times of peace from the bonobos and invented warfare because of sin, as inheriting war from chimps and learning peace from Ghandi or John Lennon. Or, since bonobos (supposed to have diverged from chimps far later than us) have fundamentally changed their behavior, we might have evolved, or invented, our behaviors entirely separately from both.

Nevertheless it's not infrequently suggested that we might do better learning (by imitation) from bonobos to be less uptight about sex and less violent (by ape inheritance). That, however, is clearly not the point—not least because human experience shows that as a race we are quite capable of customarily combining sexual promiscuity with violence inventively. Quite simply, evolution did not produce "selfish" violence in our *other* closest relative, so it is quite gratuitous to use evolution to explain human selfishness, still less to build a theology of human sin on it.

Selfish what, exactly?

Yet part of the artificiality of the whole discussion stems, it seems to me, from focusing too closely on the individual metazoan organism—the animal—as that which is to be explained by evolution. The popular paradigm of evolutionary selfishness is the bloodthirsty Tyrannosaur rampaging across the Jurassic landscape to look after Number One, or to slug it out with an equally bloodthirsty Stegosaur. I remember that image as my very first encounter with dinosaurs, at the age of five, when I saw Walt Disney's *Fantasia*. Three-toed sloths or daffodils are less often used as examples of bloody strife, though they must have evolved too.

Other units of evolution than the individual are possible, though, for as we have seen Neo-Darwinism, basing evolution on population genetics, represents that selfish individual by its selfish genome amongst those of the whole population. One should, even in that case, remember that all sexual reproduction begins by sacrificing a whopping 50 percent of one's personal genetic inheritance to one's mate's every time a sperm and an egg fuse—mutual help is at the heart of sexual reproduction, even regarding evolution. The rutting stag is fighting to best preserve the hinds' genes as well as his own.

Possible units of evolution don't end there, though. Darwin himself faced the problem of colonial insects whose members, many sterile, sacrifice themselves willingly for the good of the colony. In fact, the idea of kin selection probably started here, once it was realized that the shared traits and genes of the colony could be seen as what was being protected, an insight suggested to Darwin by Wallace.

All is not quite as inward-looking as it seems though: bee colonies, for example, need a high genetic diversity to remain healthy, which is achieved by the queen's mating with multiple external males, and by unusually large-scale (twenty times that of humans) recombination of genes. The workers sacrificing themselves, therefore, are often dying to protect the genes of different fathers from outside the colony.

So "fitness" need not be focused on the individual and its offspring even in the lowly insect. And if insect colonies can be the effective units of selection, then why not an entire species, for example, which shares a common gene pool? After all, the United Nations has labored to pass resolutions on global warming on the basis that it's a threat to humanity at large. Why should that be regarded as any more odd biologically than workers in a hive seeking the common good, or individuals laboring to survive?

But as well as looking outward beyond the individual, we might look inwards, speaking biologically rather than anthropologically. Even within our own bodies, cooperation can be seen at the level of individual cells. What is a metazoan such as a human being, biologically speaking, but a colony of cells with anything up to thirty-seven trillion members? All day, every day, our individual cells die on our behalf: skin and gut cells are shed, immune cells act as suicide bombers against bacterial invaders, and so on, and we take it for granted that they should. We even have "sterile workers" in the form of red blood cells that never reproduce, lacking even a nucleus.

Programmed cell death (apoptosis) is a sophisticated physiological process, quite different from the accidental destruction of cells, which is absolutely essential for individual development and survival.

For some reason we don't see that as the same kind of red in tooth and claw struggle and God-questioning suffering that we would attribute to an elephant fighting for her calf, a polychaete worm rupturing in egg-laying, or hard-done-by slave ants working for another species. Instead we see it, rightly, as the harmonious operation of a harmoniously constituted being.

So maybe the whole question of competition and death in the biological realm isn't usefully regarded in the sole light of "selfish" reproductive success at all, but rather in terms of various hierarchies of cooperative "commonwealth."

Include the genes in that by all means—if you can find them, since they are getting increasingly hard to define in the light of recent discoveries about the complexity of control networks in cells. Certainly there is also a level at which cells work hard to maintain their identity. Then there is the level of the organism. Then there is the level of the colony, where appropriate, or the social grouping. Then the species. But above that is the level of the ecosystem, which is an environmental construct—and is not the "environment" supposed to be the mediator of natural selection, and therefore the most obvious "fundamental" unit of evolution? And of course, even above that is the biosphere, which is to the ecosystem what a colony is to an individual bee or ant.

Above that, speaking naturalistically, would be Gaia—the self-maintaining system of the earth itself, of which life is just one part. But as Christians, maybe we need at this point to be even more aware of the providence of God—the governor of the household—as the unifying principle, since nobody seriously suggests "selfishness" to be what keeps the earth itself in equilibrium. Indeed, invoking God takes the *oikonomos* up to the level of the whole universe, and down to the level of the quark, for all the levels I have written about are, in reality, as inextricably interrelated as the systems of an individual cell or organism.

To summarize, then, since evolution, and the living world generally are found on close examination *not* to be steeped in selfishness at all, but overwhelmingly founded on cooperation and interdependence, human sin and selfishness may be seen for what they truly are—an aberration within God's good creation.

Chapter 11—On Pain and Suffering

People will not keep always in mind that pain exists in the world for a purpose, and a most beneficent purpose—that of aiding in the preservation of a sufficiency of the higher and more perfectly organized forms, till they have reproduced their kind.

—ALFRED RUSSEL WALLACE (1823–1913)[1]

·

IN THE INTRODUCTION I quoted Robert J. Russell, presenting in relatively mild terms, compared to many, the "hard truths" about natural evil that demand not only our explanation, but a setting to rights by God if he is to be considered good. Russell closed the paragraph by saying "most animals are fated to an agonizing death."[2] It's the factual basis of that sentence, so representative of modern assumptions, that I want to question in this chapter, taking a number of approaches.

The baseline—human pain

It is the experience, personal or vicarious, of human suffering that generates concerns over the sufferings perceived to exist in nature as "evil." We all ought to be aware of the truth that pain is necessary to our survival, as Wallace's quote at the head of the chapter makes clear. Those with diminished pain sensation, such as leprosy patients, suffer progressive tissue damage as a result of repeated injuries. But we're also aware of a direct link between pain and human sin, in that the most severe forms of pain are those deliberately designed as such by humans to damage or control other humans.

In fact, though, human pain is the only form about which we can be truly certain, since pain is an irreducibly subjective experience. I, like

---

1. Wallace, *The World of Life*, 375.
2. Russell, *Cosmology*, 249.

everyone else, know what it has been like to experience various degrees and types of pain only in my own life, and will return to that shortly.

My knowledge of pain in other people is founded on the same *theory of mind* that makes me able to differentiate myself *as* a self. In infancy, we human beings uniquely begin to be able to relate to other humans as beings like ourselves, making empathy and true communication possible. In turn, that ability to see others as "selves" makes it possible for us to see *ourselves* as if we were an "other": I am not only "me" but "a person like you." There is no good evidence that any other creatures gain this "theory of mind."

When our sense of self is compromised, our experience of pain may be profoundly altered. A passage in Dickens strikes me, as a doctor, as being almost certainly drawn from real life, however paradoxical. In *Hard Times* Mrs. Gradgrind, fading fast on her deathbed, is addressed by her daughter Louisa:

> "Are you in pain, dear mother?"
>
> "'I think there's a pain somewhere in the room,' said Mrs. Gradgrind, 'but I couldn't positively say that I have got it.'"[3]

But because, in normal circumstances, my sense of self is strong I can believe in your pain, inasmuch as I can compare it to mine when I suffered the same cause (an ear infection or a bruised elbow, perhaps), acted in the same way (moaning or wincing), and described the pain similarly ("I've got a dreadful earache!"). I can only gauge a pain worse than I've actually experienced (such as childbirth, being shot, or being burned alive) by using my imagination and interpreting evidence indirectly. If somebody yells louder than I remember doing, their pain is presumably worse. If constipation was painful, what must delivering a baby be like?

Yet the subjectivity of pain can play us false, and we can take for granted neither that our own pain is a reliable indicator of harm, or that other people experience pain the same as we do.

In my professional career I specialized in back pain, and for two years ran a district National Health Service back pain clinic. This led to some interesting observations. The first and most profound, and yet commonplace, is the effect of mental state on pain. A depressed patient will generally feel any pain more severely, as will someone who believes the pain has a serious cause. Conversely, adrenaline surges can virtually obviate pain, an acute stress situation often rendering even severe injuries unnoticeable. My professional friends in the hospice movement tell me the difference peace of mind makes to pain (when it occurs—often it doesn't) in terminal disease.

3. Charles Dickens, *Hard Times*, chapter 9.

Severe injury also boosts endorphin production, markedly reducing pain: the more devastating the trauma, the less suffering is often involved. The deep shock (that is, loss of effective blood circulation) of major injury also has the effect of an anesthetic. Other physical states can alter pain too—commonly back pain will get worse in those suffering an intercurrent viral infection. All these things should not surprise us for pain, as I said, is irreducibly subjective.

Chronic (or "central") pain is a very intriguing issue, because in general it is not the result of continuing tissue damage (once regarded definitionally as the cause of pain), but of autonomous pain pathways set up in the central nervous system, often after an initial injury has completely healed. Part of the treatment is to educate the patient that they are *not* harming themselves by, say, exercising a painful back.

This is one reason I am annoyed by evolutionary biologists claiming how unusually prone to injury the human spine is because of our unnatural upright gait: in fact most acute back injury comes from doing unnatural things like heavy lifting when one has already spent too much time in unnatural sedentary occupations, rather than in the upright exercise to which we are best suited by nature.

Chronic back pain occurs most often when inadequate rehabilitative exercise is done after acute injuries. It has nothing to do with mechanical failure, but (one is tempted to say) over-engineered neurological software. Central nervous software, as we are now discovering, is often reprogrammed by the higher brain centers—leading us back to the profound influence of psychology on pain perception.

Pain is also affected by such nonphysical things as culture—in hospital medicine one had to be aware that certain social groups and nationalities were unusually sensitive to quite minor sources of pain. Failure to take it into account could even lead to unnecessary acute surgery. Conversely, Alfred Russel Wallace, who had extensive experience of dwelling with hunter-gatherer tribes, reported that:

> . . . we have the well-known facts of the natives of many parts
> of the world enduring what to us would be dreadful torments
> without exhibiting any sign of pain.[4]

Neither is difference in pain perception purely psychological. The so-called *Fibromyalgia* is a condition involving generalized pains, widely believed to have a large psychological component. Be that as it may,

---

4. Wallace, *The World of Life*, 379.

neurological studies reveal spinal cord and brain abnormalities that show that such patients process pain quite differently from non-sufferers.[5]

So the subjectivity even of the common experience of human pain confirms Wallace's warning that:

> Our whole tendency to transfer our sensations of pain to all other animals is grossly misleading.[6]

He points out specific factors in the evolution of humanity that make increased pain sensitivity a likely adaptation. Not only do we have an unprotected skin prone to injury, and a lengthy period of infancy and childhood when avoidance behaviors are not in place, but we have created for ourselves unusual dangers against which pain must warn us. These include first the use of fire, then increasingly hard and sharp tools and weapons, and ultimately the complex and dangerous machinery that now forms the environment of "a large proportion of the human race." As he goes on to conclude:

> . . . it is this specially developed sensibility that we, most illogically, transfer to the animal-world in our wholly exaggerated and often quite mistaken views as to the cruelty of nature![7]

I will return both to Wallace's evolutionary viewpoint and the question of how we *may* try to gauge suffering in nature later, but first I will reinforce his warnings on the irreducible subjectivity of pain *vis a vis* the animals, by citing a modern author. Whilst we may legitimately employ our "theory of mind" to understand pain in fellow humans, we are completely unwarranted in doing the same for any other species.

Philosopher Thomas Nagel wrote a seminal paper on the "mind-body" problem, in order to show that it is quite impossible to describe subjective experience objectively (hence drawing attention to the weakness of reductive materialism). He called it *What it is like to be a bat?* He chose a bat as his example because, although a relatively advanced mammal, its lifestyle—flying and hunting by echolocation—is completely alien to us. Yet there is "something that it is like" to be a bat.

> It will not help to try to imagine that one has webbing on one's arms, which enables one to fly around at dusk and dawn catching insects in one's mouth; that one has very poor vision, and perceives the surrounding world by a system of reflected high-frequency sound signals; and that one spends the day hanging

---

5. Clauw, Arnold, and McCarberg, "The Science of Fibromyalgia."

6. Wallace, *the World of Life*, 377.

7. Ibid., 379.

upside down by one's feet in an attic. In so far as I can imagine this (which is not very far), it tells me only what it would be like for me to behave as a bat behaves. But that is not the question. I want to know what it is like for a bat to be a bat. Yet if I try to imagine this, I am restricted to the resources of my own mind, and those resources are inadequate to the task. I cannot perform it either by imagining additions to my present experience, or by imagining segments gradually subtracted from it, or by imagining some combination of additions, subtractions, and modifications.[8]

In the same way, we must conclude that it is entirely invalid to project *our* ideas of what it might be like for the bat to be caught on the wing by an owl. We can only vaguely conjecture (recognizing it is little more than an exercise of fantasy) on the basis of what scientific information we have.

But before leaving the human sphere, I want to repeat a version of "Torley's Window Test" (see chapter 8), to question to what extent pain, even in our human experience, is truly an "evil." There are certainly those whose entire life has been blighted by previous pain (one thinks of torture victims) or other sufferings like the trauma of war, of violent crime, of road accidents, or chronic illness. But for most of us, even quite severe episodes of pain are seen, in retrospect, as part of life. At the least they can make us more appreciative of the more prevalent good times, and (despite some philosophers' claims to the contrary) quite often can be viewed as enriching our life experience in numerous ways.

Personally I have (so far) been pretty fortunate in health matters. But apart from the common illnesses I have suffered very painful back injury (ironic, but also valuable, for a back pain practitioner). I have also suffered from periods of depression that, although not anything as severe as those I have treated in others, are not something I would choose to repeat. Most people I know have comparable experiences—the painful childbirth, the acute appendicitis, the crushing coronary artery thrombosis, and so on. But in a majority of cases when those episodes have passed away they seem, in retrospect, transient and even ephemeral. I have no urge whatsoever to come before God's throne and demand redress for my past sufferings, even had I done nothing in my life to deserve such troubles . . . and we must not forget that this book is written on the assumption that humankind lives in painful exile from God because of sin.

I may (and indeed should) look at the severe sufferings of others and ask "Why?"—but if I am honest I see no need to add my own quite minor,

8. Nagel, "What is it like to be a bat?," 439.

and even in some ways life-enhancing, trials to the weight of evils requiring explanation. They make perfect sense in a good world that, as yet, remains subject to mortality. This must surely relativize, to a significant extent, the "problem of natural evil" applied to human suffering.

I have a feeling that much animal suffering ought to be seen in the same way.

The evolution of pain

In the chapter on the supposed cruelty of nature in Wallace's *World of Life*, perhaps his most original contribution is in treating pain as, itself, an evolutionary phenomenon. In passing, let me mention that he quotes Charles Darwin, whose repulsion against insect parasitism in a letter to Asa Gray is oft-quoted, but whose more considered statement on natural evil in *The Origin of Species* isn't:

> When we reflect on this struggle, we may console ourselves with the full belief, that the war of nature is not incessant, that no fear is felt, that death is generally prompt, and that the vigorous, the healthy, and the happy survive and multiply.[9]

If one remembers that Darwin, like Wallace, was essentially a field naturalist, one begins to sense that such testimony is far more valuable than that of desk-bound academics engaged in theodicy or anti-theodicy.

Wallace's evolutionary argument is, as is natural given that he originated the theory, mainstream adaptationist Darwinism. No trait in evolution occurs except because of its utility, and therefore pain has evolved as far as, and no further than, it is useful to the survival of organisms. One may add from more recent knowledge that adaptations also pose a cost to the animal in terms of energy. Not only, then, would excessive pain detract from survival directly, but through the energy cost of developing and carrying around neurological mechanisms that aren't beneficial.

As for the earliest, primitive, forms of life, Wallace reasons that it is certain they evolved the minimum sensation necessary for the purpose of their short existence, and that "anything approaching what we term 'pain' was unknown to them."[10]

These organisms, being neither able (nor intended by the Creator) to avoid being ingested by higher forms, would have no reason whatsoever to

---

9. Darwin, *Origin*, chapter 3, quoted in Wallace, *The World of Life*, 370.
10. Ibid., 375.

benefit from pain sensation, and therefore do not possess it. But the same goes even for higher forms that form the basis of food chains:

> . . . it is almost as certain as anything not personally known can be, that all animals which breed very rapidly, which exist in vast numbers, and which are necessarily kept down to their average population by the agency of those that feed upon them, have little sensitiveness, perhaps only a slight discomfort under the most severe injuries, and that they probably suffer nothing at all when being devoured. For why should they? They exist to be devoured; their enormous powers of increase are for this end; they are subject to no dangerous bodily injury until the time comes for them to be devoured, and therefore they need no guarding against it through the agency of pain.[11]

Note that this is not a philosophical argument, nor one based on anatomical or physiological data open to different interpretations, but is a prediction from the logic of the very evolutionary theory that is held up (purely on the basis of the metaphor of the "struggle for existence" over deep time) as evidence for ubiquitous suffering.

In Wallace's estimation, this argument places within the realm of "painless animals"

> . . . almost all aquatic animals up to fishes, all the vast hordes of insects, probably all Mollusca and worms; thus reducing the sphere of pain to a minimum, throughout all the earlier geological ages, and very largely even now.[12]

Amongst the higher animals, he points out by the same evolutionary argument that small birds and mammals are generally less subject to injuries from falls or fighting than us, and so pain is likely to be much less developed in them. This leaves only the larger and heavier animals likely to benefit from (and therefore to suffer because of) well-developed pain sensation.

R. J. Russell's previously cited book quotes a particularly juicy piece of "creation as nightmare" prose from a Pulitzer Prize-winning book called *The Denial of Death*:

> What are we to make of a creation in which the routine activity is for organisms to be tearing others apart with teeth of all types—biting, grinding flesh, plant stalks, bones between molars, pushing the pulp greedily down the gullet with delight,

11. Ibid.
12. Ibid.

incorporating its essence into one's own organization, and then excreting with foul stench and gases the residue.[13]

Such colorful rhetoric (involving as it does, mainly the denial of life rather than death) becomes rather tedious (I could add many similar passages from J. S. Mill to Kenneth Miller). But, like the "cheap talk" in the Jimi Hendrix song, it ceases to cause any pain after a while.[14] Wallace, once more, takes a much rarer *scientific* attitude to teeth and claws: he reasons that they have evolved to catch and kill prey as quickly and efficiently as possible. The escape of a severely wounded quarry helps neither party. Neither, in fact, does the predator benefit from prolonged struggle, nor from drawing attention to the kill. The actual situation with regard to large hunters, he says, is that:

> [t]he suddenness and violence of the seizure, the blow of the paw, the simultaneous deep wounds by teeth and claws, either cause death at once, or so paralyze the nervous system that no pain is felt till death very rapidly follows.[15]

Against the previously cited statement, via Karl Giberson, that the domestic cat that teases mice cannot be a creation of God, Wallace points out that, in the wild, carnivores

> . . . hunt to kill and satisfy hunger, not for amusement; and all conclusions derived from the house-fed cat and mouse are fallacious.[16]

And so Wallace, possibly the nineteenth century's greatest field biologist, shows *from* evolution that evolution has no propensity for producing a particularly cruel nature. His conclusions are largely borne out by the study of the anatomy and physiology of animal pain.

The biology of pain

The higher animals undoubtedly feel pain. But those who work with them, such as farmers, tend to believe animals feel pain somewhat differently than do humans. That much is obvious even to pet owners. Accidentally tread on your dog's leg and she'll yelp, lick it, and carry on trotting on it, even when there is clearly ongoing injury. Tread on your child's leg and she'll grizzle

13. Russell, *Cosmology*, 235, quoting Becker, *The Denial of Death*, 282–83.

14. Jimi Hendrix, "Machine Gun" (from *Band of Gypsies*, 1970).

15. Wallace, *The World of Life*, 377.

16. Ibid.

until tempted to forget it by cuddles or treats. Tread on an adult's leg and the chances are he'll bear a grudge and get back at you somehow later on. To an extent these differences are reflected in physiology and anatomy.

Whatever philosophical views one takes on the actual perception of pain, the simple fact is that it can only exist at all in the presence of a suitable nervous system to mediate it, and some center of nervous activity to receive and process signals from damaged tissue. This immediately excludes the vast majority of the world's living organisms from the very possibility of pain or suffering.

The *Monera* (including bacteria), *Protista* (including the diatoms and dinoflagellates that alone make up 75 percent of the world's biomass and all the Protozoa), *Fungi,* and *Plantae* all lack a nervous system and so cannot possibly suffer pain in any unpleasant subjective sense.[17] And yet the danger of anthropomorphism is shown by the fact that protozoa, and even unicellular prokaryocytes like bacteria, exhibit irritability to harmful stimuli, and even plants avoid noxious agents by differential growth. But if that is evidence of suffering, one must say the same of the noise my car sensors make if I try to reverse into a wall. Our own cells exhibit such irritability responses inside us, and yet even the sum of trillions of them gives us no sense of suffering—unless those cells happen to be the right kind of pain neurons.

Ninety percent of the remaining types of organism are *invertebrates,* from sponges through to insects. The last group forms a large majority of all animal species. In the simpler types of invertebrate, such as the *Coelenterata* (jellyfish) there is, at most, a diffuse nerve network to coordinate activity. In most of the more complex invertebrate types, the neurological organization is segmental, and this is highly significant for pain sensation.

Briefly, a segmental nervous system spreads the function of coordinating responses to somewhat independent ganglia in each segment of the creature's body, with the brain being relatively insignificant. In human medicine, one effective method of anesthesia is regional nerve blockade, of various types, and this in effect imitates a segmental nervous system specifically in order to abolish pain.

In my own minor surgical work as a general practitioner, that meant a "ring block" of the digital nerves of a finger or toe, using lignocaine. But pain consultants could effectively deal with back pain using caudal epidural injections, or intractable cancer pain using regional blocks of, for example, the brachial plexus. Epidural anesthesia enabling completely painless childbirth is commonplace.

---

17. Much of the material for this and the next section is derived from the useful sources gathered by Glenn M. Miller on the *Christian Thinktank* website: Miller, *Does the savagery of predation in nature . . .*

The point is that if a source of pain is isolated from a central organ capable of recognizing "I am in pain" (our cerebral cortex, for example), there is no pain. And the higher invertebrates are all in that situation permanently by the nature of their neurological hardware.

As for their brains, pain processing just doesn't seem part of their remit. In the case of earthworms, for example, whose brain (as those of us who have dissected them can testify), is a pair of tiny supra-pharyngeal ganglia the size of pinheads,

> The brain appears to direct the movements of the body in response to sensations of light and touch. And it has important inhibitory functions, for if it is removed the worms move continuously, but otherwise their behavior is affected little.[18]

Although the insect brain is somewhat larger and more advanced, it still seems largely concerned with coordinating and inhibiting body movements—the movements themselves are organized at the segmental level, and an insect without a brain can still jump or fly, only less appropriately. The brain is responsible for more complex behaviors, and can modify them by learned responses. However,

> [t]he segmental ganglia are connected and coordinated by nerves that run in the cords, but each is an almost completely independent center in control of the movements of its respective segment (or segments) and appendages. In some insects these movements have been shown to continue in segments that have been severed from the rest of the body. An isolated thorax is capable of walking by itself, and an isolated abdominal segment performs breathing movements.[19]

Some remarkable observations demonstrate more positively that many insects, which are among the most advanced invertebrates, do not experience pain at all:

> A dragonfly, for example, may eat much of its own abdomen if its tail end is brought into the mouthparts. Removal of part of the abdomen of a honeybee does not stop the animal's feeding. If the head of a blow-fly (Phormia) is cut off, it nevertheless stretches its tubular feeding organ (proboscis) and begins to suck if its chemoreceptors (labellae) are brought in touch with a sugar solution; the ingested solution simply flows out at the severed neck.[20]

18. Buchsbaum, Buchsbaum, Pearse, and Pearse, *Animals without Backbones*, 300.

19. Ibid., 378.

20. Dijkgraaf, *Sensory Reception*.

Such (unkind) observations are relevant to Darwin's iconic example of the horrors of insect parasitism, and particularly those of the *Ichneumonid* wasps that he could not equate with the existence of God. Apart from the considerations already mentioned, insects have few *internal* nerve receptors in which pain could arise. Many parasitized insects carry on a normal life as the parasite develops, dying quickly only when the grown parasite bursts out. Some parasites paralyze their larval hosts with venom—which, of course, in a segmentally organized organism, is the equivalent of a general anesthetic.

This kind of parasitism in which the parasite (or strictly, "parasitoid") develops within a single host, eventually killing it, is common in insects, comprising around 10 percent of all insect species. But more commonly hosts are little, if at all, aware of their parasites and are not killed by them, nor hurt by them. In fact there is no clear demarcation line between parasitism, commensalism (in which the organism does no harm to its host), and symbiosis (in which host and symbiont benefit each other).

Of the invertebrates, the only other examples which might provoke difficult questions about suffering are the squids and octopi, widely regarded as intelligent and even (by some theistic evolutionists) considered an alternative candidate for the implanting of *imago Dei* had God not chosen instead an intelligent ape.[21] But their brains are still fused ganglia rather than individually developed organs, which although enabling quite sophisticated coordinated responses appear not to allow the integration of internal sensory data—and "suffering" is necessarily just such an integrated response. In other words, their nervous system is specialized in remarkable ways, but not in ways comparable to the mental "unity" experienced by ourselves, and possibly the higher vertebrates, to which we now turn.

These "higher vertebrates" constitute only around 45,000 species, somewhat less than 5 percent of the animals, amongst anything up to 10 million living species in total; it is a much lower percentage than that in terms of numbers of individuals. Before we even look at pain amongst the vertebrates, the claim that "most animals suffer an agonizing death" is already completely discredited.

The fish actually constitute several distinct taxa, and half the vertebrate species, but since the familiar *Teleostae* (such as cod or salmon) are the most developed neurologically, what is said about them should apply to the rest.

In fish the forebrain is far less developed than in other vertebrates. This, as in the invertebrates, is compensated by more autonomy at a segmental

---

21. I won't even begin to critique this understanding of what "creation" and "God's image" mean here.

level, and the delegation of roles to highly specialized cells. This leads to a wide range of purely reflex functions. For example:

> After the spinal cord of a fish has been cut, the front part of the animal may respond to gentle touch with lively movements, whereas the trunk, the part behind the incision, remains motionless. A light touch to the back part elicits slight movements of the body or fins behind the cut, but the head does not respond. A more intense ("painful") stimulus, however (for instance, pinching of the tail fin), makes the trunk perform "agonized" contortions, whereas the front part again remains calm. To attribute pain sensation to the "painfully" writhing (but neurally isolated) rear end of a fish would fly in the face of evidence that persons with similarly severed spinal cords report absolutely no feeling (pain, pressure, or whatever) below the point at which their cords were cut.[22]

Fish do have mechanical, chemical, and thermal receptors in their skin, but whereas in humans they are connected via pain fibers to the higher cortical centers, these centers are absent in fish. It is therefore likely that they are routed to more purely reflex behaviors, explaining the "agonized" response of the denervated tail of the fish. It may be added that young fish—the majority of those becoming prey items—have an even less developed nervous system.

Over recent years claims about the "consciousness," and therefore suffering, of fish and indeed of other "lower" groups have been made, seeking to separate it from the possession of an advanced brain. Yet the idea of consciousness as largely independent of the organization of the nervous system effectively takes us into a somewhat Aristotelian world of holistic "substantial forms." The arguments then become rather more metaphysical than scientific, but no less intractable.

The remainder of the living vertebrate groups—the amphibians, reptiles, birds, and mammals—become, as one would expect both on taxonomic and evolutionary grounds, progressively more like us in their neurological organization. But in the reptiles, and even more so the amphibians, the cerebrum is smaller than those of mammals by orders of magnitude, the average reptile's cerebral hemispheres being perhaps 5 percent of a typical mammal's, as a proportion of body mass. If our brain is required for consciousness, including consciousness of pain, it is hard to attribute a high degree of consciousness to reptiles and amphibians.

22. Dijkgraaf, *Sensory Reception.*

That leaves us with the birds and mammals, totaling around just 15,000 living species. Amongst the extinct species we should probably include the more advanced dinosaurs along with the birds, in view of what is now believed about their close relationship to them.

Although birds do not possess a developed neocortex like mammals, recent work suggests that a set of nuclei based on the dorsal ventricular ridge (DVR) serves the same function.[23] Birds are warm-blooded, exhibit complex and sometimes intelligent behaviors, and, most significantly, respond to painful stimuli with a set of stress responses, in the same way that mammals do.

Whilst it remains risky to attribute the same kind of awareness that mammals have to creatures with such a different neurological heritage, it seems reasonable to suggest that convergence to similar function would produce comparable levels of sensation. But we must still keep in mind that projecting our own experience even on to other mammals is unwarranted, as we have seen. A human being is, objectively speaking, a very unusual creature, even before we consider our particular position in God's creation theologically.

But the numerical point remains—whether we include the birds, and maybe the dinosaurs, with the mammals, or whether we exclude them, we are left with only a tiny proportion (much less than 1 percent) of all living species that appear even theoretically capable of experiencing agony, or even significant suffering. And as relatively large animals, though their absolute number is large (perhaps 400 billion birds and 100 billion mammals) they still constitute a very small percentage of all organisms. It is interesting how closely this conclusion matches that of Alfred Russel Wallace, working on theoretical evolutionary principles, over a century ago.

On pain of death

What proportion of "sentient creatures" (if, for the sake of a label, we use that fuzzy term for the birds and mammals which may be capable of significant pain) actually do die in circumstances that would lead to pain? Fewer than you'd think, both in numerical terms and in the degree of suffering.

One problem, which there is no space to explore fully here, is our biased impression of "life in the wild" because of our reliance on TV documentaries. The tendency to get higher ratings for violence and other emotion-stirring is longstanding. It has led, and still leads, not only to misleading editing, but to staged kills, anthropomorphic scripts, and musical manipulation of

23. Dugas-Ford, Rowell, and Ragsdale, "Cell-type homologies."

viewers' emotions. Dispassionate science doesn't sell films—even science documentary films. As one leading film producer notes:

> Far too many producers have resorted to creating "nature porn"—productions focusing solely on the blood, guts and sex of the animal kingdom. Graphic footage of shark attacks and feeding frenzies might make for thrilling entertainment, but it is irresponsible. Programs like *Untamed and Uncut* and *Man vs. Wild* depict animals as menacing at a time when these animals face constant threat. By misleading audiences and inspiring fear and terror, these TV programs are effectively discouraging conservation.[24]

Even respected documentaries like David Attenborough's *Planet Earth II* play by these rules. The editor of one, Matthew Meech, explained in an interview:

> "I'm a bit of a movie fanatic so I kind of pick things up from all over the place—big Hitchcock fan, Christopher Nolan, Scorsese Spielberg etc.," he said. "But cutting wildlife films are [sic] like cutting silent movies, it's all about action/reaction. Also timing, be it for comedy or thrills. The narration can provide some of this, but you don't want to make the pictures just wallpaper for the commentary. The shots need to speak for themselves."[25]

There may be a relatively small number of species theoretically capable of pain, but there are far fewer actually capable of *inflicting* it. For example, as a crude measure the number of species in the order *Carnivora* is just 270. It also has to be taken into account that, simply on thermodynamic grounds, a habitat can support vastly fewer carnivores than it can herbivores:

> The total mass of the animals at the top of the food pyramid, the secondary carnivores, is less than the total mass of the animals close to the plant source of food, the herbivores, because there is less energy available to the secondary carnivores. An individual secondary carnivore is usually very large. Large body size is useful to these animals, since it enables them to capture and kill their prey. However, the number of such carnivores is small.
>
> All the insects in a woodlot weigh many times as much as all the birds; and all the songbirds, squirrels, and mice

24. Palmer, *Into the Wild, Ethically.*
25. Hooton, "This Planet Earth 2 iguana v. snake scene."

combined weight vastly more than all the foxes, hawks, and owls combined.[26]

Furthermore, most herbivores are not actually targeted by carnivores at all. To begin with, nearly all carnivores will scavenge whatever they find already dead from other causes, even if significantly decomposed. Even amongst lions 10–15 percent of the diet consists of what they have found dead, not killed themselves.

But there is a general principle that herbivores holding a territory will be relatively immune to predation, whilst the killers target

> . . . the homeless, transients, the weaker animals forced out to live in sub-optimal habitats and on those suffering from disease or from wounds received in territorial fights with their fellows.[27]

This has been observed in the case of muskrats coexisting with foxes and mink in the USA, hyenas In Africa ignoring the local Thompson's gazelle, in whose territories they slept, to hunt elsewhere,[28] and even in the case of my own local foxes trotting daily past my chicken run without attempting gallicide over the last six years.

> The natural predator is not a random killer, nor does he choose trophy specimens: his selection, based on what he can most easily get, is comparable with that of the stock breeder who eliminates weaklings from his breeding herd . . .[29]

Neither does it appear that potential prey animals live their lives in fear. When I suggested in an earlier chapter that you take a look at the nature outside your own door, I doubt that many were watching lions or leopards in their natural habitat. But those who do so actually report the same general air of peace observed by those of us in less exotic locations:

> When Thompson's gazelles detect a predator, they often do not flee but move closer. They appear to be much interested and to be inspecting the dangerous creature. . . . When the predator moved, the herd followed it, evidently aware of the danger and ready to dash off at the first sign of an actual attack. The predators also seem to understand the situation and rarely attack a group of alert tommies. Predator monitoring by territorial males was especially evident. At the approach of a predator in daytime

26. Colinvaux, *Why Big Fierce Animals are Rare*, 24.
27. Ewer, *The Carnivores*, 149.
28. Griffin, *Animal Minds*, 59.
29. Ewer, *The Carnivores*, 149.

the females generally moved away, while the buck stayed in his
territory and kept the predator under close watch. As it moved
he usually followed at a safe distance until it reached the territorial boundary. Then one of the neighboring territorial males
would take over the monitoring of the dangerous intruder.
This sort of predator monitoring was so effective that predators
captured only one of fifty territorial males that Walther studied
intensively during a two-year period.[30]

Stress is not, contrary to common report, the customary state of prey
animals. What would be the evolutionary point of that anyway? Stress is
tuned to evoke appropriate responses in times of crisis: only humans make
it a way of life. The net result is that what ecologists observe (as opposed to
what theologians or evolutionary biologists suppose) is that nature is not,
after all, a chaos of suffering. Instead,

> Peaceful coexistence, not struggle, is the rule in our Darwinian
> world. A perfectly fashioned individual of a Darwinian species
> is programmed for a specialized life to be spent for the most part
> safe from competition with neighbors of other kinds. Natural se-
> lection is harsh only to the deviant aggressor who seeks to poach
> on the niche of another. The peaceful coexistence between the
> species, which results from evolution by natural selection, has to
> be understood as an important fact in the workings of the great
> ecosystems around us.
>   . . . It thus seems very likely that the larger and fiercer
> predators are not nearly so important in regulating the numbers
> of animals in nature as common sense suggests. They are really
> to be looked upon as scavengers without the patience to wait for
> their meat to die. They cheat the bacteria who would have got
> the bodies otherwise.[31]

Most animals, then, are *not* predated. But for those which are, as I
have said, it is in the interest of predators that death comes swiftly and with
minimum pain or struggle. Predators tend to have a limited range of killing
methods. A powerful bite to the neck, severing the spinal cord, kills more
or less instantly. Compression of the trachea causes suffocation in a few
minutes, and unconsciousness long before. Wild dogs and hyenas, for larger
prey, resort to sudden disembowelment that, though extremely distasteful
to human observers, kills within a couple of minutes and probably induces
shock-anesthesia very rapidly indeed.

30. Griffin, *Animal Minds*, 57.
31. Colinvaux, *Why Big Fierce Animals are Rare*, 149, 156.

Some animals, notably snakes of course, kill by using venom which is usually an anesthetic neurotoxin: prolonged and unpleasant effects in humans suffering snakebite largely result from our being too large to be prey, and so we are inadequately "dosed" in what, for the snake, is an extreme defensive strategy.

Amongst these common methods, the most prolonged is asphyxiation, and as a matter of personal testimony I can actually vouch for its lack of "agonized suffering." As a teenager at a youth camp I was involved in a play fight with a younger kid, who unwittingly and overenthusiastically locked my neck in a scissor grip. Since I was equally unwitting I had no sense of anxiety until I began to realize not so much that I couldn't breathe, as that I no longer realized what was going on. A second or two later I was unconscious.

The kid in question not being a lion, he instantly let go, and I quickly recovered without ill effects, and having even benefited from a near-death experience that need not concern us here! My own apprehension, at the time, was that waking up to a grey Welsh evening was something of a letdown compared to being strangled, though I can't say a Thompson's gazelle would see things the same way. But had my young friend eaten me, I should have been none the wiser. Ironically he's now a professor of clinical epidemiology.

Metaphysical issues

Amongst the birds and mammals, which I have loosely termed "sentient," we can measure great changes of brain structure over evolutionary history. An *Archaeopteryx* had much less mental equipment than a raven, and an early Jurassic shrew-like mammal vastly less than a border collie. Do those differences correspond to a difference in pain perception? Since we can know next to nothing about nonhuman perception, we can't say with certainty, though it would seem likely. Why else go to the problem of evolving a bigger central nervous system? But although intuitively "brain" and "pain" go together, the *metaphysical* questions of mind and consciousness are still very challenging.

There is still no clear consensus about what the link is between brain structure and function, and human consciousness, let alone the more opaque question of animal consciousness. Materialist explanations of the former tend not so much to shed light on the latter, as to try and explain it away. The reason for this uncertainty is more than hinted at in Thomas Nagel's previously mentioned paper, *What is it like to be a bat?* It is simply impossible to give an objective material account of an irreducibly subjective experience. Science has little, if anything, to say about consciousness.

The fact that this is the case leaves open the strong possibility that the mind is not a material entity at all—and that the human brain, though necessary, is not sufficient to explain our conscious experience, including the experience of pain. Whether one sees our experience as the result some kind of emergent phenomenon or as a true dualism, it still leaves the question of the difference between human and animal experience unsettled. Whether my brain is fundamentally different from an animal's through evolution, or whether I alone possess an eternal rational soul, I am still ignorant of what animals experience.

Philosophers sometimes use the *zombie* as a model for considering consciousness. A philosophical zombie is a creature in every way like a human being, only without a self. It could eat, work, walk, talk, and display appropriate emotions just like you and me, and yet would feel nothing whatsoever because it wasn't an "I."

Presumably the goal of some people involved in robotics is to produce a machine that is sufficiently like a human that, even if you are not fooled, you can suspend disbelief and treat it as a "thou" rather than an "it." Given the exasperating nature of those robotic answering machines at utility companies, repeatedly asking you if they've guessed your meaning correctly, one may doubt that this is possible.

But we are inveterate anthropomorphs, readily treating teddy bears or even old cars as people, and cuddly animals even more so. We have already seen how easy it would be to misinterpret the writhing tail end of a spinally transected fish as pain. What if animals were no more than insensate machines? Stress reactions would be no guide to their experience, for even a lifelike robot or zombie would require them in order to respond in an entirely appropriate way to circumstances, and yet would still be entirely unconscious.

At one time, not too long ago, such a view was the received scientific wisdom. The key philosophical father of the modern scientific age, René Descartes (1596–1650), reduced everything in the material world to matter in motion—except for the human mind, which he equated with an immaterial rational soul created directly by God—the original "ghost in the machine." This new approach led directly to the "mind-body problem" that has caused endless philosophical disputes since.

But although Cartesian dualism is not that popular now in philosophy, the idea persists in, for example, the belief of many scientists that they can view material events as a rational outsider, rather than being inevitably a part of the observed system. The scientific ideal of objectivity—what

Thomas Nagel calls "the view from nowhere" in an influential book of that name—is a product of the Cartesian idea of a rational soul ultimately free of time and space. This assumption becomes particularly amusing in those reductive materialists who seek to persuade us that the rational mind is an illusion, as if they themselves were an objective rational mind viewing from somewhere outside this nihilistic reality.

Dualism of this sort also persists in the still-common popular, though thoroughly unbiblical, Christian concept of the "soul" as a kind of spiritual pilot sitting somewhere in the material body and pulling its levers, whilst waiting to escape to heaven.

One conclusion from this early-modern concept of a uniquely non-material human soul was that animals, not being rational, were held to possess neither a soul nor a mind. They are, on this view, mere automata—like the modern robot or zombie. Although a purely metaphysical conclusion, this was sufficiently congruent with the atomistic science of Descartes's time to persuade many scientists that animals were entirely expendable, and insensible. The *Stanford Encyclopedia of Philosophy* says:

> Descartes himself practiced and advocated vivisection (Descartes, Letter to Plempius, Feb 15 1638), and wrote in correspondence that the mechanical understanding of animals absolved people of any guilt for killing and eating animals. Mechanists who followed him (e.g. Malebranche) used Descartes' denial of reason and a soul to animals as a rationale for their belief that animals were incapable of suffering or emotion, and did not deserve moral consideration—justifying vivisection and other brutal treatment.[32]

One can see this attitude graphically represented in the 1832 painting by Emile-Edouard Mouchy, *A physiological demonstration with vivisection of a dog*, which shows a group of indifferent students casually observing the dismemberment of a clearly distraught, but tightly pinioned, dog. Little seems to be known of the artist, but that his artistic purpose is moral appears from the presence of another dog (and hence future victim) tied up and forced to watch, as well as from the general composition.

There are, of course, true sadists among us, but only strong philosophical beliefs can turn ordinary and well-meaning people like medical students into torturers of animals. As late as 1874, when the RSPCA brought a case against a Paris physician and several British doctors involved in such a demonstration, accusations of cruelty by other experienced medical people

32. Allen and Trentsman, "Animal Consciousness."

shocked by the scene were answered by the experimental physiologists: "That dog is insensible; he is not suffering anything."

It is instructive that it was only "irrational" human compassion that eventually overcame the power of an "objectively rational" metaphysical scientific foundation that had persisted for two centuries. But my reason for mentioning this is to show how little science itself has to do with attitudes to animal pain: the metaphysical commitments underlying the science can lead to radically different interpretation of the observations. It is true that Darwin's theory stresses the continuity between human and animal (Darwin himself was strongly against vivisection on compassionate moral grounds, as was Wallace). But a Cartesian could be quite comfortable with evolution up to the point of the super-addition of a soul (the "image of God" in some theistic evolutionary parlance), and so insist on discontinuity in the matter of animal sensation.

It is true that physiological measures of stress are similar in both humans and higher animals, but that tells us no more than we learn by watching an animal in pain—a Cartesian could happily argue that the key element—a mind to hurt—was missing, and that the physiology was that of an automaton.

The fact is that the horror now expressed by scientists and other academics at suffering in the natural world, with or without considering evolution, is principally due to a shift in metaphysical, ethical, or even aesthetic *fashion* from that of Descartes. It is *metaphysical*, in that there is a current preference for seeing continuity between the beasts and ourselves because we are thought of as animals, rather than seeing discontinuity on the basis of our rationality as they did in the Enlightenment. It is *ethical*, in that suffering is now seen as an absolute, rather than a relative, evil, largely due to the relativizing of a once absolute morality (remember those mediaeval thinkers who, for the most part, simply did not believe that any suffering was undeserved). And it is *aesthetic* because our postmodern age has elevated subjectivity into a primary virtue. Those who have the right to "self-identify" as a different gender or race certainly have the same right to identify animals as people if they so choose.

Before that shift such suffering would have been self-evidently absent from the world; after it, its agony is self-evidently all-pervasive. But surely our understanding of God's creation should be based on something more solid than currently prevailing sentiment?

I suggest that a Christian ought to take a more dispassionate look at the evidence, informed by a specifically Christian worldview in which both our continuity with animal nature, and our discontinuity, is fully understood. One should add that when asking if, and how, animals feel pain, we should also fully understand our lack of any real knowledge on anything that could even make sense of the question.

Various biblical texts enjoin kindness to the higher animals, which suggests that they have real experience of pleasure and pain. God cares for the sparrow, and provides food for the ravens and the young lions, presumably because their welfare matters. For the same reason (as I have explored in this chapter) gratuitous violence is *not* actually the modus operandi of the natural world.

And yet the Noahic covenant in Genesis 9 holds animals accountable for the blood of humans, but not vice versa. Jesus sacrificed a herd of pigs by drowning in order to save one man from Satan's bondage. Animal life appears less important to God than human life, and this surely cannot be accounted for purely on the grounds of the intrinsic spiritual worth of the former, as if it were a matter of economics. Otherwise, torturing dogs to train doctors would have no moral dimension whatsoever. It is far more likely that, in absolute terms, animal suffering is significantly less severe than human suffering would lead us to believe. But that gives us no warrant to inflict it unnecessarily.

Even so, I hope I have shown that our profound ignorance of what it is like to be an animal makes it supremely arrogant to accuse God of creating a world of extreme cruelty. The evidence does not in any way support it, and as Christians we should surely default to the position that God knew what he was doing when he created the world and called it "very good."

Chapter 12—Direct Effects of the Fall on Nature

[The] link between Christ and creation means that following and living in Christ includes living in harmony with his creation. Christ's role in creation demands that we become its keepers and not its destroyers; the true Christian is someone who treats creation with reverence and respect. Creation is something that we are commanded to hold in trust as God's gift to us.

—Sir Ghillean Prance, FRS[1]

Damning creation with praise

This chapter is intended to round off this section about the evidence from the "scientific" world, which I have taken very broadly in this context to cover the world of direct observation, at all levels from that of everyday experience to that of scientific theories like Darwinian evolution.

In the first section, I sought to show that the Bible's position is that the natural creation remains God's servant, and has not become corrupted or evil because of human sin. The second section was about the witness of scholars of Scripture and theology down the years, suggesting that until recent centuries the same positive view of nature overwhelmingly predominated. The third section, up until this point, has been intended to show that what we see in the natural state of things is consistent with such a "good" creation.

You will remember from chapter 1 that this good creation is nevertheless used by God in ways that may cause us harm, and that this is not a sign of its corruption but of its continued obedience to him. It is a sign of *our* corruption that such judgements should need to occur.

---

1. Prance, *Go to the Ant*, 103.

168

In this chapter, though, I want to point out the one sense in which our sin *has* positively damaged the natural creation. This, however is not in the "spiritual" way envisaged somewhat vaguely in the "traditional view," in which by some indeterminate means, through the action of God, or Satan, or maybe nature itself, human sin made it change to become "evil." Rather our sin has damaged the innocent natural world by our rather obvious irresponsible abuse of it.

You may also remember from the examination of Romans 8 in chapter 3 that Paul introduces the idea that our sin has kept us from the proper exercise of our God-given role of ruling and subduing the earth, and so delayed the "completion" of creation into incorruptibility that has now begun through the resurrection of Jesus as the "first fruits" of the new creation (1 Cor 15:20–28; 2 Cor 5:17; Jas 1:18). This is primarily a kind of "negative" damage, in the sense of our not finishing the job we were created to perform in the world.

But I mentioned in the historical survey of views of Romans 8 that Martin Luther appears to introduce an idea of nature being damaged by humanity's misuse of it. In the relevant passage of his *Lectures on Romans* his primary thought seems to be about the putting of nature to idolatrous use by over-valuing it—a spiritual desecration, as it were. But he also hints that part of this misuse is the converse—the failure to value nature for what it actually is:

> Because man does not judge and evaluate it rightly and because he enjoys it in a wrong way, he regards it more highly than fact and truth allow, inasmuch as man . . . presumes to possess this peace and satisfaction in created things. It is to this vanity, therefore [i.e., to this wrong enjoyment], that the creature is subjected, just as grass is in itself something good and not something worthless; indeed, it is good, necessary and useful for cattle, but to man it is worthless and useless as food, yet if it were used as human food, it would be regarded and valued more highly than its nature allows.[2]

Now Luther seems to be implying in this illustration both that the grass is (in reality) devalued and abused by being put to absurd use, and also that because of its over-valuation (that is, being wrongly taken as suitable for food by humans) it becomes physically harmful instead of useful. That may be a rather convoluted way of putting things, but does actually seem applicable to many instances where human beings have harmed nature.

2. Luther, *Lectures on Romans*, 238.

Luther, in the idea of "spiritual abuse" of nature, seems to be thinking in the same broad area as the biblical idea of the land itself being polluted by bloodshed or by other human sin, which I looked at in chapter 3. If we consider the natural order as being created to glorify God through being what it is, in the role God has assigned to it, then for it to be put to a perverted human use is an offense against the creature itself.

For example, to train a creature such as a dog—or in modern times a dolphin—to carry explosives to destroy a military checkpoint or a warship is to coerce it not only into destroying itself, but into breaking the prohibition against killing humans that God gave to the animals in Genesis chapter 9. The same could be said of those wild beasts that were forced into killing Christians (and others) in the circus games in the ancient Roman Empire, sometimes apparently unwillingly.[3]

"I will demand an accounting from every animal," God says in that Genesis passage. Whilst that is unlikely to mean beasts are resurrected at the last judgement and asked to bark or roar out their case for the defense, even that would certainly be a more appropriately biblical form of anthropomorphism than either the common motif of theistic evolutionists about creation *en masse* possessing some analogy of free will, or the idea that sometimes goes with it (for example in R. J. Russell[4]) that God will need to make restitution to the beasts for the sufferings they undergo in the course of their natural way of life.

When considered in the light of a sacrilegious misrepresentation of the character and purposes of nature, then in spiritual terms the portrayal of animals as implacably red in tooth and claw in documentaries, or even in popular science or in academic theological studies, bears the same relationship to training them to kill humans that lust has to adultery in Jesus's teaching. The abuse, in other words, is mental rather than physical. Chris Palmer's

---

3. Ignatius, *Letter to the Romans* 5. "How I look forward to the real lions that have been got ready for me! All I pray is that I may find them swift. I am going to make overtures to them, so that, unlike some other wretches whom they have been too spiritless to touch, they may devour me with all speed. And if they are still reluctant, I shall use force to them." Staniforth, trans., *Early Christian Writings*, 87.

4. Russell, *Cosmology*, 266: "The challenge of evolution leads to the following criteria which eschatology must meet. First, it must include not only humanity and all the history of life on earth, but more than that: not only every species but even and most importantly the individual creatures of every species. For creatures suffer, not species, and thus creatures individually—one by one—must be the focus of any genuine Christian eschatology . . . and not as somehow included merely through human redemption." Such a theodicy makes many unwarranted assumptions, and so presents a host of problems not only theologically, but philosophically and biologically.

term "nature porn," cited in chapter 11, is a rather apposite description, and doesn't only apply to ratings-orientated documentary films.

The evils of pornography include not only the inciting of lust (with demonstrable effects on personal attitudes to others), but the demeaning and objectification of women. If it is wrong to misrepresent what human beings actually are, in God's eyes, in their sexuality, is it not a similar wrong to nature to make it what it is not? Luther seems to have seen more than he realized in this respect.

Just as it is unlikely that the Genesis 9 talk of creatures being held to account for shedding the blood of humankind refers to a court scene with talking animals, it is equally unlikely that the creatures will, on the last day, literally cry out their offense at their natures being misrepresented by humanity, rather than appreciated and enhanced. I doubt also that Abel's blood *literally* cried out from the ground, and have already suggested in chapter 3 that the "groaning" of creation in Romans 8 is a literary personification rather than a literal statement.

But surely the point is that nevertheless creation has a defender and spokesman in its Creator, Jesus Christ the *Logos* of God, just as do the poor and unheard amongst humankind. If the creatures cannot speak on their own behalf at the judgement, then the Judge will.

The long history of trashing the planet

The idea of damage to the environment was probably not really appreciated in Luther's time, but that is not to say such damage had not occurred before, on a large scale, or that it had not been noticed. It is commonplace to blame Paleolithic hunting for the extinction of large mammals like the mammoth, but the evidence for that is seldom compelling. What is more evident is the damage that has occurred in historic (i.e. unequivocally post-fall) times.

In a 1980 essay, Anne and Paul Ehrlich describe several such early ill effects of human intervention. They begin with the desertification of Mesopotamia from the inevitable silting up of the irrigation channels used to increase agricultural production. They go on to say how Plato, in 360 BCE, recorded the historical deforestation and soil erosion of his own Greek state of Attica:

> And, just as happens in small islands, what now remains compared with what then existed is like the skeleton of a sick man, all the fat and soft earth having wasted away, and only the bare framework of the land being left. But at that epoch the country was unimpaired, and for its mountains it had high arable

hills, and in place of the "moorlands," as they are now called, it contained plains full of rich soil; and it had much forestland in its mountains, of which there are visible signs even to this day; for there are some mountains which now have nothing but food for bees, but they had trees no very long time ago, and the rafters from those felled there to roof the largest buildings are still sound.[5]

It's not clear from Plato's text that the Ehrlichs are correct when they suggest he was aware of the human origin of the degradation: he seems mainly (if you read the original text) to blame earthquakes. But they appear accurate to suggest that deliberate deforestation itself was the biggest genuine cause:

> The Greeks inherited a land covered by rich stands of oaks, pines, and other trees with thick, drought-resistant leaves . . . called a "sclerophyllous forest," in the jargon of plant ecologists. But, as the Greek population expanded, it progressively destroyed the forests for firewood, charcoal (needed in firing pottery and other industrial processes), and lumber. The great trees were often burned by accident, too . . . or as part of a military operation, or simply to create more open pastureland.[6]

Now, maybe most of those uses for timber seems legitimate to us, and the "unsustainability" merely the result of an understandable lack of knowledge. We should, though, remember that God's true wisdom was the very thing first forfeited by the fall, and so such ignorance is, in fact, culpable.

In any case keeping warm and making pots was not the most destructive activity of the Greeks. When I was on holiday in the Attic peninsula of Greece some years ago, my guide, like the Ehrlichs, said that the bare limestone hills resulted from ancient deforestation, but suggested that the greatest depredation of trees came at the time when Greece acquired the maritime military power that gave it world domination in the fifth century BCE. The iconic Greek ship called a *trireme* was first designed in the seventh century, and apart from the tons of timber needed for the 120-foot hull *each one* of its 170 oars was made from a single fir tree:

> [I]mmense quantities of suitable timber were required. It is probably impossible to estimate the weight of a trireme or the amount of timber needed, but as they were turned out almost in hundreds it needs little imagination to realize that there must

5. Plato, *Critias.*
6. Ehrlich and Ehrlich, *Ecoscience.*

have been plenty of forests from which the necessary timber could be obtained. Mount Ida in Phrygia was famous for its pines, but the mainland and islands of Greece must have contained vast areas of forest. The demands of the Peloponnesian War alone must have caused considerable deforestation. How many pine trees were needed for the oars of a fleet? . . . At Aigospotami there were 380 ships in the two sides together. If each vessel had its full complement of oars, this means . . . a total of 76,000 oars! (76,000 men!) What acreage of pines would be needed to supply the necessary trees?[7]

Given that Plato wrote just forty-five years after that battle, the last major engagement of the Peloponnesian War, then in describing the denudation of the soil of Attica he was actually writing, at least in part, about the ill effects of Athens's war effort on its own well-being—ill effects that persist 2,400 years later, and which may even be a contributory factor to Greece's parlous economic state in recent years.

Translating this example into Luther's mind-set regarding Romans 8, we can suggest that trees, intended by God as good both in their natural situation and for housing, firewood, and charcoal for pottery, became overvalued by humans as a means to inflict violence on other humans. The trees therefore became instruments for evil rather than good, and were also irreversibly destroyed, together with the now unstable soil in which they had grown.

The Ehrlichs go on to show how the Romans, both ruthlessly exploitative and lacking any real environmental concern, extended deforestation empire-wide, and furthermore caused the extinction of large animals in many countries, in many cases for thoroughly evil reasons:

Huge numbers of beasts were pitted against each other (and against human beings) in lethal combats. Titus, for example, had some 9,000 wild animals slaughtered during the three months' dedication of the Colosseum, and Trajan's conquest of Dacia (modern Romania) was celebrated by games in which 11,000 beasts were killed. When one considers that tens or even hundreds of lions, leopards, rhinos, buffalos, and so on must have died—or been killed—in transport or captivity for every one that lived to entertain the citizens, the probable scale of the Roman impact on wildlife staggers the imagination.[8]

7. Horn, *The Fall of Athens.*
8. Ehrlich and Ehrlich, *Ecoscience.*

When you consider that the present population of lions in the whole of Africa is some 30,000, and of rhinos maybe 25,000, those figures are sobering. Perhaps we need fewer reminders about the environmental degradations closer to our own time, given the laudable concern for ecological issues over recent decades, sadly in the face of even more thorough destruction of our natural world than in many millennia before. Loss of trees in Greece has given way to the wholesale felling of continental rainforests with worldwide effects. Destruction of large game species in Upper Egypt by the Romans scarcely compares to the wanton extermination of bison, wolves, or passenger pigeons across nineteenth-century America, and the threatened or actual extinction of major species nowadays, through African or Indian poaching and habitat destruction. Localized soil erosion has now (arguably, admittedly) given way to global climate change, endangering whole nations.

Herman Melville, writing in 1851 about the industrial-scale commercial whaling of his time (mainly for lamp oil from their blubber—a hugely wasteful pursuit which discarded the rest of the carcass), knew of the collapse of bison populations and its cause. He also knew of the increasing difficulties whalers were experiencing in finding their quarry. Yet he assumed, against the fears of the more prescient "philosophers of the forecastle" he mocked, that whales were immune from extinction.[9] But in his day, whaling voyages were long and extremely hazardous, and the odds were at least a little more evenly balanced in the whales' favor. The invention of motorized factory ships and explosive harpoons increased the rate of killing dramatically, but not for generations was there any willingness to see the devastating effects on nature of such progress. Whaling was becoming less commercially viable anyway by the time it was banned in 1982, but several species came perilously close to extinction and are still endangered.

These are familiar stories, though probably they are still not sufficiently appreciated by most Christians as being a central component of the heinousness of human sin, involving as they do the desecration of the "cosmic temple" of God's earthly creation and the abandonment of our own creation ordinance to maintain it on God's behalf. This blindness is decidedly odd when so many believers are willing to blame many of the features of that creation itself, in all its God-given wonder (even "glory" in Paul's words in 1 Corinthians 15), on sin.

All of the same human vices that caused the ancient environmental problems have contributed to our present ones. As amongst the ancient Greeks valuable natural resources are still used to create weapons that, in

9. Melville, *Moby Dick*, chapter 105.

turn, destroy more natural resources as well as human lives. That happens on the large scale of nuclear weapons, and on the smaller, but much more destructive, scale of cheap, mass-produced landmines.

Like the Romans we tend to see the world only in terms of its utility for us, and greedily exploit it for the sake of profit or convenience. We consider ourselves far-sighted if we can budget for resources like oil lasting another century or two. Even my own recorded family history is twice as long as that—it is myopic to think ahead no farther.

In this profligacy we differ markedly from nature itself. The soil of the earth had been renewed without human care for billions of years before it was entrusted to us. The Mesopotamians, Greeks, and Romans managed to undo that conservation work in centuries. Later, American deep ploughing created the Dust Bowl in just a century of farming the prairies, and more recently the adoption of intensive agriculture worldwide has continued the process in China, Russia, Africa, Central America, and elsewhere, in even less than that time. In fact the United Nations reports that:

> SOLAW [State of the World's Land and Water Resources for Food and Agriculture] provides for the first time ever a global assessment of the state of the planet's land resources. Fully one quarter are highly degraded. Another 8 percent are moderately degraded, 36 percent are stable or slightly degraded and 10 percent are ranked as "improving." The remaining shares of the earth's land surface are either bare (around 18 percent) or covered by inland water bodies (around 2 percent). (These figures include all land types, not just farmland.)[10]

We saw in the last chapter how carnivores tend to take out the old, weak, and socially marginalized herbivores, in this way maintaining healthy ecosystems. It is interesting to compare this to human hunting: the idea of "conservation" a century ago was to rid the environment of "evil" carnivores altogether (before proceeding to hunt the herbivores). Even now the hunter's aim is often to bag the trophy specimen—the dominant lion, or the seventeen-point stag: in other words the individuals most important to the success of the breeding population. Perhaps that had some point when hunting involved the courage of single-handed combat, but now that the killing is done at a distance with a hi-tech rifle, trophy hunting is a particularly pathetic activity, whether in US forests or on Scottish estates—or even by Maltese and Northwest African "traditionalists" who decimate the migrating songbirds annually in a pointless shooting spree.

10. Food and Agriculture Organization, *Scarcity and degradation.*

But the scientific management of the land often pays no more real attention to the ecology than do private individuals. It seems hard to credit that a policy of creating genetically-resistant patented monocultures, and then blitzing everything else that lives with glycophosphates, owes anything whatsoever to the science of ecology. The dangers of losing genetic diversity have, after all, been known for at least two generations (during which time commercial farming has single-mindedly increased the loss of crop varieties).

We have historically exhibited, in our management of nature, a most misguided knowledge of what is good, and what is evil. Some might call such Promethean wisdom crass ignorance.

The health risks of Bacon

But we also have a longstanding, though ambiguous, *intellectual* basis for such self-centeredness, though it is often blamed on the Genesis 1 creation ordinance regarding humankind's rule of creation. There are undoubtedly current streams of popular Christianity, especially in the West, that take the idea of human domination of the world as a tenet of faith without any real consideration of how the fall affects it, or what it meant in the first place. It's sometimes hard for an outsider to understand the gung-ho insistence of some American Christians that fossil fuels are there for us to squander as we please, with no thought for current pollution or future depletion. But no doubt it's equally hard for rural Indian Christians to understand why British believers really feel the need to drive large four-wheel drive off-roaders on flat streets in towns, and fly across continents to sit by a hotel pool in Goa, spreading jet-engine exhaust across the local people who cannot afford such things.

Such a conscious attachment of the Divine Right of Humanity to Exploit is, whatever may be said in its defense, radically out of kilter with historic Christian teaching, and seems rather to be an offshoot of an attitude that arose in early modern intellectual circles in Europe, and which is expressed in the Baconian concept of science.

In the section on historical theology (chapter 7), I referred briefly to Cameron Wybrow's book, *The Bible, Baconianism, and Mastery over Nature*. In this he makes out a detailed case for how natural philosophers like Francis Bacon (1561–1626) co-opted the language of Genesis to justify a completely non-biblical and actually quite new approach to studying the world, based on a strong sense of human domination over all things. Because this proceeded from a radical *desacralization* of nature, that had come to regard it as an entirely inert and passive work of God, it then became legitimate to plunder it for any resources or secrets it held that might benefit humanity.

Before this, although Christianity clearly perceived nature to be the work only of God and subordinate to his will, there was some sense that it possessed an organic unity, analogous to a living being rather than a mere object. But the early modern scientific trend towards atomism paved the way for an entirely mechanistic view of creation as mere matter. Because that idea is central to our worldview, we forget how recent, local, and aberrant it is.

The ruthless attitude to animal experiments we saw in the last chapter is one graphic instance of this, as perhaps is this extract from Bacon himself on the supposed resilience of nature in general under any kind of experimentation:

> But if any skilled minister of nature shall apply force to matter, and by design torture and vex it, in order to its annihilation, it, on the contrary, being brought under this necessity, changes and transforms itself into a strange variety of shapes and appearances; for nothing but the power of the Creator can annihilate, or truly destroy it; so that at length . . . it in some degree restores itself, if the force be continued. And that method of binding, torturing, or detaining, will prove the most effectual and expeditious, which makes use of manacles and fetters; that is, lays hold and works upon matter in the extremest degrees.[11]

So the victim *likes* it, really (Wybrow draws attention to the prevalence of rather troubling analogies to rape and torture in some of this early scientific literature). Since that time, there have really been two broadly different ways of doing science: the first involves primarily a respectful observation of nature, in order to understand its ways. But the second, which one might call the Baconian stream, is a largely utilitarian effort to manipulate nature to make it do useful new things for us, with an optimistic expectation that those new things will ultimately do good.

Obviously enough of the second of these has a greater capacity to cause the kind of damage to creation that I have been discussing, whether that damage come through ignorance of the unforeseen effects of one's science (such as the over-use of fertilizers, insecticides, or antibiotics), greed (such as allowing unnecessary industrial pollution in order to provide greater profit) or malice (such as high explosives, the hydrogen

---

11. Bacon, *Proteus, or Matter,* quoted in Wybrow, *The Bible, Baconianism, and Mastery,* 180.

bomb, nerve gases, defoliation agents and a host of other such products of progress in the science of killing).

Underlying all of these is an unstated assumption that the world is merely a machine-like arrangement of interchangeable parts, which may legitimately be dismantled and put back together in any order we choose. On this understanding the job of creation was badly bodged in the first place, sad to relate. But Bob (Bacon) the Builder says, "Can we fix it? Yes we can!"[12]

Only such a mind-set could make it even *conceivable* to manufacture animal-human chimaeras in accredited Western universities. Yet the United States' National Institutes of Health, like similar agencies elsewhere, has had to step carefully back and forth between ambitious research applications from powerful scientific lobbies, and ethical objections. As of September 2015, it has decided not to fund such research—but only pending "a deliberative process to evaluate the state of the science in this area, the ethical issues that should be considered, and the relevant animal welfare concerns associated with these types of studies."[13] The research continues in any case with funds from elsewhere, and one wonders what new ethical considerations can be brought to the table at this late stage, since the sanctity of human life from conception was negotiated away long since.

But in all cases, it's interesting how the same unquenchable optimism exhibited in the Bacon quote above seems to be maintained: "Well, maybe the last three centuries' progress is threatening the whole planet, but *this* century's progress is bound to put it right again." Indeed, it seems to be a characteristic of the scientific community seldom to acknowledge the role of science in *creating* massive problems at all, but only to wave flags for its role in their solution—or at least, its role in the brave *efforts* to solve them against the unscientific forces of ignorance.

By way of example, consider the causes of the increased production of greenhouse gases implicated in climate change. There are two major factors. The first is increased industrialization, the direct result of the Enlightenment science project to tame the uncouth world for rational humankind, whose ill effects are now somehow blamed on politicians and consumers.

The second is the unprecedented exponential increase in the world's population over the last century from 1.5 billion to 7 billion, which according to a classic article in *Nature* is largely to be attributed to the work

12. *Bob the Builder* is a British children's TV show. His Baconian optimism is usually, fortunately, restricted to vernacular architecture and things people have broken, rather than God.

13. National Institutes of Health, *Research Involving Introduction of Human Pluripotent Cells.*

of chemists Fritz Haber and Carl Bosch.[14] The Haber-Bosch process of nitrogen fixation was developed to enable the mass production of high explosives in World War 1, a questionable and world-changingly costly project in itself. But it also led directly to the production of artificial fertilizers and that was, it is argued, by far the biggest cause of the population growth of the twentieth century.

The process itself is highly dependent on fossil fuels, thus contributing directly to climate change. Nanotechnologist Professor Richard Jones pointed out in a BBC radio discussion that that there is no current fix for this vicious circle—higher population requires more artificial fertilizer, and so more fossil fuel dependence—not to mention more soil degradation from humus depletion, as we saw above.

And yet this science-initiated problem is seldom brought to public attention, and instead the blame is laid at the feet of Roman Catholics in the developing world opposing the almost certainly inadequate Baconian "fixes" of artificial birth control and abortion. It does appear, nevertheless, that populations begin to level off as economic development leads to *voluntary* limitation of family size.

But it may not solve the problems. 2016 saw the publication of a paper by a multidisciplinary team of twenty-two authors in *Science*,[15] endorsing the thesis that, since the 1950s, the world has entered a new geological age, the *Anthropocene*, as a result of human activity. As the abstract says:

> The appearance of manufactured materials in sediments, including aluminum, plastics, and concrete, coincides with global spikes in fallout radionuclides and particulates from fossil fuel combustion. Carbon, nitrogen, and phosphorus cycles have been substantially modified over the past century. Rates of sea-level rise and the extent of human perturbation of the climate system exceed Late Holocene changes. Biotic changes include species invasions worldwide and accelerating rates of extinction. These combined signals render the Anthropocene stratigraphically distinct from the Holocene and earlier epochs.

Perhaps it is rather unfair to call such a new era the "Anthropocene," since it has only been caused by a particular, very recent, *subset* of humankind. Would *Technocene* or *Scientocene* be more accurate terms, or perhaps *Illuminocene* (after the Enlightenment project)? My own suggestion, given arguments earlier in this book, might be the *Prometheocene*. For the word "scientist" was coined by William Whewell only in 1834, marking,

---

14. Smil, "Detonator of the population explosion."
15. Waters et al., "The Anthropocene."

at least symbolically, the much-celebrated blossoming of the scientific age. If one looks at the specific factors mentioned in the *Science* abstract, *every single one*—from nuclear fallout to pollution by non-biodegradable hydrocarbons, is the fruit of little more than a century of that professional scientific enterprise.

It all seems more than ironic when you consider the gall of those like the late New Atheist particle physicist Victor J. Stenger, who wrote:

Science flies you to the moon. Religion flies you into buildings.[16]

Why has that become so much quoted, rather than "Science flips you into a new geological age"? The latter is, after all, the more important, if uncongenial, truth.[17]

One could multiply instances of the way humankind has damaged, and still damages, God's natural creation, and apportion specific responsibility in each case. But there would be few, if any, of us who could claim to be innocent, for the world is not damaged because people are scientists, politicians, soldiers, industrialists, jihadists, Catholics, air passengers, or anything else, but because they are sinners exiled from God's wisdom by sin, and believers instead in their own wisdom.

The next question is, what difference does it make to realize that creation is an innocent damaged by our violation, rather than a monster, red in tooth and claw, fanatically bent on violence against us? What implications for Christian faith does belief in a good, rather than a fallen, creation have?

16. Stenger, *The New Atheism*, 59.

17. Incidentally, it's more accurate to say that "religion gets you to the moon," if you consider that nearly every landmark scientist involved was a believer: Bede (discoverer of gravitational effect of tides, Catholic), Copernicus (heliocentrism, Catholic), Tycho Brahe (planetary motions, Lutheran), Galileo Galilei (heliocentrism, Catholic), Johannes Kepler (elliptical orbits, Lutheran), Isaac Newton (gravitational laws, Arian), Wernher von Braun (NASA rocket scientist, evangelical) and Sir Bernard Lovell (radio-astronomy, Anglican/Methodist).

Section 4—The Application

Chapter 13—What Difference Does It Make, Anyway?

Glad that I live am I;
That the sky is blue;
Glad for the country lanes,
And the fall of dew.

After the sun the rain,
After the rain the sun;
This is the way of life,
Till the work be done.

All that we need to do,
Be we low or high,
Is to see that we grow
Nearer the sky.

—Lizette Woodworth Reese (1856–1935)[1]

Beliefs have consequences

Beliefs, of course, do not exist in a vacuum but inevitably result in consequences. They make up the mind-sets that inform worldviews. Worldviews (traceable from the German *Weltanschauung* of Immanuel Kant), are best seen as the narratives that more or less unconsciously shape our lives. Sociologist Peter Berger[2] helpfully described these in terms of *plausibility structures*, that is to say things that seem self-evident, or else unbelievable,

1. Reese, "A Little Song of Life," 51.
2. Berger, *The Sacred Canopy.*

in particular sociological contexts. That, of course, was why Deuteronomy enjoined that Israelites should become *immersed* in their *torah* in a world whose prevailing value system was very different to God's:

> [18] Fix these words of mine in your hearts and minds; tie them as symbols on your hands and bind them on your foreheads. [19] Teach them to your children, talking about them when you sit at home and when you walk along the road, when you lie down and when you get up. [20] Write them on the doorframes of your houses and on your gates, [21] so that your days and the days of your children may be many in the land the LORD swore to give your ancestors, as many as the days that the heavens are above the earth.[3]

The faithful Israelite was, then, essentially someone whose worldview was molded by *torah*. In the same way, when Luke lays out the priorities of the members of the new church in Acts, the formation of a thoroughly Christian worldview (in the face of unconverted Judaism in the first place and Gentile paganism and philosophy later) was central:

> [42] They devoted themselves to the apostles' teaching and to fellowship, to the breaking of bread and to prayer.[4]

When beliefs involve such a core doctrine of Christianity as creation, they cannot fail to affect the life of the believer—and on the larger scale, of the church—profoundly. Peter Berger, in a recent interview, points out how easily Christianity can be subverted by ideas from secular worldviews:

> [T]he main mistake of Mainline Protestantism, . . . is to replace the core of the Gospel, which has to do with the cosmic redefinition of reality, with either politics or psychology or a kind of vague morality, which is not what I think the Christian Gospel is basically about. The Christian Gospel is about a tectonic shift in the structure of the universe, focused on the events around the life of Jesus.[5]

Likewise it makes a huge difference whether one believes the "traditional view" that the natural creation is fallen and corrupted or whether, as I have argued in this book, it retains the same "goodness" that was accorded it by God in the beginning. It makes far less difference whether that beginning

---

3. Deut 11:18–21.

4. Acts 2:42.

5. Thuswaldner, "A Conversation with Peter L. Berger."

was just a few thousand years ago, or back in deep time long before there were humans to lapse into sin, than whether it is "very good" now.

What you do not love, you will not value, and if God values not only "Nature," as an abstract concept, but each creature, to the extent that "not one sparrow is forgotten by God,"[6] there is a mismatch of values if we love them any less.

> [24] How many are your works, LORD!
>   In wisdom you made them all;
>   the earth is full of your creatures.[7]

In practice, the goodness of the natural creation has seldom been denied outright within orthodox Christianity, but instead has been relativized by the stultifying assumption that it isn't really as it should be. This leads to a kind of dampening of the natural human sense of the beauty and glory of the world, an unspoken conditional upon every experience we may have of it.

We saw this earlier in the book in such quotes as that of Spurgeon: "Creation glows with a thousand beauties ... yet ..." or of Wesley: "[H]ow little shadow of good, of gratitude, of benevolence, of any right temper, is now to be found in any part of the brute creation!" Have you ever been told, "I love you, but ..."? That conditional "but" makes all the difference between rapture and misery.

In contrast, there sometimes has been a recognition that we should see more goodness, not less, in the world the closer we come to God's way of seeing. For 150 years evangelicals have sung the words of the Irish Congregational minister, George Wade Robinson:

> Heaven above is softer blue,
> Earth around is sweeter green;
> Something lives in every hue
> Christless eyes have never seen:
> Birds with gladder songs o'erflow,
> Flow'rs with deeper beauties shine,
> Since I know, as now I know,
> I am His, and He is mine.[8]

This seems to be, for many people, one of those risky hymns to sing, since the nature lover is often taught, if indirectly, to doubt the goodness

6. Luke 12:6.

7. Ps 104:24.

8. Robinson, George Wade (1838–1877), "Loved with Everlasting Love."

of creation, not exult in it, after coming to Christ. But surely Robinson's words must be taken as a true expression of spiritual insight, rather than as a Christian version of the hyperbolic sentimentalism of secular songs about falling in love. Vera Lynn notwithstanding, and however true the true love, nightingales have probably never sung in Berkeley Square, and any angels at the Ritz keep a pretty low profile. But it is no hyperbole to say that "the heavens declare the glory of God; the skies proclaim the work of his hands."[9] It should be affirmed more often, and unreservedly, than it is.

Joy in creation

The sheer sense of *joy* in natural things is, perhaps, the first thing to be restored when the idea of their fallenness is seen as the unbiblical fiction it is. To be able to look, at one extreme, at the Milky Way arching across a winter sky and, at the other, at any small creature poking its head out from under a log and to say, without conscious or unconscious reservation, "My Father made that!" is restorative of the human spirit. We are beginning once again to see things as God does.

Whether one's fear of doing so stems from a theological teaching that nature fell with Adam and Eve, or from one of the more modern notions that God made matter and evolution autonomous so that its corruption derives from the very business of creation, is immaterial. The witness of Scripture and traditional Christian theology, and the instinctive and natural appeal of our hearts, is that it is suffused with God's wisdom and goodness.

[1] LORD, our Lord,
> how majestic is your name in all the earth!
You have set your glory
> in the heavens.
[2] Through the praise of children and infants
> you have established a stronghold against your enemies,
> to silence the foe and the avenger.
[3] When I consider your heavens,
> the work of your fingers,
the moon and the stars,
> which you have set in place,
[4] what is mankind that you are mindful of them,
> human beings that you care for them?[10]

One of those who seems most to have apprehended the importance of this sense of joy is the Anglican clergyman and metaphysical poet

---

9. Ps 19:1.

10. Ps 8:1–4.

Thomas Traherne (1636–1674), whom I mentioned in chapter 7. He specifically set out to discover the joy promised in Christian faith, and found it by remembering and devotionally refocusing his (natural) childhood delight in the created order.

He saw that the creation stemmed (paradoxically, it may seem) from God's insatiable *desire* to spread his love beyond himself into everything he made. In particular Traherne perceived that, in making Adam the focus and culmination of his work, the whole cosmos was a gift for one person, and was intended to stir up the same sense of joyful desire in us. This burning desire was not *for* what was created (which would be idolatry), but *through* its rich variety, its goodness, and its being freely *given*, to desire the God who made it and gave it.

Traherne reasoned that the gift of creation was not in any way diminished or divided by the subsequent increase in the human race, but that God has given the whole of creation to each one of us. The sense of joy and desire for God that creation can give us is therefore no less than it could be for Adam. From this primary, and overwhelming, sense of natural joy stems a due sense of all the other truths of Christianity, whether that be love for our fellow humans—each of whom shares the creational privileges of Adam—or even central theological matters like sin:

> Till you see that the world is yours, you cannot weigh the greatness of sin, nor the misery of your fall, nor prize your redeemer's love. One would think these should be motives sufficient to stir us up to the contemplation of God's works, wherein all the riches of His Kingdom will appear. For the greatness of sin proceedeth from the greatness of His love whom we have offended, from the greatness of those obligations which were laid upon us, from the great blessedness and glory of the estate wherein we were placed, none of which can be seen, till Truth is seen, a great part of which is, that the World is ours. So that indeed the knowledge of this is the very real light, wherein all mysteries are evidenced to us.[11]

A high view of creation, then, is the key to a fuller appreciation of salvation teaching. This is thrown into relief when one considers the effect of its opposite. The reverse of joy is misery or despair, and if that is the settled state of the world around me, then I am not much to be blamed for taking on its faults and griefs *before* conversion (so much for original sin) but also even afterwards. If God himself is miserable about his world, what warrant have I to rejoice in it? What is more, if God cared so little about our existence that he left the world to evolve autonomously, contingently, and even viciously,

---

11. Traherne, *Centuries*, 80.

there is little motive for contrition on my part, and rather more for the questioning of his goodness that appears so prevalent today.

Consequently if I have any hope of relief from the deplorable state of things, it must be in some other world, at some other time on the other side of the evil of death. The love of God is not to be seen in the "softer blues and sweeter greens" of the hymn, which are likely rather to be dangerous snares of Satan to "worldliness," but only in what filters down, through the fog of earthly corruption, from heaven.

If in this way I give up on the present creation (to whatever extent I buy into the idea), I will see my relationship with God not as a deepening of my bond with his cosmos, but as a divorce from it. Several things follow from this, and the first is in the sphere of *thanksgiving*.

Thanksgiving for creation

Giving thanks to God is, self-evidently, directly proportional both to the degree to which you believe things come from him, and the degree to which you believe them to be good. Scripture is unequivocal in affirming the universality of both:

> [33] Oh, the depth of the riches of the wisdom and knowledge of
> God!
>> How unsearchable his judgements,
>> and his paths beyond tracing out!
> [34] "Who has known the mind of the Lord?
>> Or who has been his counselor?"
> [35] "Who has ever given to God,
>> that God should repay them?"
> [36] For from him and through him and for him are all things.
>> To him be the glory forever! Amen.[12]

Now Paul's doxology is in the context of the mysterious, even disturbing, outworking of God's providence in salvation history. All, though, is from God. But it is virtually axiomatic of the material things in the world:

> [4] The Spirit clearly says that in later times some will abandon
> the faith and follow deceiving spirits and things taught by de-
> mons. [2] Such teachings come through hypocritical liars, whose
> consciences have been seared as with a hot iron. [3] They forbid
> people to marry and order them to abstain from certain foods,
> which God created to be received with thanksgiving by those

12. Rom 11:33–36.

who believe and who know the truth ⁴ For everything God created is good, and nothing is to be rejected if it is received with
thanksgiving, ⁵ because it is consecrated by the word of God
and prayer.¹³

Paul is either referring to Jewish food laws (superseded in Christ) or to
abstention from food which may have been offered to idols (points of conscience for Jews and ex-pagans alike), but the basis of his open attitude is the
fundamental doctrine of creation: everything God created is (not *was once*)
good, and is to be accepted as such with thanksgiving. Abstention from what
God has made, on the grounds of some kind of intrinsic evil associated with
it, would appear to be taught not by God, but by demons.

This surely applies to more than just what we eat and drink—though
it's hard to see how we can give very sincere thanks even for that, if we
believe it either to be corrupted by sin or the product of a mindless (and
flawed) evolution.

What's your favorite food? How can I truly give thanks to God for,
say, fresh salmon if I believe the diet of herring and krill that imparts its
flavor (and color) is the result of its disobedience to a creation ordinance
to eat only vegetables? Or if I believe that its spawning activity is a test case
for the wastefulness and cruelty of an evolution that it would be blasphe-
mous to attribute to God? In that case would it not really be blasphemy to
say grace before meals?

Or who is the love of your life? Can you *really* give thanks to the Lord
for the line of his manly chin or the graceful curve of her neck if both alike
are signs of the poor design of the jaw and the human spine respectively?
Are you going to thank God for the fruit of the womb when, according to
some calling themselves believers, the whole human reproductive tract is
a botched design?

How can you be grateful for any beautiful countryside scene you love
and remember, when you can be quite certain that it would not exist but for
the interplay of predation, parasitism, and sheer misfortune that (you believe) wouldn't exist but for the sin of Adam? Or else that God did not plan
those exquisite details at all, but just made them possible with a few simple
laws? Are you going to thank God for the weather if he does not control it?
Or for the beauty of clouds if it is fortuitous?

Evolutionary ingratitude is, as far as I can see, even more pernicious
than fundamentalist belief in natural evil from the fall. For God is, both
by the preferred science of undirected Darwinian processes and on the

13. 1 Tim 4:1–5.

principle of distancing him from all that suffering, almost infinitely removed from the actual things for which we want to thank him.

In my house we have a standing joke (the result of our strange sense of humor, I'm afraid) that whichever of us is thanked for cooking the meal replies, "No—thank Tesco!"[14] Behind the quip are some half-serious garbled ideas about how big business seems to replace the Lord of the harvest in most people's minds nowadays as the source of food, and also about the absurdity of displacing one's thanksgiving away from the particular to some distant entity with no knowledge of our existence, let alone any real interest in, or care for, the details of our cuisine.

One can give intellectual assent to the Deist God as First Cause, but one cannot thank him as a Father for the individual gifts that life affords. The man with an iPhone app for ordering birthday gift vouchers from Amazon.com automatically is not in any way comparable to the one who makes your present himself in his workshop. Yet James teaches:

> [17] Every good and perfect gift is from above, coming down from the Father of the heavenly lights, who does not change like shifting shadows.[15]

If belief in natural evil makes us hesitant in our thanksgiving for natural gifts that bless us, we will certainly not see adversity as part of his good provision for us. And yet this kind of thanksgiving was instilled into new believers in the early church, based, of course, on the creation doctrine that God remains sovereign over all things for our good, including even the "powers and principalities" that might threaten our well-being. The *Didache*, possibly dating from the mid-first century, says:

> Accept as good whatever experience comes your way, in the knowledge that nothing can happen without God.[16]

A significant part of their experience, at that period, would be persecution by the authorities—let alone the common hazards of poverty and early death from infectious disease. It's quite impossible to follow that advice to "give thanks in all circumstances"[17] if one believes that natural events "just happen" beyond the providential reach of God, or else that they are signs of nature in revolt against God. In the same way Paul's words become nonsensical:

14. For non-Brits, Tesco is the largest supermarket chain over here.

15. Jas 1:17.

16. *Didache*, 3, in Staniforth, trans., *Early Christian Writings*, 192.

17. 1 Thess 5:18.

[28] And we know that in all things God works for the good of those who love him, who have been called according to his purpose.[18]

God cannot work *for good* in all things unless he *works* in all things ("all things" in the passage being applied to everything in all creation). And if he is, indeed, working in all things created, they are his servants for our good, and worthy of thanksgiving. The basic Christian prayer of thanksgiving, then, depends on belief in the goodness of God's creation, or suffers the death of a thousand qualifications.

Prayer within creation

Since thanksgiving, when considered, requires the creation to be fully obedient to God's purpose for it, then the very same applies to prayer, on similar grounds. If nature is in revolt against God, is it going to be any more submissive to him because we pray to him? If we pray for the bane of disease to be turned to the blessing of health, are we (in fact) asking God to pit his strength to *oppose* his own creature (the bacteria or whatever), or are we asking him to command his servants to spare us? If we cry out in distress from a ship foundering in a storm, are we whistling in the wind because storms are "just a natural phenomenon"?

Some theistic evolutionists object to God's "interventions" on the grounds that God could not pit himself against his own works without being self-contradictory (though more often they're thinking about past evolution, and are sketchy on whether the same strictures apply to present prayer). They have a valid point, but if they imply that, therefore, God does not act in his world, then they are denying the massive weight of biblical testimony to the contrary and, effectively, denying prayer to have any more than psychological effects. In the sinking ship, or in my hospital bed, I am not asking primarily to accept that nature will continue as normal and for me to realize that my demise is in line with God's eternal will (though a good number of Christians nowadays would deny even that), but to be saved. One does not need prayer in order to be fatalistic—a Deistic conception of God will do the same job with less effort.

Philosophical theologians, such as the Jesuit Luis de Molina (1535–1600),[19] have reasoned in detail about how God may cooperate, or decide not

18. Rom 8:28.

19. "If God did not cooperate with secondary causes, He clearly would not have been able to bring it about that the Babylonian fire did not burn the three young men except by opposing it, as it were, and impeding its action either (i) through some

to cooperate, with secondary causes in the world (the weather, wild beasts, fire, *etc.*) and so govern the outcomes of "natural" events. As a philosophical position, this "concurrence" has, historically, been the preferred option for orthodox theologians over the alternatives.[20] But whilst philosophy can support and explain Christian truth, having a fully worked through theory of divine action is secondary to the core biblical truth—God is sovereign over all he has made, and especially the "nonrational" realm. It is not in rebellion against him, and it is not autonomous of him.

So, to ground this in a contemporary example, is climate change part of our individual prayer life, or that of our churches? Do we pray only that people will act more wisely, or do we pray that God will change the weather? Why would he be less sovereign over his servants the elements than over sinful humankind's wisdom? Yet even in those churches that have treated it seriously enough to take action, there seem to have been few, if any, calls for *prayer* regarding global warming. And the same seems to be the case for the other events of nature which may affect us for good or ill. It is only the truth of God's continued sovereignty within his universe that makes the discipline (and joy) of prayer that Jesus practiced and taught worthwhile, or even rational. What *did* Jesus teach about God in creation when he commanded us to pray "Give us this day our daily bread"?

Worship on behalf of creation

One sign of the continuing goodness of creation is its own participation in the worship of God:

> [19] The LORD has established his throne in heaven,
>   and his kingdom rules over all.
> [20] Praise the LORD, you his angels,

---

contrary action or (ii) by placing something around the young men or conferring on them some resistant quality which would prevent the fire's impressing its action upon them. Therefore, since this derogates both the divine power and also the total subjection by which all things submit to and obey that power, one should claim without doubt that God cooperates with secondary causes, and that it was only because God did not concur with the fire in its action that the young men were not incinerated by it." (Molina, *Concordia* pt. II, disp. 25, §15).

20. The alternatives (simplistically put) are *occasionalism*, in which no real powers exist in nature, and God acts directly in everything; and *conservationism*, in which they act independently, but only exist by his power—unfortunately, since the Enlightenment this last view has often been simply assumed, and still in practice underpins much theistic evolution , nature being seen as a closed system of cause and effect in which prayer makes little sense. This denies the all-important aspect that God *governs* the world, and does not merely maintain it.

> you mighty ones who do his bidding,
>   who obey his word.
> [21] Praise the LORD, all his heavenly hosts,
>   you his servants who do his will.
> [22] Praise the LORD, all his works
>   everywhere in his dominion.
> Praise the LORD, my soul.[21]

In itself the irrational creation is, metaphor apart, only capable of giving God praise by being what it is. That in itself, given that Scripture in many places says it *does* praise him, is firm evidence against its fallenness. The sea and everything in it resounds, the rivers clap their hands, and the mountains sing together for joy.[22] But do the hyena, the shark, or the flea keep surly silence whilst the rest of creation worships?

Yet one major creation role of humankind, coming under the command to rule and care for the earth as those formed in the image of God, is to express its worship in rational form. I am always a little wary of claims by philosophers that, with the arrival of humankind, the universe became self-aware. We are not the universe. But in a sense it is true, in that (hypothetical extraterrestrials aside) we are the only race to be able to *comprehend*, rather than simply experiencing, physical reality. We are, at least, self-aware on *behalf* of the universe, by being rationally aware of its wonders.

The mediaeval thinkers had a profound (if dangerous) insight when they conceived of the person as a *microcosmos*. Through our reason, they said, we can encompass the universe in our minds, as it were bringing everything we perceive within ourselves—or perhaps extending our souls out to enfold all things. It's a deep idea—and not even that metaphorical, either, according to some interpretations of scientific quantum theory. Thomas Traherne, again, gives us a sense of this mystery:

> Alas the WORLD is but a little center in comparison of you. Suppose it millions of miles from the Earth to the Heavens, and millions of millions above the stars, both here and over the heads of our Antipodes: it is surrounded with infinite and eternal space. . . . The Omnipresence and Eternity of God are your fellows and companions. And all that is in them ought to be made your familiar Treasures. Your understanding comprehends the World like the dust of a balance, measures Heaven with a span,

---

21. Ps 103:19–22.

22. Ps 98:7–8.

and esteems a thousand years but as one day. So that Great, End-less, Eternal Delights are only fit to be its enjoyments.[23]

We alone of all material creatures, seeing even the trees of the field that "clap their hands"[24] in worship, can appreciate their strength, beauty, and utility, their age and mystery, and offer thanksgiving and rational praise to God. And so on for all of creation. In that way humankind was created to be a priesthood to creation—in God's cosmic temple to be those who bring sacrifices of praise worthy of the God who has made all things.

This priestly work is the calling of every human being, for everyone can admire the grandeur of the heavens, feel the warmth of the sun, taste the flavor of fruits, appreciate the devotion of a dog, or any of the billions of other blessings built into our daily, created world.

Yet it is also the work of everyone who develops particular crafts and skills—the farmer who knows the particular ways of livestock or crops, the woodworker who understands which woods may benefit which tasks and how their grain behaves, the glider pilot who learns the secret ways of thermals and winds, the musician who knows how to create beauty out of wood or metal or electronics.

This too is the primary *theological* role of the scientist. The scientist can study anything from quarks to the whole vast cosmos, from Planck time to the duration of all things. In this he models the immensurability of God. Apart from the utility of knowledge of the natural world to human-ity, there is a sacerdotal function in uncovering truths hidden in nature and offering the very specialized form of worship that only they can. That may involve appreciating the beauty of a mathematical equation that most of us can't understand, or the detailed classification of a thousand closely related species of mosquito that most of us wouldn't *want* to understand. The scientist who is able to *share* the thrill of knowledge is a double bless-ing to the world—as is the layperson who cares enough about God's world to find out what the scientist has been up to.

One of the objections to deep time made by a certain sort of Creation-ist is that God would be wasting his time to create all those extinct plants and animals that nobody has ever seen. But of course, we *have* seen them, or at least many of them, through their study and reconstruction by pale-ontologists. And the more science progresses, the more we can understand of their departed world, both in the beauty and wonders of the individual forms, and in their ecological interactions. We can give praise to God for

23. Traherne, *Centuries*, 1/19, 12–13.

24. Isa 55:12.

those things, and for continental drift, and for the taxonomic relationships between the different forms, and for the molecular glories of DNA.

But what you don't love, you don't value. And what you don't value does not become part of your priestly concern. If we are ambivalent in our thanksgiving for the food on our plate or the weather outside, how likely are we to engage in worship on behalf of Permian *Pelycosaurs* or distant quasars? I wonder how many believing scientists nowadays see their job as glorifying God as Creator through their discoveries simply *as* discoveries, quite apart from any practical application they may have? I wonder how many nonscientists see science as that kind of spiritual pursuit, or even see that of their own particular vocation, or their daily commute into work, through the glories of God's world?

Relating science to creation

Whilst we are thinking of science, the biblical belief that creation is both good and subject to God dethrones the still-common Enlightenment principle that the universe is a closed causal system, in which God cannot act and, by implication, on which only science has the final say concerning physical truth. In Christian circles linked to science, that prohibition on God's power has often been theologized into an idea that it would be *wrong* of God to act within the space-time world, and for a number of reasons.

In the first place, it is said, it would deny the importance of faith by "showing God's hand" and so "forcing" people to believe in him. This supposes that belief in God is a kind of hide-and-seek game—which has only ever been true because of the very Enlightenment principles I am calling into question. Outside that localized (within both geography and history) movement, the existence of God has never been in doubt—it is fundamental human knowledge, and implied in the teaching of Genesis 1 of the universe as a temple.[25]

---

25. Philosopher Alvin Plantinga has been a leader in arguing that belief in God is as "properly basic" a belief as belief in other minds, or the past, or an external world. See Plantinga, *God and Other Minds*, Part III.

St. Athanasius, among several other early Christian authors including Tertullian,[26] Novatian,[27] Basil,[28] and Chrysostom,[29] saw the very *purpose* of the creation as making the invisible God visible:

> 35. *Creation a revelation of God; especially in the order and harmony pervading the whole.*
>
> For God, being good and loving to mankind, and caring for the souls made by Him—since He is by nature invisible and incomprehensible, having His being beyond all created existence, for which reason the race of mankind was likely to miss the way to the knowledge of Him, since they are made out of nothing while He is unmade—for this cause God by His own Word gave the Universe the Order it has, in order that since He is by nature invisible, men might be enabled to know Him at any rate by His works. For often the artist even when not seen is known by his works.[30]

"Faith" has actually *never* been primarily about believing in God's existence, but about committing oneself in covenant relationship to the God of Israel, and of the Lord Jesus Christ, on the very *basis* of witnessing his historical actions in the space-time world, most notably the exodus and the resurrection—and of course, his creation as (in Tertullian's words) the "primary witness."[31]

Secondly it is claimed that God would be cheating the freedom and dignity of his own creation by "breaking its laws." Support is sometimes sought from selective use of Thomas Aquinas's teaching on secondary causes in this (though in most other discussions he is viewed as an Aristotelian muddying the waters of true science). Space forbids a full rebuttal of this, but the short reply is that, post-Enlightenment interpretations of Aquinas notwithstanding, the biblical God, Aquinas wrote, is one who delights to be *involved* with his world, and not merely to "set it a-going," as the deist Leibniz wrote in criticism of Newton's theistic science, in "a perpetual motion."[32]

---

26. Tertullian, *Against Marcion* V.XVI (Roberts and Donaldson, *Ante-Nicene Library*, Vol VII, 455).

27. Ibid., Vol. V, 304–5.

28. Basil, *Homilies on Creation*, I VI.

29. Chrysostom, *Homily 14 on Romans*, 8:19–20.

30. Athanasius, *Against the Heathen* III 35.

31. Tertullian, *Against Marcion* V.XVI (Roberts and Donaldson, *Ante-Nicene Library*, Vol VII, 455).

32. "Sir Isaac Newton and his followers have also a very odd opinion concerning the work of God. According to their doctrine, God Almighty wants to wind up his watch from time to time: otherwise it would cease to move. He had not, it seems, sufficient foresight to make it a perpetual motion." Clarke, *A Collection of Papers*.

The Deist, and semi-Deist, complaint that a God who acts within nature is showing the incompetence of a model-maker who has to keep pushing his engine to get it going is missing the point entirely. When God told Moses at the burning bush *"Ehyeh asher ehyeh"* ("I will be what I will be") he was not making a Scholastic statement about eternal Being, but speaking about immanence and action, perhaps with the implication, "I am there (for you)." He was going to do dirty business with Pharaoh on behalf of his people. A skilled mechanic can make a player piano that will execute piano rolls unattended, but the man who both builds a violin and performs great music on it in real time is scarcely to be considered less great—especially if in his playing he interacts with other musicians and an audience to transform their souls. That is more like the Christian picture of God.

Thirdly, some people complain that were God to be actively involved, he would be deceiving scientists in their pursuit of predictable natural causes and laws. One has to be astonished by the self-serving arrogance of thinking that way. It was a small number of humans, not God, who set themselves the task of exploring his hidden ways through science. It was they, not God, who determined that his ways were to be found in constant patterns that they, on their own initiative, likened to his biblical laws. And finally it was they, not God, who declared that *only* such lawlike processes were worthy of God, and therefore that the whole of creation could and must be understood through them.

God is no person's debtor—so he certainly owes nothing in particular to scientists. The most amusing example of such a mentality of God as "cheat" is the kind of double-bluff implied in too much theistic evolution. The original cover of Richard Dawkins's *Blind Watchmaker* read:

> Natural selection is the blind watchmaker, blind because it does not see ahead, does not plan consequences, has no purpose in view. Yet the living results of natural selection overwhelmingly impress us with the appearance of design as if by a master watchmaker, impress us with the illusion of design and planning.[33]

Dawkins proceeds to show that this overwhelming impression of design is an illusion because of the powers of the blind process of Neo-Darwinian evolution. Theistic evolutionists frequently endorse the effective blindness of that process, and thus the illusion of design, and *then* say that behind it all stands the inscrutable creative power of God. The illusion of design itself is therefore a cunning illusion.

One could draw an analogy with someone who insists that a book, whilst it appears full of meaning, is in reality just a physical artifact produced by printing machines—and then declares that, hidden behind that

33. Dawkins, *The Blind Watchmaker*, cover.

mechanical process is an author. In truth, of course, the design of the author is obvious in the meaning of the words, and is inherent in the very physical form of the book. There is one continuous process of creation at work between the author's intent and the reader's comprehension, not three independent processes.

In summary, to recognize that science is just one useful source of provisional truth, rather than the arbiter of truth, even in the physical and material realm, is a necessary corrective for our scientistic age, and this is greatly encouraged by the knowledge that creation is not only good, but God's servant for governing the world. This in no way denies any scientific evidence, though it may involve being skeptical about certain scientific theories in their metaphysical aspect—for one of the achievements of philosophy of science is the understanding that all theories are the products of cultures and their largely unevidenced worldviews.

Care over creation

Long before creation was widely viewed as "fallen" a certain "gnosticizing," or perhaps more charitably a "platonizing" tendency was widespread in the church, which viewed the Christian hope as the escape of the soul from the physical world to the "spiritual" realm of heaven. The theological error of this view has, thankfully, been fully explored in recent conservative theology, for example by N. T. Wright[34] and J. Richard Middleton.[35] Such a tendency is only exacerbated once it is seriously considered that the physical creation has been ruined by sin, and I will return to the effect of this on spiritual matters later. But the direct effect on our God-given role to rule and care for the creation is even more obvious. Briefly, if one believes that the natural world is God's good provision for us, one will care for it. If it is bad, and doomed to be swept away altogether at the return of Christ, one may as well give up on it: who starts repainting their house if they believe the world is ending (or even if they believe it has dry rot)?

It has been one of the scandals of recent decades (akin to the former evangelical retreat from social and political action in reaction to the liberal social gospel) that Christians are widely seen as not only unconcerned about conservation, but a hindrance to it through the false claim that the Bible teaches domination over nature. Wrong though that representation of the Bible is, it gains credence from what has been a general lack of concern, particularly amongst evangelicals, to rejoice in creation by caring for it.

34. Wright, *The Resurrection of the Son of God,* and Wright, *Surprised by Hope.*
35. Middleton, *A New Heaven and a New Earth.*

There are notable exceptions to this, one being an organization started a number of years ago by a university friend of mine, Peter Harris, and now operating worldwide: the conservation group A Rocha. In the abstract of a paper first presented to the Lausanne Movement's Theology Working Party under the chairmanship of Dr. Christopher J. Wright, Harris wrote:

> Evangelical theology has already made great progress in rediscovering the doctrine of creation. A similar effort is urgently needed in order to mainstream the care of creation within our missiology, but this must be rapidly followed by concerted global action. Nothing less can do justice to the biblical proclamation that Jesus is Lord, and so address the human and biodiversity crises we face.[36]

Care for creation, then, is part of Christian mission—given the truth of Genesis 1:28, it is actually the original part of that mission. Fortunately this work has attracted the support of leading scientists as well as theologians and church leaders, which at the very least is a testimony to society that this is God's world and that his people recognize it. It goes without saying that one is much more likely to wish to preserve what one loves because it is God's good handiwork, than if one views it as irretrievably corrupted by evil.

But there is more to it than that, because the Christian hope engendered by the resurrection of Christ is the *renewal* of all things in heaven and earth, not their complete replacement and, still less, a mass evacuation from earth to heaven prior to its annihilation. Instead, the Bible teaches a coming together of heaven and earth in imperishability, which is why we read that

> [13] But in keeping with his promise we are looking forward to a new heaven and a new earth, where righteousness dwells.[37]

There is the same kind of continuity, as well as discontinuity, in creation as there is between our present body and the resurrection body (the archetype being, of course, the risen body of Jesus). It is similar, come to that, to the fact that all the work we do for God's kingdom here will, in some strange way, continue to bear fruit in the age to come.[38] It is no less a part of Christian living to cherish this present natural realm than it is to cherish our bodies, and to live by kingdom values.

---

36. Harris, "Towards a Missiology of Caring for Creation," 220. Prepared for The Lausanne Movement's Theology Working Party in Beirut, Lebanon (February 2010).

37. 2 Pet 3:13.

38. 1 Cor 15:58.

Creation and resurrection

The valuing of the material creation as "good" also affects our understanding of eschatology, as I have already hinted. The Gnostic dualism of corrupt matter versus pure spirit, which began to infect Christianity in the second century as it lost touch with its Jewish root, leads to the idea (held rather vaguely nowadays, in the absence of much substantial pulpit teaching) that the Christian hope is that our "souls" leave our bodies at death to "go to heaven." By implication the world we leave, like the hopelessly damaged *Titanic*, sinks into the abyss of oblivion. But in Scripture the state of disembodiment after death is, for us, no more than a waiting time for our true hope, which is resurrection to eternal life.

The unique Jewish concept of resurrection arose in the context of the equally distinctive biblical belief in the goodness of God's material creation. Because there was no idea in Judaism that the immaterial was superior to the material, the hope of second temple Jews was that there would be a resurrection of the righteous to life *on earth* at the end of the age. Cleared of evil people, it would be the land of promise for which Abraham had hoped, where God would dwell with his people in prosperity and blessing.

Jesus' resurrection endorsed this view, though it modified it by actually delivering on the resurrection in the person of Jesus as a deposit (or "firstfruits"), and by clarifying that the final resurrection would be part of a complete renewing of the original physical creation, rendering it imperishable. That which had been "naturally empowered" (*psuchikos*) would at the coming of Christ be swallowed up by the "spiritually empowered" (*pneumatikos*).[39]

But the very promise of that transformation affirmed that it had been "very good" from the beginning. To put it bluntly, if there is a significant continuity between the world in which we live, and our physical bodies, and the world which is to come, which we shall also inhabit in the body, then it is important to see eye to eye with God on its status now.

This has much to say, too, to those who picture God's creation of humankind as (effectively) an evolutionary accident to which God has condescended to add his image, or a "soul." This too is inherently dualistic, reducing the true work of God to the "spiritual" realm of the soul. One would hope, in that case, either for eventual escape from this jerry-built evolutionary body, with its badly designed jaws, spines, eyes, appendices, and so on, or at least for God to do a completely new design job to celebrate

---

39. 1 Corinthians 15:53–57: The "empowerment" idea is well set out by N. T. Wright in *The Resurrection of the Son of God*.

our resurrection to a life that we will have to live within the same body forever.

But that is not possible, for the resurrection of Christ has already set the pattern, and the resurrection pattern is that of humankind as it is, as it was created to be—the biped who walks, talks, and eats (in Jesus' case, at least, fish caught using his own five-fingered vertebrate hands). At the incarnation, the Son of God became human. As Wright says concerning John's Gospel:

> [T]he Word who was with the one God, who was identified with this God, is now also and forever flesh. There can be no sense that the flesh has been turned back simply into word and spirit. The resurrection matters for John because he is, at his very heart, a theologian of creation. The Word, who was always to be the point at which creator and creation came together in one, is now, in the resurrection, the point at which creator and new creation are likewise one.[40]

The resurrection confirms God's love for, and approval of, the human body, and that it is physically, as well as in any other sense, made in the image of Christ—himself the true image of God even now, as a man, as much as before his incarnation. Currently there is a man in heaven, and he will dwell in the same body on earth in the age to come. Perhaps one should, in the light of that, reconsider one's low view of the human body, for it will be around a long time.

But there is, as well as continuity, also a discontinuity between our present bodies and the resurrection body, as both Paul in 1 Corinthians 15 and the resurrection appearances of Jesus in the Gospels make plain. If, as John writes, "what we will be has not yet been made known,"[41] then it's even less clear in what ways the physical world to come will resemble ours, and in what ways it will show discontinuity. But the possibilities are a lot more open when we dispense with the notion that it needs to be purged from evil, and will instead be welcomed as it is "into the freedom and glory of the children of God."[42]

There are no doubt other implications, both for present living and for future hope, in recognizing that God's natural cosmos remains his holy temple, for through this understanding we see that the whole message of Scripture becomes more integrated, and makes more sense of the true history of the world.

40. Wright, *Resurrection of the Son of God*, 667.
41. 1 John 3:2.
42. Rom 8:21.

This understanding will demand, for many of us, some fundamental readjustments of beliefs and attitudes, but we may take comfort in the fact that we are not, by making those changes, moving away from the faith of the Bible and the church of Christ, but closer back towards both.

And we get to enjoy the world more too—it's a win-win situation.

Conclusion

Down by swirling streams

The creation seems to enfold our souls

In a pool of your brooding love,

Giving good, in love, to a world you fill
with renewal.

Over hilltops we wandered, pleased to stand by
deep valleys,

The creases of your hands.

And as I look upon all that your arm has done

Wonderment freezes me, and a thrill seizes me

That hill and meadow are nothing but shadows
and representations

Of a greater creation to come.[1]

I WILL LEAVE THE reader who is persuaded by the case set out in this book to work out the full application to their own faith, and their own science. It is a valuable exercise to ask this question, whatever one chances to encounters in nature: "What does it mean for my heavenly Father to have pronounced this 'very good'"? The answer can have some far-reaching implications.

Richard Bauckham, in a book justifying the eyewitness testimony of the Gospels against the skepticism of the Higher Critics,[2] quotes a poignant Holocaust memory from a Jewish woman, named Edith P., in transit from

1. Jon Garvey, *The Eye of the Beholder,* 1973. http://www.jongarvey.co.uk/download/beholder/The%20Eye%20of%20the%20Beholder.mp3.

2. Adam was judged by God's word—Prometheus, practicing Higher Criticism, turns the tables!

Auschwitz to a labor site. Deliberately consigned to living hell by those committed to burning away God's genetic mistakes (and, of course, to building a Promethean empire that would last a thousand years), she hoisted herself painfully on another prisoner's starving shoulders to see, through a crack in the railway wagon, where their train had stopped. She looked out:

> "And. . . I. . . saw. . . Paradise! The sun was bright and vivid. There was cleanness all over. It was a station somewhere in Germany. There were three or four people there. One woman had a child, nicely dressed up; the child was crying. People were people, not animals. And I thought: 'Paradise must look like this!'"[3]

The story, of course, has much to say about human sin and unjust suffering which must challenge any superficiality in our theology. But it also has something to say about nature—that it is all too possible, through familiarity, to lose sight of what it really is. In this case, it was privation that first stole away, and then momentarily revealed, the paradisiacal vision of our present creation. But it is also possible for a strong delusion to lead us to believe a lie.[4] Such a delusion seems to have affected the vision of a great part of the Christian world for half a millennium, and maybe it is time to expose its Promethean sources.

Much of the impetus for people to do so much hard work on a theodicy of nature comes from the complaint of unbelievers, back to Darwin himself, that a good God could not have made the natural world we see. But beauty is in the eye of the beholder, and our eyes have, perhaps, been dimmed by a debased theology of creation, so that we see nature with doubting eyes rather than with God's. When we consider how the pessimistic attitudes of paganism were swept away by the persuasive arguments of the early Christians and their joyful assertion that our world is the *good* creation of our heavenly Father, perhaps our best strategy is to seek to recover their vision. "If your eye is good, your whole body will be full of light."[5]

I will just add a word of personal testimony. In the time since I began to suspect that what I had assumed about creation's corruption all my life was mistaken, I've begun to see the world with new eyes. When I look out of my study window, I find I can admire the beauty of what I see without a subconscious "Yes but . . . " imposing itself on the view. I can love the freedom of a soaring buzzard without thinking, "Yes, but it's spoiled by the evil suffering that sustains it." I can rejoice in a gorgeous metallic red and

3. Quoted in Bauckham, *Jesus and the Eyewitnesses*, 494.

4. 2 Thess 2:10–12.

5. Matt 6:22.

blue parasitic *Chrysis* wasp on the patio and leave its lifestyle in God's wise hands, rather than accept uncritically Darwin's jaundiced assessment.[6] If I pick up an ammonite from the beach, or read about a newly discovered function for DNA, I find that what I see and experience leads me, in a new way, into expressing worship on the creation's behalf; a role for which I myself was created. The more of nature I appreciate, the more of it I may bring into the sacred space of God's temple of creation. Practically, I will be more its steward and less its exploiter. Finally, I will rejoice as much to see its new, yet familiar, face, come the transformation of the end of the age, as I shall at the sight of my own new face in the mirror.

That, in a very real sense, is to return to Eden, and to extend its borders.

> To think well is to serve God in the interior court: To have a mind composed of Divine Thoughts, and set in frame, to be like Him within. To conceive aright and to enjoy the world, is to conceive the Holy Ghost, and to see His Love: which is the Mind of the Father. And this more pleaseth Him than many Worlds, could we create as fair and great as this. For when we are once acquainted with the world, you will find the goodness and wisdom of God so manifest therein, that it was impossible another, or better should be made. Which being made to be enjoyed, nothing can please or serve Him more, than the Soul that enjoys it. For that Soul doth accomplish the end of His desire in Creating it.[7]

"And from the crew of Apollo 8, we close with good night, good luck, a merry Christmas, and God bless all of you—all of you on the good Earth."

—FRANK BORMAN, DECEMBER 24, 1968

6 "I cannot persuade myself that a beneficent and omnipotent God would have designedly created the Ichneumonidae with the express intention of their feeding within the living bodies of caterpillars." Letter to Asa Gray (22 May 1860).

7. Traherne, *Centuries* 1/10, 7.

Appendix: Prometheus Abridged

IN CHAPTER 7 I make the case for the profound influence of the Greek Prometheus myth on the change in attitude towards creation about the time of the Reformation. Readers may feel they know less about the myth itself than they would like, so I summarize it here.

Greek theogony (how the gods came to be gods) is actually a story of dynastic struggle between generations of deities. But at its heart is a univocal idea of the world, for the gods' origin is in the same world, and from the same kinds of causes, as the origin of humankind. This means that the privileges and powers of gods, compared to the poverty and struggles of mankind, are somewhat fortuitous. This idea has a bearing on the role of Prometheus as some kind of champion of humankind against the gods. It means that reverence for the gods seems to have more to do with the fact that they hold the reins of government, rather than because of their intrinsic worthiness.

The story that follows is a simplified and composite one, based on several centuries of adaptations and retellings, which is my attempt to give the general "feel" of the Prometheus story, and how it became linked to Renaissance ideas of human autonomy.

The forerunner of the gods is Uranus (Ouranos), the heaven itself. His children are called Titans, who subsequently usurp his rule. The generation after that are the Olympians, led by Zeus, who fight against, and eventually conquer the Titans, consigning them to Tartarus (under the earth) and taking over the world. Being Greek mythology, and adapted from generation to generation, the family history is actually more complicated than that!

One complication is that Prometheus, descended from Titans, is still regarded as a Titan rather than an Olympian. But note that this makes him by nature equal to the Olympian gods—he just comes from the losing family in the struggle for power. Note also that his name implies "Forethought," and that of his dull brother, Epimetheus, signifies "Afterthought."

Maybe because of this forethought, Prometheus takes the side of the Olympians against his own kind, and actually helps secure their victory. Accordingly, Zeus spares him (and his brother) their kinsmen's fate, and assigns him the task of creating humankind. Nevertheless, you'll see that from the start, Prometheus has a "history" with Zeus—the latter has wiped out his family, and Prometheus himself has only survived by cunningly changing sides.

The role as humankind's originator is the basis for Renaissance Europeans' transference to him of the role of Adam. But that's to reach ahead of ourselves. The dull brother, Epimetheus, is responsible for handing out attributes to all the worlds' creatures, and as a result of imprudence has nothing left to give humankind in the way of claws, wings, and so on. So Prometheus decides to make him walk upright, like the gods, and also gives him the divine gift of fire.

Not long after this, a meeting is called between the gods and humanity at Mecone, in order to decide who gets what when humans sacrifice an animal. This, in fact, is probably an etiological tale to explain why, in Greek sacrifices, the gods get the fat and bones, and the worshippers the rather more enjoyable remainder. Prometheus gets to organize the event and, presumably to get even with Zeus for his family's defeat, wraps the bones of the sacrificial ox in a tasty piece of fat, and the best of the carcass in its unappetizing stomach, and gets Zeus to choose his portion, setting a precedent for all time. Zeus is fooled into taking the fat and bones, and takes out his anger on humankind by withdrawing fire from them (and in some accounts, the very means of subsistence).

Prometheus, in the most famous bit of the cycle, then steals fire back from heaven for humankind out of compassion for his creation (and continuing spite against the Olympians). I should add that though the earliest source, Hesiod, presents Prometheus as a "lowly trickster and semi-comic foil to Zeus's authority,"[1] in Aeschylus's later play *Prometheus Bound* he also teaches humanity "all the civilizing arts, such as writing, medicine, mathematics, astronomy, metallurgy, architecture, and agriculture."[2]

Zeus punishes Prometheus by binding him to a rock and having an eagle devour his liver each day, only for it to regenerate, according to the Titan's immortality, each night. In fact, Zeus has another motive for this torture, in that Prometheus knows of a prophecy about a potential overthrower of Zeus's rule, whose name he refuses to reveal: the torture is intended to extract the name to secure his release. In the event, you'll be pleased to know that Zeus's alternative escape route is eventually fulfilled

---

1. Wikipedia, *Prometheus Bound*, https://en.wikipedia.org/wiki/Prometheus_Bound #Departures_from_Hesiod.
2. Ibid.

when the centaur Chiron offers his life in return for that of Prometheus, and Herakles kills the marauding eagle.

Meanwhile, Zeus also extracts a penalty from humanity, by procuring the creation of a woman, Pandora (= every gift), and sending her to earth with a jar of troubles, whose contents are unknown to her and which she is forbidden to open. Despite Prometheus's warnings (presumably between hepatectomies) not to accept any gifts from Zeus even if they have fluttering eyes, Epimetheus lodges her at his place, and as we all know curiosity overcomes her, she looks inside the jar, and all the troubles in the world are released.

In the earlier versions, foresight alone is left in the jar, preventing humankind from avoiding trouble and so adding to its woes; in the later versions, hope remains hiding under the rim as a kind of consolation.

In mediaeval times, the limited portions of the Prometheus cycle then available were used as an example, like Icarus, of those who reach too high and come a cropper—rather in the vein of the biblical Adam. As I have shown in chapter 6, this was slowly transformed into something more like its role in ancient Greece. So Prometheus became the benefactor of mankind, unjustly punished for bringing knowledge and self-sufficiency, against the malevolence and self-interest of the gods. In Renaissance Europe the target was not Zeus, the usurper of supreme power by force and intrigue, but the God and Father of the Lord Jesus Christ, Creator of all things from nothing and author of life and love. That fact makes the use of the myth far more subversive.

Bibliography

A Kempis, Thomas. *The Imitation of Christ.* Translated by Betty Knott. Glasgow: Fount, 1978.

Aldo, Leopold. "Thinking Like a Mountain." In *A Sand County Almanac and Sketches Here and There.* Oxford University Press, 1949. http://www.uky.edu/OtherOrgs/ AppalFor/Readings/leopold.pdf.

Alighieri, Dante. *The Divine Comedy.* Translated by Robin Kirkpatrick. London: Penguin Classics, 2012.

Allen, Colin, and Michael Trestman. "Animal Consciousness." In *The Stanford Encyclopedia of Philosophy* (Summer 2015 Edition). http://plato.stanford.edu/ archives/sum2015/entries/consciousness-animal/.

Anselm. *Monologion.* http://jasper-hopkins.info/monologion.pdf.

Aquinas, Thomas. *Summa Contra Gentiles.* http://dhspriory.org/thomas/Contra Gentiles.htm.

———. *Summa Theologiae.* http://www.newadvent.org/summa/.

Arminius, Jacobus. *Disputation XXIV.* Works of Arminius—on Creation. http://www. godrules.net/library/arminius/arminius67.htm.

———. *The Providence of God.* Works of Arminius—The Providence of God. http:// www.godrules.net/library/arminius/arminius153.htm.

Athanasius. *Against the Gentiles.* http://www.newadvent.org/fathers/2801.htm.

———. *On the Incarnation of the Word.* http://www.copticchurch.net/topics/theology/ incarnation_st_athanasius.pdf.

Augustine, Aurelius. *Confessions, City of God, On Christian Doctrine.* Great Books of the Western World 18. Chicago: Benton, 1989.

———. *On Genesis against the Manichees.* Translated by Edmund Hill. New York: New City, 2002. https://books.google.co.uk/books?id=AXDYAAAAMAAJ&pg=PA21 &source=gbs_toc_r&cad=3#v=onepage&q&f=false.

———. *On the Grace of Christ and Original Sin* Vol 2. http://www.newadvent.org/ fathers/15062.htm.

———. *On the Literal Meaning of Genesis, Vol 1.* Ed. Johannes Quasten et al. Mahwah, NJ: Paulist, 1982. https://books.google.co.uk/books?id=_sokIgDonCcC&printsec =frontcover&source=gbs_ge_summary_r&cad=0#v=onepage&q&f=false.

Ayala, Francisco. *On Reading the Cell's Signature.* Science and the Sacred. http:// biologos.org/blogs/archive/on-reading-the-cells-signature/#sthash.eRxVDoa5. dpuf.

Barcella, Susanna. "The Myth of Prometheus in Giovanni Boccaccio's Decameron." *Modern Language Notes* 119:1 Supplement (2004) S120–S141. http://muse.jhu. edu/journals/mln/summary/v119/119.1abarsella.html.

Barfield, Owen. *Saving the Appearances*. Middletown, CT: Wesleyan University Press, 1988.

Barth, M. *Ephesians 4–6*. The Anchor Bible Commentaries. New York: Doubleday, 1976.

Basil of Caesarea. *Homilies on Creation*. https://www.fisheaters.com/hexaemeron.html.

Bauckham, Richard. *Jesus and the Eyewitnesses*. Grand Rapids: Eerdmans, 2006.

Beale G. K. *The Temple and the Church's Mission*. Downers Grove, IL: InterVarsity, 2004.

Becker, Ernest. *The Denial of Death*. New York: Free, 1973.

Benton, M. J. "The quality of the fossil record of vertebrates." In *The Adequacy of the Fossil Record*, edited by S. K. Donovan and C. R. C. Paul, 269–303. New York: Wiley, 1998.

Berger, Peter L. *The Sacred Canopy*. Garden City, NY: Doubleday, 1967.

Berkhof, Hendrick. *Christ and the Powers*. Scottdale, PA: Herald, 1962.

Berry, R. J. *Christians and Evolution*. Oxford: Monarch, 2014.

Block, Daniel I. "Eden: A Temple? A Reassessment of the Biblical Evidence." In *From Creation to New Creation: Biblical Theology and Exegesis (Essays in Honor of G. K. Beale)*, edited by Daniel M. Gurtner and Benjamin L. Gladd, 3–30. Peabody, MA: Hendrickson, 2017.

Buchsbaum, R., M. Buchsbaum, J. Pearse, and V. Pearse. *Animals without Backbones*. 3rd ed. Chicago: University of Chicago Press, 1987.

Caird, G. B. *Principalities and Powers: Study in Pauline Theology*. Oxford: Oxford University Press, 1956.

Calvin, John. *Commentary on Genesis*. http://biblehub.com/commentaries/calvin/genesis/1.htm.

———. *Commentary on Psalms* (104). http://biblehub.com/commentaries/calvin/psalms/104.htm.

Cassirer, Ernst, and Mario Domandi. *The Individual and the Cosmos in Renaissance Philosophy*. Chicago: University of Chicago Press, 2010.

Catholic Church. *Catechism of the Catholic Church*. 2d ed. Vatican: Libreria Editrice Vaticana, 2012. http://www.vatican.va/archive/ccc_css/archive/catechism/ccc_toc.htm.

Chrysostom, John. *Three Homilies on the Devil*. http://www.newadvent.org/fathers/1919.htm.

———. *Homily 11 on the Statues*. http://www.newadvent.org/fathers/190111.htm.

———. *Homily 14 on Romans*. http://www.newadvent.org/fathers/210214.htm.

Church, Leslie F. *Matthew Henry's Commentary on the Whole Bible in One Volume*. London: Marshall, Morgan, and Scott, 1973.

Clarke, Samuel. *A Collection of Papers, Which passed between the late Learned Mr. Leibnitz, and Dr. Clarke, In the Years 1715 and 1716*. London: 1717. The Newton Project. http://www.newtonproject.sussex.ac.uk/view/texts/normalized/THEM00226.

Clauw, D. J., L. M. Arnold, and B. H. McCarberg. "The Science of Fibromyalgia." *Mayo Clinic Proceedings* 86 (2011) 907–11.

Colinvaux, Paul. *Why Big Fierce Animals are Rare—an Ecologist's Perspective*. Princeton, NJ: Princeton University Press, 1978.

Cosmas Indicopleustes. *Christian Topography*. Early Church Fathers—Additional Texts, Roger Pearse, ed. http://www.tertullian.org/fathers/cosmas_00_2_intro.htm.

Coyne, Jerry. *Mimicry: The nefarious cuckoo.* Why Evolution is True. https://whyevolution istrue.wordpress.com/2011/03/04/mimicry-the-nefarious-cuckoo.

Cunningham, Conor. *Darwin's Pious Idea.* Cambridge: Eerdmans, 2010.

Cyril of Jerusalem. *Catechetical Lectures 9.* http://www.newadvent.org/fathers/310109. htm.

Dalley, Stephanie. *Myths from Mesopotamia: Creation, The Flood, Gilgamesh, and Others.* Oxford: Oxford University Press, 2000.

Darwin, Charles. *Origin of Species and Voyage of the Beagle.* London: Vintage, 2009.

Davies, Brian. *The Reality of God and the Problem of Evil.* London: Continuum, 2006.

Dawkins, Richard. *The Blind Watchmaker: Why the Evidence Reveals a Universe Without Design.* New York: Norton, 1987.

———. "God's Utility Function." *Scientific American*, vol. 273, no. 5 (November 1995) 80–85.

———. *The Greatest Show on Earth.* New York: Simon and Schuster, 2009.

Dembski, William A. *Being as Communion—A Metaphysics of Information.* Farnham: Ashgate, 2014.

———. *The End of Christianity: Finding a Good God in an Evil World.* Nashville: Broadman & Holman, 2009.

Dembski, William A., and Michael Ruse, eds. *Debating Design.* Cambridge: Cambridge University Press, 2006.

Dickens, A. G. *The German Nation and Martin Luther.* New York: Harper and Row, 1973.

Dijkgraaf, Sven. *Sensory Reception: Mechanoreception.* Encyclopedia Britannica. https:// www.britannica.com/science/mechanoreception.

Dilley, Stephen. "Charles Darwin's use of theology in the *Origin of Species.*" *British Society for the History of Science* (2011) 29–56.

Doyle, Robert C. *Eschatology and the Shape of Christian Belief.* Carlisle: Paternoster, 1999.

Dugas-Ford, J., J. J. Rowell, and C. W. Ragsdale. "Cell-type homologies and the origins of the neocortex". *Proceedings of the National Academy of Sciences* 109.42 (2012) 16974–79.

Eddington, Arthur Stanley. *The Nature of the Physical World.* London: Dent, 1942.

Ehrlich, A., and P. Ehrlich *Ecoscience: The Greeks and Romans Did It, Too!* Mother Earth News, 1980. http://www.motherearthnews.com/nature-and-environment/greeks-and-romans-zmaz80mjzraw.aspx.

Eldredge, N., and S. J. Gould. "Punctuated Equilibria: an alternative to phyletic gradualism". In *Models in Palaeobiology*, edited by T. J. N. Schopf, 82–115. San Francisco: Freeman Cooper, 1972.

Erasmus, Desiderius. *Adages 1.* http://www.people.virginia.edu/~jdk3t/ErAdPref.pdf.

Ewer, R. F. *The Carnivores.* Ithaca, NY: Cornell University Press, 1973.

Food and Agriculture Organization of the United Nations. *Scarcity and degradation of land and water: growing threat to food security.* 2011. http://www.fao.org/news/story/en/item/95153/icode/.

Fretheim, Terence E. *God and World in the Old Testament.* Nashville: Abingdon, 2005.

Furneaux, Holly. *An introduction to In Memoriam A. H. H.* https://www.bl.uk/romantics-and-victorians/articles/in-memoriam. The text in this article is available under the Creative Commons License, https://creativecommons.org/licenses/by/4.0/.

Ghiselin, Michael T. *The Economy of Nature and the Evolution of Sex*. Berkeley, CA: University of California Press, 1974.

Giberson, Karl. *Evolution and the Problem of Evil*. Science and the Sacred. http://www.beliefnet.com/columnists/scienceandthesacred/2009/09/evolution-and-the-problem-of-evil.html#pXc57RSzUCV76hHZ.99.

———. "Living with Darwin's Dangerous Idea." In *Christians and Evolution*, edited by R. J. Berry, 153–73. Oxford: Monarch, 2014.

Gilson, Etienne. *From Aristotle to Darwin and Back Again*. San Francisco: Ignatius, 2009.

Gleason, John B. *John Colet*. Berkeley, CA: University of California Press, 1989. https://books.google.co.uk/books?id=PgYuN5XKS6IC&printsec=frontcover&source=gbs_ge_summary_r&cad=0#v=onepage&q&f=false.

Goffman, Erving. *The Presentation of Self in Everyday Life*. Harmondsworth: Pelican, 1971.

Gordon, B. L., and W. A. Dembski. *The Nature of Nature*. Wilmington, DE: ISI, 2011.

Gould, S. J. "The origin and function of 'bizarre' structures: antler size and skull size in the 'Irish Elk', Megaloceros giganteus." *Evolution* 28.2 191–220.

Gray, Asa. "Darwin and his Reviewers". *The Atlantic Monthly* 0006.36 (October 1860). https://www.theatlantic.com/magazine/archive/1860/07/darwin-on-the-origin-of-species/304152/.

Green, Michael. *I Believe in Satan's Downfall*. London: Hodder & Stoughton, 1981.

Gregory of Nazianzus. *Second Theological Oration*, XXI. http://www.tertullian.org/fathers2/NPNF2-07/Npnf2-07-43.htm.

Griffin, Donald R. *Animal Minds*. Chicago: University of Chicago Press, 1992.

Hannam, James. *God's Philosophers*. London: Icon, 2010.

Harris, Peter. "Towards a Missiology of Caring for Creation." *Evangelical Review of Theology* 34.3 (July 2010) 220–32.

Heiser, Michael. *The Unseen Realm: Recovering the Supernatural Worldview of the Bible*. Bellingham, WA: Lexham, 2015.

Hesiod. *Theogony*. http://www.sacred-texts.com/cla/hesiod/theogony.htm.

———. *Works and Days*. http://www.sacred-texts.com/cla/hesiod/works.htm.

Hick, John. *Evil and the God of Love*. New York: Harper & Row, 1966.

Hooton, Christopher. "This Planet Earth 2 iguana vs. snake scene plays out like a chase from The Bourne Identity." *Independent* 11/08/2016. http://www.independent.co.uk/arts-entertainment/tv/news/planet-earth-2-ii-episode-1-iguana-snake-chase-scene-a7404201.html.

Horace. *Carmina I.3*. http://www.poetryintranslation.com/PITBR/Latin/HoraceOdes BkI.htm#anchor_Toc39402009.

Horn, Theodore. *The Fall of Athens: Selections from the Hellenica of Xenophon*. London: Macmillan, 1962. https://cliojournal.wikispaces.com/Greek+warships.

Hughes, Philip Edgcumbe. *The True Image—the Origin and Destiny of Man in Christ*. Leicester: InterVarsity, 1989.

Hume, David. *Dialogues Concerning Natural Religion*. 2d ed. London, 1779. https://ia800503.us.archive.org/28/items/dialoguesconcern1779hume/dialoguesconcern1779hume.pdf.

Huxley, Thomas. *The Struggle for Existence in Human Society*. Collected Essays IX. https://mathcs.clarku.edu/huxley/CE9/Str.html.

Ignatius. *Letter to the Romans*. http://www.newadvent.org/fathers/0107.htm.

John of Damascus. *Exposition of the Orthodox Faith*. http://www.orthodox.net/fathers/exactidx.html.

Kent, Bonnie. "Evil in Later Medieval Philosophy." *Journal of the History of Philosophy* 45.2 (2007) 177–205.

Kidner, Derek. *Genesis*. Tyndale Commentaries. London: Tyndale, 1968.

Kingsley, Charles. *The Natural Theology of the Future* (1871). The Literature Network. http://www.online-literature.com/charles-kingsley/scientific/7/.

Kitchen, K. A. *On the Reliability of the Old Testament*. Grand Rapids: Eerdmans, 2003.

Kuhn, Thomas S. *The Structure of Scientific Revolutions*. Chicago: University of Chicago Press, 1970.

Lane, Belden C. *Ravished by Beauty*. Oxford: Oxford University Press, 2011.

Levenson, Jon D. "The Temple and the World." *Journal of Religion* 64 (1984) 275–98.

Lewis, C. S. *The Magician's Nephew*. London: Fontana Lions, 1984.

———. *Out of the Silent Planet*. London: Pan, 1963.

Lovejoy, Arthur O. *The Great Chain of Being*. Cambridge, MA: Harvard University Press, 2001.

Luther, Martin. *Bondage of the Will*. Translated by J. I. Packer and O. R. Johnston. London: James Clark, 1957.

———. *A Critical and Devotional Commentary on Genesis*. Translated by Wilhelm Pauck. Philadelphia: Westminster, 1961.

———. *Lectures on Romans*. Translated by Wilhelm Pauck. Philadelphia: Westminster, 1961.

———. *Table Talk*. Translated by W. Hazlitt. London: H. G. Bohn, 1862.

———. *Luther on the Creation: A Critical and Devotional Commentary on Genesis [1–3]*. https://archive.org/details/LutherOnTheCreationACriticalAndDevotionalCommentaryOnGenesis1-3.

Maier, Paul L. *Josephus—the Essential Writings*. Grand Rapids: Kregel, 1988.

Malthus Thomas R. *An Essay on the Principle of Population*. http://www.esp.org/books/malthus/population/malthus.pdf.

Marks, Jonathan. "What is the viewpoint of hemoglobin, and does it matter?" *History and Philosophy of the Life Sciences* 31.2 (2009) 241–62.

Mauriac, François. *Oeuvres Romanesques, vol. 2*. Paris: Flammarion, 1965.

———. *Knot of Vipers*. Translated by Gerard Hopkins. London: Eyre & Spottiswoode, 1951.

Mazur, Suzan. *The Paradigm Shifters*. New York: Caswell, 2015.

McElreath, R., and R. Boyd. *Mathematical Models of Social Evolution: A Guide for the Perplexed*. Chicago: University of Chicago Press, 2007.

McGrath, Alister E. *The Re-enchantment of Nature*. London: Hodder & Stoughton, 1988.

———. *A Scientific Theology. Vol. 1: Nature*. Grand Rapids: Eerdmans, 2001.

McLelland, Joseph C. *Prometheus Rebound: The Irony of Atheism*. Waterloo, ON: Wilfrid Laurier University Press, 1988.

McElreath, R., and R. Boyd. *Mathematical Models of Social Evolution : A Guide for the Perplexed*. Chicago: University of Chicago Press, 2007.

Melville, Herman. *Moby Dick*. London: Penguin 1994.

Middleton, J. Richard. *A New Heaven and a New Earth*. Grand Rapids: Baker Academic, 2014.

Miller, Glenn M. *Does the savagery of predation in nature show that God either isn't, or at least isn't good-hearted?* A Christian Thinktank. http://christianthinktank.com/ predator.html.

Miller, Keith B., ed. *Perspectives on an Evolving Creation.* Grand Rapids: Eerdmans, 2003.

Milton, John. *Paradise Lost.* London: Penguin, 1989.

Molina, Luis de. *Concordia* Pt 2, Disp 25. https://www3.nd.edu/~afreddos/translat/ molina25.htm.

Nagel, Thomas. "What is it like to be a bat?" *The Philosophical Review* LXXXIII.4 (1974) 435–50.

National Institutes of Health. *Research Involving Introduction of Human Pluripotent Cells into Non-Human Vertebrate Animal Pre-Gastrulation Embryos.* (Notice Number: NOT-OD-15-158, September 23, 2015.) https://grants.nih.gov/grants/ guide/notice-files/NOT-OD-15-158.html.

Packer, J. I. *Fundamentalism and the Word of God.* Grand Rapids: Eerdmans, 1958.

Palmer, Chris. *Into the Wild, Ethically: Nature Filmmakers Need a Code of Conduct.* Documentary Magazine. http://www.documentary.org/magazine/wild-ethically-nature-filmmakers-need-code-conduct.

Patte, Daniel, and Eugene TeSelle. *Engaging Augustine on Romans.* London: Continuum-3PL, 2003.

Philo. *Questions on Genesis.* http://www.earlychristianwritings.com/yonge/book41.html.

Plantinga, Alvin. *God and Other Minds.* Ithaca, NY: Cornell University Press, 1967.

———. *God, Freedom and Evil.* Grand Rapids: Eerdmans 1989.

———. *Where the Conflict Really Lies.* Oxford: Oxford University Press, 2011.

Plato. *Critias.* http://classics.mit.edu/Plato/critias.html.

———. *Protagoras.* http://www.bard.edu/library/arendt/pdfs/Plato-Protagoras.pdf.

Pope Francis. *Laudato Si'.* http://w2.vatican.va/content/francesco/en/encyclicals/docu ments/papa-francesco_20150524_enciclica-laudato-si.html.

Postell, Seth D. *Adam as Israel: Genesis 1–3 as the Introduction to the Torah and Tanakh.* Eugene, OR: Pickwick, 2011.

Prance, Sir Ghillean. *Go to the Ant.* Glasgow: Wild Goose, 2014.

Premack, David, and Ann Premack. *Original Intelligence.* New York: McGraw-Hill, 2003.

Prothero, Donald R. "Fossil Record." In *Encyclopedia of Palaeontology,* edited by Ronald Singer, 490–92 . Chicago: Fitzroy Deerborn, 2000.

Reese, Lizette Woodworth. "A Little Song of Life." In *Wayside Lute,* 51. Portland, ME: Thomas B Mosher, 1909.

Roberts, Alexander, and James Donaldson. *Ante-Nicene Christian Library.* 24 vols. Edinburgh: T&T Clark, 1867–1885.

Rose, Seraphim. "Genesis and Early Man—The Orthodox Patristic Understanding." Orthodox Christian Information Center. http://orthodoxinfo.com/phronema/ evolution_frseraphim_kalomiros.aspx.

Russell, Robert J. *Cosmology from Alpha to Omega.* Minneapolis: Fortress, 2008.

Sailhamer, John H. *The Meaning of the Pentateuch.* Downers Grove, IL: InterVarsity, 2009.

Schneider, Robert J. *Theology of Creation: Historical Perspectives and Fundamental Concepts.* Perspectives on Christianity and Science. http://community.berea.edu/ scienceandfaith/essay02.asp.

Schopf, T. J. N., ed. *Models in Palaeobiology.* San Francisco: Freeman Cooper, 1972.

Sharpe, A. "Evil." *The Catholic Encyclopedia.* New York: Robert Appleton Company, 1909). New Advent: http://www.newadvent.org/cathen/05649a.htm.

Shinn, Roger L. *Man: The New Humanism.* New Directions in Theology Today VI. London: Westminster, 1968.

Smil, Vaclav. "Detonator of the population explosion." *Nature* 400.6743 (1999) 415–16.

Spurgeon, Charles Haddon. *Creation's Groans and the Saints' Sighs.* Sermon 1–3–1868. http://www.biblebb.com/files/spurgeon/0788.htm.

Staniforth, Maxwell, trans. *Early Christian Writings.* London: Penguin, 1988.

Stenger, Victor J. *The New Atheism: Taking a Stand for Science and Reason.* Amherst, NY: Prometheus, 2009.

Stott, John. *The Cross of Christ.* Leicester: InterVarsity, 1986.

Surin, Kenneth. *Theology and the Problem of Evil.* Eugene, OR: Wipf and Stock, 2004.

Swinburne, Richard. *Providence and the Problem of Evil.* Oxford: Oxford University Press, 1998.

Tennyson, Alfred Lord. *Works.* Ware: Wordsworth, 1994.

Thuswaldner, Gregor. "A Conversation with Peter L. Berger : 'How My Views Have Changed.'" *The Cresset* LXXVII.3 (Lent 2013) 16–21. http://thecresset.org/2014/Lent/Thuswaldner_L14.html.

Tice, Mike. *Oxygen and Co-Creation.* Science and the Sacred. http://biologos.org/blogs/archive/oxygen-and-co-creation.

Tilley, Terrence W. *The Evils of Theodicy.* Eugene, OR: Wipf and Stock, 2000.

Torley, Vincent. *God: Lawgiver or Hypocrite?* Uncommon Descent. http://www.uncommondescent.com/intelligent-design/lawgiver-or-hypocrite-loftus-attacks-divine-command-theories-of-ethics/.

Traherne, Thomas. *Centuries of Meditations.* New York: Cosimo Classics, 2007.

Tyndale, William. *The Obedience of the Christian Man.* London: Penguin Classics, 2000.

Wallace, Alfred Russel. *The World of Life.* London: Chapman & Hall, 1910.

Walton, John H. *Ancient Israelite Literature in its Cultural Context.* Grand Rapids: Zondervan, 1989.

———. *Genesis 1 as Ancient Cosmology.* Winona Lake, IN: Eisenbrauns, 2011.

———. *Genesis.* NIV Application Commentary. Grand Rapids: Zondervan, 2001.

———.*The Lost World of Adam and Eve.* Downers Grove, IL: InterVarsity, 2015.

Ward, P. D., and D. Brownlee. *Rare Earth—Why Complex Life is Uncommon in the Universe.* New York: Springer, 2004.

Waters, C. N., et al. "The Anthropocene is functionally and stratigraphically distinct from the Holocene." *Science* 351 (2016). DOI: 10.1126/science.aad2622. https://www.researchgate.net/publication/289670932_The_Anthropocene_Is_Functionally_and_Stratigraphically_Distinct_from_the_Holocene.

Wenham, Gordon J. *Genesis 1–15.* Word Biblical Commentary. Nashville: Nelson, 1987.

———. "Sanctuary Symbolism in the Garden of Eden Story." In *I Studied Inscriptions Before the Flood: Ancient Near Eastern, Literary, and Linguistic Approaches to Genesis 1–11*, edited by Richard S. Hess and David Toshio Tsumura, 399–404. Winona Lake, IN: Eisenbrauns, 1994. http://www.godawa.com/chronicles_of_the_nephilim/Articles_By_Others/Wenham-Sanctuary_Symbolism_Garden_of_Eden.pdf.

Wesley, John. *The General Deliverance Sermon 60.* Wesley Center Online. http://wesley.nnu.edu/john-wesley/the-sermons-of-john-wesley-1872-edition/sermon-60-the-general-deliverance/.

Westminster Assembly of Divines. *Westminster Confession of Faith and Larger and Shorter Catechism.* Edinburgh: Swinton and Brown, 1671.

Whiteley, D. E. H. *The Theology of Paul.* Oxford: Blackwell, 1972.

Wilcox, David L. *God and Evolution.* Valley Forge, PA: Judson, 2004.

Wink, W. *Naming the Powers: The Language of Power in the New Testament.* Philadelphia: Fortress, 1984.

Wordsworth, William. *The Prelude.* Oxford, 1970.

Wright, N. T. *Jesus and the Victory of God.* London: SPCK, 1996.

———. *The Resurrection of the Son of God.* London: SPCK, 2003.

———. *Surprised by Hope.* London: SPCK, 2007.

Wright, Nigel Goring. *A Theology of the Dark Side.* Downers Grove, IL: InterVarsity, 2003.

Wybrow, Cameron. *The Bible, Baconianism, and Mastery over Nature.* New York: Peter Lang, 1991.

General Index

Moltmann, Jürgen, xvi
mortality, 25, 83, 85, 135
Moses, 4, 23n6, 55, 57, 92, 197
Mouchy, Emile-Edouard, 165

Nagel, Thomas, 150–51, 163–64, 165
natural evil, xiii, xiv-xix, 30, 36, 45, 82,
    83, 86, 88, 89, 92, 94, 105, 112,
    115, 147, 152, 189–90
natural selection, xv, 101, 121, 124, 127,
    142–3, 145, 146, 162, 197
Needham, Nick, xi, xvii
Neo-Darwinism, xiv, xv, 142, 145, 197
new creation, xixn20, 49, 52, 54, 58, 67,
    169, 201
new heavens and new earth, xix, 48, 50,
    51, 54, 169
Newton, Sir Isaac, 180n17, 196
Nietzsche, Friedrich, 114
Noah, 24, 28–30, 38–40, 95, 167

open theism, 98, 113
Origen, 46
original sin, 74, 86, 93, 187

pain, xiv, 27, 41, 96, 98, 100, 121, 123–
    24, 125, 126, 147–67
Paley, William, 80
Palmer, Chris, 160n24, 170–71
Pandora, 110–12, 209
parasitism, xiii, 8, 28, 39, 120, 123,
    133–34, 152, 157, 189, 205
Paul, 10, 11–12, 15, 23, 42–49, 54,
    57, 61–68, 80, 135, 169, 174,
    188–90, 201
Philo, 23, 72–73
Plantinga, Alvin, xvi, 195n25
Plato, 108n12, 127, 171–73
powers and principalities, 8, 42–43,
    60–68, 190, 192
Prance, Sir Ghillean, 168
predation, xiv, 31, 33, 39–40, 74, 76, 79,
    81, 92, 106, 123, 131–32, 143,
    154, 161–63, 189
Premack, David and Ann, 138
principle of plenitude, 127
Prometheus, 103–115, 203n2, 207–9
Prothero, Donald, 127

providence, 12, 15, 76, 82, 92, 98, 120,
    146, 188
punctuated equilibria, 128–29

Rahab, 12–13, 54
ransom theory, 61–62, 64–65
redemption, xix, xx, 44, 48, 108n13,
    170n4
Renaissance, 107–112, 207–9
resurrection, 24, 25, 42–48, 51, 62, 135,
    169, 199, 200–202
Robinson, George Wade, 185
romanticism, 125–26
Russell, Robert John, xiv, xv, 120, 147,
    153–54, 170

sabbath, 7
Sailhamer, John, 57
Satan, xv, 11, 13, 15, 21, 26, 41, 59,
    60–61, 63–68, 74–75, 85, 112,
    115, 167, 169, 188
selfish genes, xv, 138–45
selfishness in evolution, xv, 137–46
semi-deism, xvi. 197
serpent, xiii, 25–26, 30, 50–51, 60, 65,
    72–74, 78
SOLAW, 175
sovereignty of God, 4, 8, 10, 11, 13, 77,
    97, 192
Spurgeon, Charles Haddon, xiii, xiv, xv,
    21, 60, 100, 119, 185
Stenger, Victor J., 180
Stott, John, 62–63
suffering, xiv, xv, 27, 34, 36, 41–42, 74,
    90, 119–28, 146, 147–67, 170,
    190, 204
Surin, Kenneth, xvi, xviii, 83n28
Swinburne, Richard, xvi
symbiosis, 157

temple, 5, 20, 37, 51, 54–56, 97, 174,
    194–95, 201, 205
Tennyson, Alfred Lord, 101–2
theistic evolution, xiv, xv, xix, 21, 103,
    120–21, 133, 142, 157, 166, 170,
    191, 192n20, 197

Index of Ancient Sources

35915401R00153

Made in the USA
Lexington, KY
08 April 2019